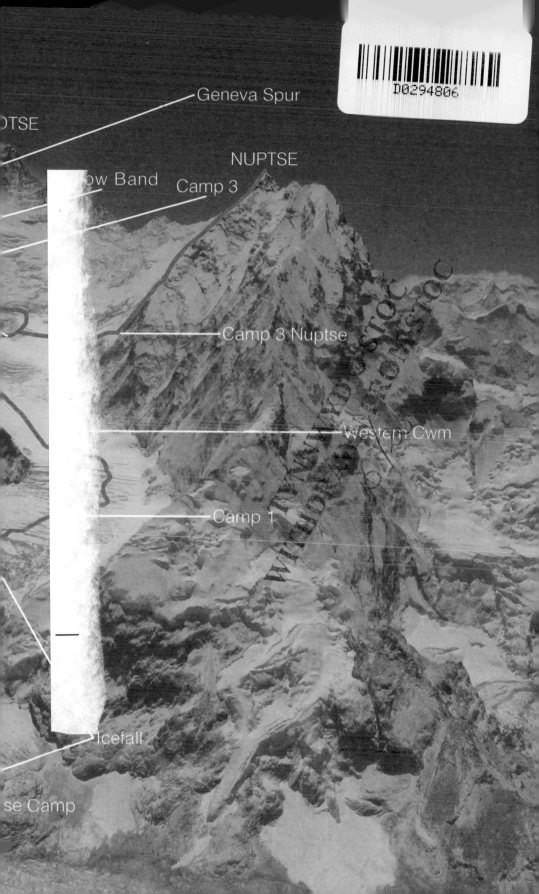

Geneva Spur

OTSE

NUPTSE

ow Band

Camp 3

Camp 3 Nuptse

Western Cwm

Camp 1

Icefall

se Camp

ONE MAN'S EVEREST
KENTON COOL

preface
publishing

1 3 5 7 9 10 8 6 4 2

Preface
20 Vauxhall Bridge Road
London SW1V 2SA

Preface is part of the Penguin Random House
group of companies whose addresses can be found at
global.penguinrandomhouse.com

Penguin
Random House
UK

First published by Preface in 2015

www.randomhouse.co.uk

A CIP catalogue record for this book
is available from the British Library

ISBN 9781848094482

Everest image on endpapers © Keith Partridge, 2015

Typeset by Palimpsest Book Production Ltd, Falkirk, Stirlingshire

Printed and bound by Clays Ltd, St Ives plc

Penguin Random House is committed to a sustainable
future for our business, our readers and our planet.
This book is made from Forest Stewardship Council®-
certified paper.

For the Three Amigos:
Jazzy, Saffy and Wilbs.

25 April 2015, a Saturday

Around 8.30 a.m. I was making pancakes for my children Saffy and Wilbs at home in Gloucestershire with my wife Jazz. The children were in their pajamas running amok in the conservatory when the phone rang. It was Shweta Poddar an old friend who works for the King's Challenge, a bespoke travel company, and lives on the Indian–Nepalese border.

'Kenton, have you heard about the earthquake in Nepal? I immediately thought of you and your friends and wanted to make sure you were okay.'

A little later the news was reported on the BBC and the full horror of what had happened that morning began to reach the rest of the world. The earthquake was a magnitude of 7.8, the most violent to strike Nepal for many decades. A second one struck couple of weeks later of a similar magnitude, adding yet more misery to an already desperate situation. Over the next days the death toll rose and rose and is now, as I write, estimated to be above 8,000 with countless others injured.

Nepal is one of the poorest countries in the world and when

the quake struck there were very few structures built to withstand an earthquake of such size, even though one had been expected for quite some time. Great swathes of the country have been levelled and hundreds of thousands of people are still living in makeshift shelters.

Eighteen people were killed at Base Camp, three of the Sherpas my good friends: Pasang Temba, Kumar and Tensing. Quite rightly, no climbing will take place on any part of Everest until 2016 at the earliest as the country picks itself up – as it surely will.

I would like to dedicate this book to the people of Nepal, to thank them for the hospitality and kindness they have shown me over many years. As a people they have made me feel a privileged and welcome guest and I would never have been able to climb Everest without their help and collaboration.

CONTENTS

PROLOGUE
EVEREST, 2004

We take the last few footsteps of our approach, over the Hillary Step, 8,750 metres above sea level, a mere 100 metres from the summit of Everest. It is my first time on the mountain, so I really have no idea how far it is from here to the top. We are the first up of the year, on either the south side or the north side of the mountain. I pull ahead a little bit from my client Clive Jones, while Pemba Norbu, my powerful but tiny Sherpa, pushes on with me.

From the Hillary Step we traverse the ridge on the last push. Luckily, the angle on the southern side is not steep, and we trot up the slightly undulating slopes. By now, even with supplimentary oxygen, we are gasping for breath.

Then we round a little rocky outcrop, and slowly rise up, and that's when I can clearly see the summit for the first time. That's the point where you can start to believe it's really going to happen.

It is like an early spring day at home in Gloucestershire . . . Blue skies, with just a little bit of wind, not a cloud in the sky except for a patch of white way off behind me, hundreds of miles away in India somewhere. Underfoot, conditions are perfect: just enough snow to make progress easy. And, of course, as we are the first, there are no footsteps. It is pristine, just as Tenzing Norgay and Edmund Hillary would have found it way back in May 1953.

We are now climbing in the Death Zone, above 7,500 metres, where the air pressure is so low that life is unsustainable, and I am trying hard to focus. I have to look after Clive and make sure he is never too far behind me. From where we are standing it first flattens out then rises steadily again, then it's just a little kick on over the last 50 metres. As I walk I try to suck in the view, just as I am attempting to suck in the much-needed oxygen. What do I remember? Everything. It is as clear to me now as it was then – the view, the feelings, the emotions welling up at the staggering sight of the whole earth at my feet.

I gaze across the surrounding mountains, attempting to work out what they are, not really paying attention to where I am going. Pemba eases off a little bit for the last 20 metres. I don't really notice he's doing so at first – and I never got the opportunity to thank him for this consideration, because he died a couple of years later* – but with hindsight I can see that he is allowing me to arrive at the summit on my own.

I take the final three or four steps, watching my feet making marks in the snow. Here I am, laying down the path for the season, my efforts opening up the route for others to follow, literally, in my footsteps. In my mind these footsteps become Hillary's, they become Tenzing's. I am standing as they had done fifty-one years before.

*

* Pemba Norbu died north of the Annapurnas, working with a French team. It was quite a high-profile accident at the time: a huge avalanche swept away a base camp and the ex-head of ENSA, the Ecole Nationale de Ski et d'Alpinisme, the French guides school, died, along with about fifteen people all told.

Their story and the stories of those who came after are the stories that inspired me to become a climber. As a boy, I loved the images of them: the photographs of Tenzing, taken by Hillary, on Everest in 1953; or Dougal Haston and Doug Scott in 1975 – that picture of Doug on the top, which he had to plead with Dougal to take, because Dougal *never* took photographs. Apparently Doug turned round and said, 'Come on, youth, take one for my mother!' From the age of about fifteen or sixteen, I wanted to be a climber like Dougal or Doug.

Of course, there's no photograph of Hillary at the summit because Tenzing didn't know how to operate a camera! I always wondered whether Hillary regretted not having a record. But of course he knew he was there, in the same way that I knew I was there. Why do we need a selfie? You take the moment away in your mind. It becomes part of you, precious and life-affirming.

Hillary and Tenzing kept their secret – the secret of who was first to reach the summit. I remember listening to Hillary when he was being interviewed once and he was asked, as he must have been thousands of times, who got to the top first. 'Let's just say I wasn't second,' he said. At the time I thought he'd given the secret away, but I realised, standing there myself for the first time, that he hadn't. You can walk shoulder to shoulder on that last little bit, so I like to believe they walked to the top together like the team that they famously were.

I too have a secret. My secret is that I have never actually stood on the very top of Everest. To be a purist, neither did Hillary and Tenzing nor, indeed, did hundreds of others who say they have. In my eleven climbs of Everest I have never stood on the true summit. The true-true summit is actually very small, and drops steeply on all sides; it's only about the size of a break-fast tray. I have touched it, but I have never stood on it.

I don't want to conquer Everest. You can stand on the top if you like but she won't submit to you even if you do. You can sneak round her side, and crawl up her flanks, very humbly showing suitable respect, and if she's in a good mood she'll allow you to reach the top safely. And if she does you should run away quickly, feeling very proud of what you've achieved – and a little lucky. One never conquers Everest – or any other mountain, for that matter – you are simply allowed to be part of the mountain's history, if only for a fleeting moment. And that is a privilege.

I worry that respect doesn't exist in some climbers these days. Okay, I was the first to send a tweet from the summit, I've made telephone calls, and been filmed from the top, which you could say was disrespectful, but I've never taken a huge banner up there, I've never danced a jig there. I've never left anything up there to mark my moment. If the Sherpas want to leave prayer flags or pictures of the Dalai Lama, that seems to me a little different. They are recognising the spirit as well as the meaning of the place, not the ego of the person.

Pemba had summtited once before, and that was another reason why he hung back, letting me have that moment. It only comes once, that first summit, the knowledge that you're the highest person on the planet, that there's no one else above you on the face of the earth.

So here I am: standing at the top of a mountain I always said I didn't have an interest in climbing. All the commercialism surrounding it, the costs, the hubbub, the attraction to the non-climber – it is everything that I'm not, but here I am and, well, what a hypocrite! I love it, and I can admit to myself that I love it – that I want to be here and nowhere else. I am fulfilling this secret desire of mine, and it feels wonderful. I am walking in the footsteps of some of my heroes. Then I slump to the ground.

I'm not really a spiritual person, but like the astronauts looking back from space to our 'blue marble' in a sea of blackness, at that moment I feel humble and grateful to be alive. I can't begin to do justice to the uninterrupted 360-degree panorama. It is an unbelievably clear day, and gazing out at scenery that stretches out for hundreds of miles into the distance, I feel as though somebody has punched me in the stomach, taking my breath away. The Chinese believe that mountains connect earth and heaven. Standing on top of Everest, who would disagree?

Pemba comes up and sits down too, and we hug one another. I dig my crampons into the snow more securely – I don't fancy scooting off down the south-west face. Pemba and I are looking straight down into the Khumbu Valley, the valley everyone approaching Base Camp treks through. I think, 'I've got to take this all in. What a great opportunity to look at all these mountains that I could climb in the future.' Trying to pick out peaks that would make good climbing objectives, I find myself looking at one nearby and thinking, 'Wow, that's an amazing mountain, really interesting.' It's pyramid shaped with these beautiful-looking ridge lines. Then it dawns on me: this is Ama Dablam, the mountain that dominates the view when you walk up towards Base Camp. Trekking up the Khumbu Valley, you can't see Everest – she's hidden behind Nuptse and Lhotse – it's Ama Dablam that dominates. I'd climbed it in 2001 at 6,800 or so metres – it was my introduction to high-altitude mountaineering.

From the peak I remember looking across and up at Everest. You get an amazing view from Ama Dablam, but to me it was just 'that mountain over there'. And now I'm looking down – two vertical kilometres down – at its summit, and that's when it really hits me just how extraordinarily high we are. Suddenly I understand how fragile human beings are. Nature makes us insignificant. Sitting on top of the world it feels sensational, but at the same time it is scary. There we are, so far above sea level, so high in the thin atmosphere, in a place human beings are not meant to be.

I look out over the Himalayas, and it feels as though the range stretches for ever, mountain after mountain after mountain. I can see Kanchenjunga and Makalu to the east, Cho Oyu and Shishapangma to the west. Looking to the north I see the Tibetan Plateau, where the Himalayas end abruptly, and then south down into India. I can see it all, sitting there at the pinnacle of everything. If I jump off at that moment it will mean nothing in the span of life and of time. At that moment I am not even a grain of sand.

I shake myself. Where's Clive? And then he appears, coming up with his Sherpa guide Pema Tshring. And the next thought that strikes me is: 'I've got to phone Mum and Dad.' I whip out the sat phone. My parents are aware I am going for the summit today; I have to tell them I've made it. I dial, it rings, and it rings and it rings, and I think, 'They're not going to pick up.'

There is a four-and-three-quarter-hour time difference. I am at the summit at seven o'clock in the morning, so it's 2.15 a.m. at home. Then my mother answers, and says, 'Hello. Is that you, Kenton? Hello, dear.' (She knew it would be me, which is something.)

'Mum, Mum.' I'm choking back tears. 'Mum, Mum.'

And she interrupts: 'How are you?'

'Yes, yes, I'm good, great, very good.'

'Now, how's that chest infection of yours, dear?'

I am completely taken aback; she's asking me about a chest infection and I'm at the top of Everest and I find myself saying, 'Yes, the antibiotics seem to be working, thanks, Mum, much better, do I sound—'

'You do sound better.'

'Oh, great, Mum, great.'

'So, where are you?' she says, like I'm about to ask if she'll pick me up from the local chip shop.

And I burst into tears. 'Mum, Mum, I'm on the top . . . I'm on the summit of Everest.'

I'll never forget her reaction: 'Oh, that's nice, dear. Now you probably want to speak to your dad as well, don't you? He couldn't sleep so he's taken the dog for a walk. Is there any chance you can call back?' I'm not making this up.

'Well, maybe I'll call from the top camp,' I suggest.

'Oh, well, that would be a real shame. I think your father would like to talk to you at the top.' At which point I lost the sat link.

I look at Pemba as I hang up. I've been in this little bubble, consumed by a feeling of euphoria coupled with being physically and mentally exhausted. Then, suddenly, I'm back to the real world – my father's walking the dog and my chest infection is better – and the moment has gone. And I have a client to think about.

Clive is a great guy, and a great client to have on my first Everest trip. We celebrate together, but not for long, because I am very anxious about getting back down. We take a few photographs, amid some big hugs and a few tears. There's so much wrapped up in the success of getting to the top – the hard work that's gone into it, the planning, the fulfilment of dreams for myself and, when I'm guiding, for others. I love expedition life, but I always find summits are mixed with sadness, because a summit represents the start of an expedition drawing to a close. Although there is celebration it's tinged with anxiety, because, obviously, we've still got to get down safely.

For me, that first summit was the end of the beginning. I am still in contact with Clive, eleven years later, and indeed Nick Brooke, my other client that year, who summited about a week later. It was Nick who, much later, inadvertently introduced me to my wife. But that's another story.

PART ONE

CHAPTER 1
PRIDE AND THE FALL

We all think it will never happen to us.

I was twenty-two years old. It was the glorious summer of 1996 and I had left Leeds University a couple of years earlier, buzzing with expectation and passion, my future rolling out before me. The Euro '96 Championships, held in England, had kicked off, with the Atlanta Olympics just around the corner. Along with some great climbing friends and colleagues, I was shortly to embark on my second trip to Pakistan, to attempt the mighty (then) unclimbed south-west ridge of The Ogre.

A week before we were due to leave, a group of us had come together to nip up to North Wales to collect a load of sponsorship kit. We had decided to combine the trip with a spot of climbing around Llanberis, on the northern edge of the Snowdonia National Park. I was living in London at the time, and I drove up to North Wales on the Friday evening with my girlfriend Carolyn, my friend Richard Spillett, who, like me, was a member of the North London Mountaineering Club, and his wife Sara.

The weekend weather forecast was so-so, but we were familiar with the area because the North London club had a hut in Capel Curig, which meant we were always climbing there, and so we looked forward to the weekend whatever the weather.

The plan was to climb on Saturday and meet up with Andy McNae later. At that time Andy was the National Officer of the British Mountaineering Council, and one of the guys on the Pakistan expedition. He had gone ahead of us, to pick up all the sponsorship kit for the trip. We were going up there to make sure all the sizes were right, and to drink some beer.

On Saturday morning we were on the twenty-minute drive into Llanberis from the club hut, looking out of the car windows at grey skies. All the way there the rain was on and off, and I was having second thoughts about climbing. On days like that we would often end up in the disused slate quarries above Llanberis. I was not totally fit for rock climbing, as I'd broken my wrist not long before, taking a tumble climbing Right Wall on the Cromlech in North Wales. Right Wall is super classic, one of the most sought-after climbs in the area, but I had managed to fall off and fracture my wrist. In any case, I'd arrived in Llanberis with my head in expedition mode. I had been training hard, been doing a lot of running and cardio, and it was only seven days until I'd be sitting on a plane going to Pakistan. I've always found it difficult to swing from one type of climbing to the other. I'm either in expedition mode or I'm in rock-climbing mode. To be frank, on that June day I wasn't really that psyched – what I actually wanted to do was to nip off to the café for a cup of tea and a second breakfast. 'God, wouldn't it be great if it rains? If it really rains?' I thought. 'Then I won't need an excuse not to climb, because the decision will be made for me.'

As we got closer to Llanberis, it began to brighten up a little. Spillett was really keen to get up there. Spillett is always super keen, that's his charm. We parked at the bottom of the Dinorwic

Quarry and started walking the half-mile or so up the inclines. The slate quarry is quite a surreal place, a bit like Mordor in the *Lord of the Rings* movies: bleak and dead-looking, almost post-apocalyptic. It's as if the quarry workers of 1969 have just upped and left the day before, leaving everything behind them. The rail tracks are still in place on the inclines, as are the blast shelters. When we were students, and had no cash, we used to bivouac in these shelters, often spending the evenings in the warmth of the pub and staggering up there in the dark of night, once the pub had shut. It's hardly better in daylight, the dark slate bearing down on you from all sides in the gloom. Almost every climb in the quarry is up steep slabs, with very small holds and, as you would expect from slate, it's slippery. It's very technical, which never really suited my style of rock climbing. Slate is also quite friable, hence the reason it makes good roof tiles, as it's easy to cleave.

We decided to go to the area called Colossus Wall, a 50-metre-high sheer face, an unusually steep wall for slate. It's south-facing and it's exposed to the weather, meaning that although it gets the sun when it's out, the Welsh rain that falls all year round is usually seeping out of the wall somewhere, making the already slippery slate even trickier. Spillett was raring to go and wanted to do a route called Ride the Wild Surf, which is an E4 – testing but nothing drastic. I decided I'd do an easy E1 or E2 warm-up route called Bella Lugosi is Dead with Carolyn, but it didn't go well from the start. I wasn't feeling the movement; instead, I was feeling awkward and clunky.

I don't regret anything, but I look back on it now and I kick myself. I should have cooled it. I should have been sensible, weighed up the situation, said to myself, 'I'm off to Pakistan next week: I don't need this.' But I was young, I had a rabid competitive spirit and at that time I would pick up any gauntlet.

Spillett, geared up and launched up Ride the Wild Surf quickly, which upped the ante for the day. Nearby there was an E5 route called Major Head Stress: aptly named, in retrospect.

We were looking it over when a couple of climbing friends, Chris Barnes and a guy everyone knew as Mad Max, appeared. I quizzed them about the climb. They said it had some very widely spaced expansion bolts in it, so it was not super hard, but quite bold, which is my forte. So that was it. I decided I was going to do Major Head Stress. I was going to do it – or rather we were going to do it, myself and Carolyn – and that was that. I had made up my mind and when that's done I'm immovable. Get this done. Bragging rights for later, and then straight back to the café for a mug of tea.

I sat down and pulled on my boots: Boreal Lasers. All these years later I still think they were my favourite boots – I loved them. I racked up with the equipment I thought I'd need. I wouldn't need a lot with the bolts in.

An E5 is a hard route for me; at least, it was at that time. But the start was really pretty easy. I was at around 13 feet high, nothing much in the scheme of things, and there was a very obvious crack in front of me. Above, at maybe 30 feet, was the first bolt winking at me, egging me on; just one or maybe two tricky little moves and then I'd be on an easy-looking ramp line, stretching up to the bolt. I tried to get to the slight broken ramp, teetering on small holds with my feet. Carolyn was belaying below me, holding the ropes. I grabbed the big nuts, which always sit on the right-hand side of my harness, looking at the crack to assess the size. I grabbed the nut, the one I thought was the right size, and offered it up to the crack. It was too big.

What I should have done then was swap the nut for the slightly smaller size nut. I distinctly remember thinking, 'I'll just swap it for a smaller one.' But then the confidence demon on my shoulder whispered, 'You don't need it; just two moves and you're on the broken ramp and it's easy up to the bolt.' I put the wires back on the harness and, committed, made one move. I reached up and pulled on the hold above. I was just making the move . . . And then I was airborne.

It was so slow. I was maybe 12 to 14 feet up, no higher, but it seemed to take for ever to hit the ground. On the way down I was just thinking, 'This is going to hurt.' I had no idea.

There was an explosion of pain as my heels hit the rocky ground.

Nineteen years later it still hurts.

I hit the ground and crumpled, and, weirdly, immediately got back to my feet before slumping back down to the ground. Pains shot up both of my legs; it was as if somebody was ramming hot pokers through my heels, through my knees and into my thighs. I lay there on the floor, looking up at the grey sky. The first thing going though my mind was 'I've fallen off!' I couldn't believe it. I had fallen off! Then I saw Carolyn peering over me.

Spillett was still climbing, high up on Ride the Wild Surf, he might even have been at the top. But very quickly Chris and Max were there. (Years later, over a beer, Max and I were reminiscing about the fall. Max, who happens to be a doctor, said, 'Mate, I took one look at the state of your feet and thought, "He's fucked."')

I immediately went into denial. I didn't want to believe I had seriously injured myself. 'How can I possibly be hurt? I fly to Pakistan next week!' I thought. I was going to be climbing an amazing mountain called The Ogre. An outrageous climb. There was no way that I was not going to be on that plane.

I'm not sure who called the ambulance, because, as I lay there, the pain was unbelievable, blotting out everything around me. About the only thing that I was conscious of was that I was wearing my boots, and I really liked those boots, and if my feet swelled up too much by the time I got to hospital, they would cut them off, and I wasn't having that. I sat up to remove them, but as soon as the boots came off, my ankles ballooned. It wasn't the cleverest thing to do. Max, Chris and Carolyn made me comfortable. By now, Richard Spillett had come down the incline with his wife, and between them all they made a nest for me out of blankets, and raised my feet. We were quite high up in the quarries so we had to wait a considerable time for the ambulance guys to arrive. It wasn't a massively easy place to get down from. There was some chat about exactly how they were going to do it and it seemed to take for ever for anyone to make a decision. When the ambulance crew finally got there, we had to make our own way down to the road as the terrain was too tricky for them.

Chris, Max, Sara, Spillett and Carolyn carried me down, literally in relays. Two of them linked arms and they carried me. It took them a long time to negotiate the inclines. Somehow, in amongst the howling pain, I kept it together. They finally got me to the road after a huge effort and handed me over to the ambulance guys. 'At last, the professionals,' I thought. The first thing the professionals did was bash my ankles against the ambulance door and it felt as though I'd just fallen off the bloody route again. They slid me into the back of the ambulance, Carolyn jumped in, and then they put me on gas and air to help with the throbbing, intolerable pain. It had an amazing, immediate effect, the pain suddenly easing off.

The ambulance took me to Bangor Hospital, and I was rushed into A&E and immediately taken through to X-ray. I must have looked slightly mad because I was sitting there with a big smile on my face as the rather attractive radiographer came in. 'What on earth have they given you?' she said. I didn't care; I was away with the fairies.

When the consultant appeared, both of them started to study the X-rays. I didn't like the silence. 'How do they look?' I asked, desperate to find out what the damage was. 'I've just sprained them, haven't I? I know it's probably a bad sprain but I'm going to Pakistan next week on this expedition . . .'

What with the effects of the gas and air wearing off, and the pain now coming back, a fear started to grow inside me that this was a pretty major thing, but I seemed to think I could talk my way out of it. 'Well, if they are broken, maybe it's just a hairline fracture and I can go to Pakistan anyway, because, you know, I can sit on the back of a donkey or something to get to Base Camp, because it is a really long walk in and it's going to take us two weeks to get there. That's going to be long enough, isn't it, long enough for my feet to heal?'

The consultant looked up from the X-rays and stared at me as if I was crazy, which I suppose I was a bit by that stage.

'No. You've smashed them. You have smashed your heel bones.' He showed me the X-rays, which made no sense to me at all. He pointed to the heel bones as if I should know what I was looking at and shook his head. 'I'm really sorry, you're not going anywhere. You've pulverised both of your heel bones.'

By this point I was utterly confused, bewildered and frightened. Not frightened about my injuries but frightened about not being able to climb. I was given all sorts of injections, put into a hospital bed and wheeled to a small ward of maybe eight beds. I had never been in hospital before.

Carolyn appeared, and then the Spilletts turned up, and Andy McNae – the guy that we had gone to meet who had all the sponsorship kit – and they were all hanging around the end of my bed. I remember being really anxious that no one should go anywhere near my feet; I didn't want anybody knocking them – maybe it was a throw-back to the ambulance men. I wanted them anywhere but the end of the bed. There was a Euro '96 match on that night. I remember Andy's big grin as he said, 'I've got to go. I want to see the footie.'

My world was spiralling out of control but everybody else, it seemed to me, was just carrying on as normal. They all disappeared for an evening in the pub, while I was left there not quite knowing what had happened or what to do. I kept thinking, 'It's going to be fine; bones heal, that's not an issue. It will be fine.' But then a wave of anxiety and despair washed over me, the dark realisation that things might not be fine. At this stage, I thought, 'Oh God, I suppose I had better contact my parents.'

On Sunday evening everyone had to go back home, leaving me completely on my own in a Welsh hospital. I didn't know anybody, I had no visitors, so I had no distractions from my thoughts. I'm a very positive person, but this was completely out of my control. Cracks were appearing as the reality of the situation started to sink in.

I lay there in bed, wondering how this had happened to me, what had I done wrong. How had I ended up here? With nothing to do but stare at the ceiling, waiting for Mum and Dad to ring, I thought back to home.

I was brought up in a small house in a corner of a farm field in a village in Buckinghamshire. My father was unemployed for much of my teenage years so we didn't have very much money, which meant my younger sister, Meredith, and I became very good at entertaining ourselves in and around the farm – she on the horses, me in the rivers and fields surrounding us. My father being very good at field craft, he was never happier than when he was outside in the fields or woods with me, passing on his knowledge of the wildlife around the farmland. I spent hours lying low, crawling through the undergrowth stalking a rabbit, or trying not to be noticed by the farmer in his tractor at the end of a field. My father knew the names of all the flora and fauna (although to my shame the names never stuck with me); he knew which had healing properties, which could be eaten or made into tea. Simply put, he instilled in me a love of the outdoors; he introduced me to walking the small hills and footpaths close to our home. Although we lived inside the M25 we were really blessed in having considerable open space around us, totally ideal for an adventurous-minded boy. My father also happened to be a Scout leader, so I became a Scout as soon as I was old enough, having progressed through the Cubs first.

Moel Siabod in Snowdonia was my first mountain, if you can call 872 metres a mountain. I was fifteen years old, one of the youngest there. I'd been selected to go to the World Scout Jamboree in Australia, to be held over a ten-day period over the New Year of 1987–8, and those of us who had been selected to represent the county of Buckinghamshire came together for a weekend up in North Wales. Part of the weekend was to climb Moel Siabod, which means 'shapely hill' in Welsh. It was raining most of the time, the terrain was hard, I was wearing all the wrong gear – a cagoule that was too long, a sodden pair of tracksuit bottoms and cotton socks inside my wet boots that gave me blisters – but I utterly loved it. When I got to the top I was king of the world. It was never really a case of being hooked there and then, but certainly something had bitten. The whole weekend gave me a huge sense of freedom. The hill-walking element was just one little part of a bigger adventure then, but it did appeal to my sense of competitiveness. Looking back now it's hard to believe that that humble hill sprouted such an obsession.

I started doing my own little adventures with a dear friend, Chris Lockyer, who lived down the hill from my family and also went to the Jamboree. We started taking ourselves off. We walked the Pembrokeshire footpath on our own, aged sixteen or seventeen, and we went up to Scotland, walked over Cairn Gorm and Ben Macdui, some 1,300-odd metres, dropping down to the Linn of Dee, a monster of a day. We were way out of our depth – seventeen-years-olds with no experience, and weather conditions nothing short of horrendous. Ben Macdui is infamous for a school disaster back in 1971: five school-children were killed when they became disorientated and got lost. It's a dangerous place with the weather changing constantly, so I guess we were lucky.

About the same time I went on a Venture Scout summer camp near Ashover in the Peak District. Back then, my idea of a great camp was to locate the biggest hill nearby, find the steepest route up it, strap on the biggest rucksack, and be the first up – sod everybody else. I must have been such a pain in the arse for anyone who didn't share the same outlook; luckily, Chris Lockyer saw things my way, so I always had a partner in crime. There I was, forging my way up at the front, a long line of people trailing behind me, wondering what the hell they were doing there: wasn't this meant to be fun? I didn't care, I loved it.

After one particularly gruelling two-day hike we were being picked up near Chee Dale, so we ended up walking through Water-cum-Jolly. This is a beautiful limestone valley with the river Wye bubbling away through it. It was a rare, wonderfully sunny day, and, as we wandered though the valley, we went underneath a cliff called Raven Tor, which is home to arguably some of Britain's hardest rock climbs, though I didn't know it at the time.

We got to the pick-up point a little bit early, so being seventeen we all hit the nearest shop to see if we could buy some beer. While the others attempted to pass themselves off as mature eighteen-year-olds, I found myself by the news rack, looking at the front cover of a climbing magazine. There was a photograph of a guy called Ben Moon. Ben had just climbed something called Hubble, which is considered even today to be one of the world's harder rock climbs; back then it was setting new standards by being the world's first 8C+ climb (it has since been upgraded to 9A because it is so hard). Completely unbeknown to me, I'd just walked underneath Hubble because it was on Raven Tor; I'd literally been about 20 metres away from where this now-iconic picture had been taken. The photo is taken from above, Ben had dreadlocks at the time, and he's pulling incredibly hard, with his muscles bulging. To the seventeen-year-old me he looked the coolest bloody thing known to mankind, with no big rucksack, no big boots, he was wearing Lycra, he had dreadlocks. He was dripping cool. I thought, 'I want some of that.'

Soon after that I was offered my first rock-climbing opportunity. Actually, it was more a case of me grabbing the bull by the horns. A guy called Andy Fowkes was in the same year as me at school in High Wycombe, but we didn't really know each other, being in different classes. It also did not help that at this time in my life I spent every spare minute playing hockey which I was mad keen on, and it had completely taken over my life. I knew that Andy climbed and I plucked up the courage one day and blurted out, 'I know you climb; can I come along sometime?' His reaction was great: 'Yes, sure. We go to Brunel University a couple of nights a week– why don't you come?' So that's what I did: I started climbing indoors. After a few weeks, he happened to mention he was thinking about going down to the south coast to do some outdoor climbs, and did I want to come? 'We can take my mum's car,' he added. So that weekend, as I was building up to my A levels, we jumped into Andy's mum's car, chucked all the camping and climbing kit in the boot, and drove down to Swanage in Dorset. Her car was an Astra SRi, which was pretty nippy, so needless to say we got stopped for speeding.

The weather was glorious on the morning of my first real climb. Andy did a couple of easy routes for us both to warm up, with me enthusiastically following him up. Then we got to an area called Subluminal, which sits on a platform perched above the waves. Standing underneath this steep limestone cliff, Andy asked if I wanted to give it a go first, or to lead the next climb, as climbers would say. I was chuffed. 'Can I?' Andy gave me all the dangly stuff that goes onto the harness – I had no idea what all this stuff was, or, least of all, what it was for, so Andy gave me a tutorial at the base of the cliff. 'You put it in the crack like this, and you get the karabiner and you clip that to there.' I tried to pay attention but the sun was warm, the sea was lapping gently against the shore below us, and I was itching to get started.

At last, I was off. The sun was glaring off the limestone, intensifying the heat as I began to climb. I found it relatively straightforward to start with, mainly because I'd been getting reasonably good on the indoor walls (which, like the limestone, are pretty steep) and I had a good base level of fitness from all my hockey.

I got about a third of the way up, and I started thinking, 'I better get some of this paraphernalia I'm carrying on my harness into the rock and secure myself to the cliff in case I fall.' I managed to get the tips of my toes onto some relatively comfortable ledges jutting out of the steep cliff, which gave me enough stability to try to fix some gear. I wiggled a nut into a crack and pulled it a little bit, not too hard as I was scared that it may pull out and unbalance me; it stayed fast. I took the quickdraw (a short webbing sling with two karabiners attached) and I clipped that to it.

If you're not used to doing all this sort of thing, it takes a wee while and when you're 30 or 40 feet up a cliff face it feels somewhat precarious. Then you've got to pull the rope up and clip it into the bottom karabiner of the quickdraw. On that first climb, I almost certainly dropped the rope two or three times while trying to clip it into the karabiner; when you fluff the clip like that you have to hang on that little bit longer to repeat the process, burning up valuable strength. As you get more experienced, you find better, less stressful body positions in which to stand, and making the clip becomes more fluid until it becomes second nature. That day I finally got it clipped, breathing a silent sigh of relief, and climbed higher.

The moves didn't feel hard. I carefully picked my way up the rock, slowly unlocking the puzzle that the rock presented, trying various options before committing and gaining more height. The whole process felt wonderful, until, all of a sudden, the realisation that I was a good 50 feet up flooded into my mind. I hadn't even thought about the height – that I was hanging off a cliff higher than the roof at home – until that moment. I do worry about heights, everyone does; I think it's a healthy fear to have, it means we're always careful.

'God, this is a bit naughty,' I thought, looking at the sharp rocks underneath. 'If I fall off here, I might hit the deck.'

All of a sudden, the wonderful feeling that the day had seduced me with evaporated and it felt a little bit serious. Deciding to place some more gear in the rock, I tried to take my hand out of the crack to get the nuts off my harness. Every time I did so, I found myself 'barn-dooring' – swinging out into the air. I was naturally off balance by the way I had my feet and my hands in the crack, so every time I reached for anything I swung out and almost toppled off. I got scared, really scared. 'Shit, if I fell off now this would be my first and last attempt at a lead climb.' I felt that I didn't have the strength to hold on and get the nuts off my harness, let alone select the right size, wiggle it into the crack, clip a karabiner to the nut and finally pull up the rope and clip this into the krab. Instead, I decided to do what seemed to be the next best thing: make for the top. In my mind the top represented safety. I knew I couldn't retrace my steps down so I looked up and thought, 'Just climb.'

I figured I'd done the hard stuff (what this was based on I'll never know) so now it was just a case of 'don't fall off.' Simple as that: just don't fall off, don't let go. The top of the crag slowly shelved out and I ended up scrambling up the last little bit, pulling the rope up behind me. A few metres back from the edge there was a big iron spike that had been bashed into the rock to use as a belay. I looked over my shoulder. What a view! I was dripping in sweat – partly from the heat of the sun, partly from the physical effort, and partly from the stress of the whole affair – but a feeling of euphoria was also washing over me. The sun was up high, the sea glittering, it was idyllic, a fabulous day. I pulled myself up the last little bit, grabbed the iron spike and every ounce of energy evaporated through my fingers and down into this spike. I just collapsed, like a big jelly man.

Quickly pulling myself together I realised I had no idea how to secure the rope to the spike. I was embarrassed about what

Andy, the expert, might say, as it seemed a rather schoolboy thing not to be able to do. In the end, I simply looped the rope around the spike a few times and pulled it tight, hoping it would hold, and gingerly walked back to the edge. I was 75 feet up, and I'd climbed the last 20 or 30 feet with no gear due to my incompetence. I sat down with my legs over the edge and shouted to Andy that he could start to climb. I looked out to sea, the sun glistening on the water, the boats bobbing on the perfect blue. My muscles sang with a dull ache of contentment; my breathing finally calmed down. I thought this was the best thing ever. I couldn't think of anywhere I would rather be. I sat there, my fingers bleeding, sweat dripping from my chin while my mouth was so dry I could hardly swallow, yet, surveying the scene, for a brief moment it was perfection. I was now a rock climber. I saw myself standing shoulder to shoulder with Ben Moon. I was one of the clan.

Andy quickly appeared over the edge of the cliff, a little too quickly for my ego, looking annoyingly cool and calm, with his trademark headband. He had these big golden curls and always seemed in control. We used to call him Goldilocks. 'Wow, good climb. Really, well done – that was really good.' Then he grinned. 'You could have put more gear in, though. I was looking up thinking, "Jesus, what am I going to tell his mother?" I was willing you to put some more gear in, and you didn't, you just kept going. Wow, you know, that was pretty way out there,' he said.

In those early days I was certainly not technically the best climber (I never have been) but I was bold. I'd like to think it was a calculated boldness but if I'm honest sometimes I was too reckless, bordering on stupid. What I did that day at Subluminal was reckless. In mitigation, I didn't know any better: is that recklessness or just naivety? But at that moment, I sat there with

Andy with a feeling of utter contentment, basking in his praise, which to me meant the world.

That, my first ever lead, was the start. I owe a lot to Andy Fowkes for allowing me up first that afternoon. Andy and I climbed a good deal together after that, in the Peak District and North Wales. My first time to Llanberis was with Andy. Later I did my first Alpine and Himalayan trips with him.

As soon as I finished my A levels I headed away with Andy, his brother Roger and Chris Lockyer to Chamonix in the French Alps for a month or so. We drove down in Andy's dad's car this time, an old Hillman Imp that was a lot slower than his mum's, and stayed on the infamous Pierre's Field – which used to be called Snell's Field – a somewhat legendary location to Brit climbers. It was the last year that it was open as it was closed down as a health hazard after that – nothing to do with us, honest.

We thought we were laying siege to the Alps that season but, of course, what we were doing was so minor. We actually had no idea what was going on in the Alps, its standards were way, way, way beyond anything we could have comprehended at the time. But it didn't matter; we were there. We were The Boys. Well, we *thought* we were The Boys, but what we really were was a complete catalogue of cock-ups. Just how green we were was unbelievable.

We planned to climb up the Forbes Arête. We were going to do this on a budget by walking up the valley and not paying to use the cable car. I had bought myself some salopettes (high-waisted trousers with braces) in a jumble sale for a £1 back home. My £1 salopettes were padded – skier's salopettes – and were nothing like those used for climbing. The Alps in summertime are really hot and here I was wandering around in a pair of insulated salopettes . . . How I didn't sweat to death I don't know.

The Forbes Arête is a classic climb on the Aiguille du Chardonnet. I've guided it subsequently with Sir Ranulph Fiennes – it's such a beautiful climb. All four of us were walking up with big rucksacks, aiming to bivouac when we got somewhere near the glacier as we didn't have the money for the hut. We were lying out at our bivy spot; the sun was beginning to go down, and to my salopette-clad relief it was finally cooling down just a bit. Andy let out a big theatrical yawn . . . and his mouth locked open. He sat up, panic-stricken, speaking like a ventriloquist's dummy with his mouth wide open and only his tongue moving. 'I can't crose ma mouf! I can't crose ma mouf!' We were rolling around laughing, thinking it was hilarious. Then we realised he was actually in real pain and he really couldn't close his mouth. It was locked wide open. It dawned on us that we had no idea what to do. Eventually we walked down to the hut and the hut guardian called the rescue services and out came a chopper to pick Andy up, carting him down to hospital, and the three of us were, like, 'Well, shit. What do we do now? He's the only one that can drive.'

We walked back down the mountainside and, although Roger couldn't legally drive, he knew how to, so off we went to find Fowkes in hospital. By now it was dark and well into the evening. It transpired that Andy was sorted pretty quickly under anaesthetic, but the episode set the tone for the rest of the trip. If it *could* happen, it *would* happen and *did* happen.

We went up to the Aiguille du Midi cable car, which rises to 3,800 metres; it's one of the highest lifts in Europe, climbing more than 2,700 metres up towards Mont Blanc from the valley floor and giving access to a wealth of fabulous climbing. It was so expensive we decided to do the trip up on the cable car only once, taking our massive rucksacks with as much food as we can carry. We planned to stay up there, dig a snow cave and spend the week climbing, in an attempt to justify the vast cost of the cable car. In retrospect it was a crazy plan – nobody digs a snow cave, everyone just puts a tent up. But remember, we were The Boys.

Coming out of the top of Aiguille du Midi cable car, you walk down a ridge that defines the glacial basin; it's pretty spectacular, and in wintertime there's always a handrail and a path dug into the ridge making it accessible for skiers. But in summertime, it's a knife-edge. Down one side there is a 1,200-metre drop straight down the sheer north face towards Chamonix. On the other side it's another sheer drop of a mere 300 metres or so. I say sheer; it's probably not quite that but it's certainly very steep, and if you're unlucky enough to fall off you'd go the distance, so it might just as well be.

Our idea had been to spend all week up there, and it worked out pretty well for the first few days . . . until we ran short of food. I don't how it happened, but I found myself volunteered to go back down to replenish the camp with supplies. We pooled our cash, and I went down on the cable car to get the stuff from the supermarket. So far so good, until near the top of the mountain on my return journey, when it became really stormy, and the car just stopped and hung there, swinging as if it was about to tumble headlong into the valley. This went on for what seemed like an age, and I began to feel really dizzy until – without warning – I passed out. I fainted in the cable car. It was really busy, packed with people, and when I came to I was lying on the floor of the cable car with a gaggle of people peering over me speaking French, and I don't speak a word of French. They sat me up and started offering me peanuts, which I worked out are meant to be good in such situations. Eventually the car finished the journey and with great relief we all disembarked. I still felt a bit weak and wobbly, but more that that I was immensely embarrassed by what had happened, so I made light of it, and smiled, telling my concerned fellow-passengers that I was okay.

I rushed out onto the arête with a rucksack on my back and a full shopping bag in each hand, and for some reason – to this day I don't know why – I decided I didn't need crampons on, even though the arête was covered in snow and ice. If I'm honest, I think I probably left the crampons behind deliberately so I could get more food in the rucksack, but what happened next probably put that thought out of my mind. I took about four steps and I slipped, and started to head down the side where you end up – many painful and scary seconds later – a couple of thousand metres below with no stops in between. I didn't have an ice axe, I didn't have crampons on, I didn't have a harness. I started sliding and instinctively let go of the bags, desperately digging into the snow with my hands and heels. Luckily, I stopped before I accelerated too fast and travelled beyond the point of no return. So there I was, perched a few feet down from the edge, looking between my feet at a humungous drop. I very gingerly pushed myself up and, because the snow had been in the sun all day, it was soft enough for me to slowly claw my way back up the slope. When I got back to the snow hole, the boys were there, hungry and momentarily jubilant that their saviour has returned. Their cheerful faces turned quickly to confusion when they saw I'd returned with only half the food expected. Andy looked at me. 'So where's the rest of the food?' By now, of course, it was halfway down the north face of Aiguille du Midi, some poor climber completely showered in saucissons and cheese. 'Mate, you will not believe what just happened . . .'

The whole episode was just typical of that first season; we were a liability: starting too late, underestimating the difficulties, overestimating our ability. I was climbing with Chris Lockyer one day, we were on the north face of Mont Blanc du Tacul; having never ice climbed before, we hadn't got a clue. We had these ice screw things but we had no idea how they worked. We didn't even own a rope, so we had borrowed one from a friend before we left the UK. Chris was climbing while I was anchored to the face and letting out the rope (which was the standard 50 metres), and as he climbed I shouted up that he only had a few metres of rope left and he needed to stop. Only he didn't stop, but carried on moving up. I kept screaming at him, 'What's going on?' Frantically, I untied my anchor and started moving up as well until he finally found a belay and made himself safe. I got up to him and I started tearing strips off him.

'What do you think you're doing?'

'I was so scared. I've got these ice screws, I couldn't get any in, the ice was too hard and the screws suck. I was shitting myself so I just kept going until I found this rock.' He'd clipped himself to it and was hanging on, gibbering away to himself.

I look back on that trip now and it's bathed in a wonderful rosy glow. It was a brilliant time, utterly brilliant. We were learning by our mistakes, which, despite all those self-help guides, is so *not* the way to do it. It really isn't. But we were immortal, young and carefree, everything was so simple.

Eventually, Chris and I had to leave to go to the Ardennes because we were doing our Duke of Edinburgh Gold Expedition. When we arrived, we discovered that we were expected to troop around wooded hillsides with big rucksacks for four or five days for what we perceived to be no apparent reason. It felt so beneath us all of a sudden. Having to jump through hoops, filling in forms, writing out route descriptions and adding in the timings. Didn't they know we'd just been shoulder to shoulder with Ben Moon?

Not that Ben Moon ever climbed there; he had no interest in Alpine climbing.

I was in Bangor Hospital for four or five days before the decision was taken to transport me to Wexham Park Hospital, which was closer to home and had better facilities. By then I was feeling pretty low but the two ambulance drivers who transported me were great, doing everything they could to make me laugh as well as be comfortable.

We arrived at Wexham Park Hospital and soon a very arrogant consultant appeared with a registrar. He was like Sir Lancelot Spratt in that 1950s film *Doctor in the House*. He bustled in with an air of self-importance. He was quite a small man (shades of a Napoleon complex maybe?), which made me giggle, because the registrar was a huge bear of a man, maybe 6 foot 4 or 5. They were like Little and Large. The consultant looked through my notes and X-rays.

'Well, your feet are pretty bad, so what we're going to do is have you in for surgery, and try to rebuild them.'

'Great. That's great news. How long before I can climb?'

'What do you mean?'

'When will I be able to climb? Soon?'

He looked like someone who wanted to chuckle in a benign way at this foolish patient, but didn't know how. 'Climb? No. You're never going to climb again. You're not going to run. You won't be able to walk across rough ground, and the chances are you will walk with a stick for the rest of your life.'

I couldn't take in the brutality of what he was saying. I literally couldn't make sense of it. My whole life revolved around climbing. I had found my purpose, my passion. It wasn't enough to say I was in love with it – at the time it felt as though it was what I was born to do.

And now somebody was telling me it was all over. In a mere thirty seconds this man had torn away everything that had meaning to me, crushing my life and throwing it into the bin, in such an offhand way, as though he was telling me I had a bad cold. He made no attempt to see things from my point of view. That was it, it was so final. I was stunned. Clearly unable to think of anything to say, he simply left. The door shut behind him and I was left in silence yet again. This empty room, with an empty human being in it. My future, my life had just walked out of the door with that thoughtless man. The enormity of what he had said hit me, and the walls started to close in, closer and closer. I couldn't breathe. Then I burst into tears. Huge sobs of despair. I just didn't know what to do. I was utterly destroyed. This man, this arrogant, insensitive man, had the audacity to come in and tell me that life as I knew it was over, then walk out leaving me to get on with it.

After fifteen or twenty minutes, I started to pull myself together and tried to phone my parents, but, typically, I couldn't get through.

Then a small act of kindness happened that I will always remember. The registrar came back into my room and apologised for his boss's manner. Some time later, when I mentioned it to people, I discovered that Sara Spillett, who had been there when I had the accident, knew the registrar from when she had trained as a physio in London. At the time he was at St Mary's medical school and their paths had crossed. It transpired that he had made this amazing decision in life: he had a pro rugby career ahead of him but had to make a choice – rugby or medicine – because he couldn't balance the two, and he had chosen medicine. Maybe that's why he understood; maybe that was why he came back, and said, 'You know, don't take that to heart. Don't listen to that man. It is what it is, and it is what you make of it.' I don't think I saw him again. He might have made a good rugby player, for all I know, but I have little doubt that he is an exceptional doctor.

Maybe that was a turning point, one of those times in life when things had gone right. Here was someone trying to help. Someone trying to understand. Someone with a level of empathy. I remembered back to the last time I'd been at school in High Wycombe, when I'd returned home after that Duke of Edinburgh trip to the Ardennes, and had gone to collect my A-level results. I had walked up Marlow Hill, something I had done every single day of my school life, only now I was doing it for the last time. It was about three o'clock in the afternoon; I was the only one there as everyone had picked up their A-level results first thing in the morning. I followed the signs – *A-level results this way* – and found the boards and the right form group, then scanned down the list of names: *Ahmed, Bignal, Burrows, Carter, Cool...* I followed the line across.

It was a big thing. If I didn't get the right grades, all of a sudden life would be derailed. I had been offered a place at Leeds University. It was another glorious summer day with the sun belting down. I'd come back from the wilderness of the Alps, and now I was surrounded by the red bricks of John Hampden Grammar School. I was looking at the board and in a rush I realised school was all over, finished, for ever. I know I'm strange and unusual, but I loved school, I truly did – I realised that even back then – but now there I was standing looking at my future and wishing my past would never end.

The headmaster strode out of the school to find me standing alone in front of the board. We were all terrified of Mr McTavish, an ex-Royal Marine who ruled the place with an iron rod. As usual he was smoking a pipe, puffing smoke out like a bonfire. I stood to attention. 'Did you get what you need?' he said gently.

I was shocked, 'Oh, hello, sir. Yes, sir, yes, I did, thank you.'

'So, what's next?'

'I'm off to Leeds, sir. To Leeds University. To study Geology.'

'Good luck,' he said, smiling sweetly as he shook my hand. That was the last time I ever saw Mr McTavish, a man who played such a pivotal role in my younger days, and the last time I walked through the school gates for nearly twenty years.

I spent three weeks in Wexham Park Hospital. Carolyn was great, and made the effort to come to see me once or twice a week from London. My somewhat arrogant consultant did the first operation that I needed, and as the anaesthetic wore off and I came round, the pain in my left foot was unbelievable. Clawing at the side of the bed in agony I called one of the nurses over. 'Jesus Christ, why does that one hurt like hell but the other one doesn't?'

'Oh,' she said, 'it took him so long to operate on the first one, he hasn't even looked at the second one.'

The consultant came in a little later, so I asked him what was happening with my right foot. Without missing a beat he replied, 'Oh, I'm not going to touch that one. It's too difficult. The left one was tough enough.'

I was moved to a different ward while everyone decided on the best course of action. Opposite my bed was a roofer, quite a young guy, who had fallen off scaffolding and done the same thing as me, broken his calcaneus. Every day his girlfriend would bring him a four-pack of beer and, once all the doctors' rounds were over, she'd wheel him outside. I used to join them, wheeling myself into the hospital grounds. We'd break open the beer in the afternoon sunshine; by then it had shaped up into a beautiful summer.

One afternoon I decided I had to break out. Carolyn and some of her friends came and they helped to wheel me and my new chum down to the pub. It was probably completely out of order, against all the rules, but getting out of the hospital was a real treat. I had five or six pints of Guinness, and I was more than a little bit inebriated. When I sneaked back onto the ward – it's tricky to sneak about in a wheelchair, but we thought we'd got away with it – I noticed a big sign hanging on the wall behind my bed: *Nil by mouth*, which meant I was due to have an operation the next day. I didn't know anything about any operation, but as it didn't seem sensible to ask questions when I was breathing alcohol over anyone I spoke to, I didn't know what to do so I just pretended nothing had happened and waited for the consultant to come round and tell me what was going to be done the following day.

The next morning I woke up with a horrible hangover, my tongue stuck to the roof of my mouth. I called over a nurse. 'Do you know what time I'm due in theatre? When's the operation?'

'It could be anytime today,' she said.

'Can I have something to drink please?'

'You can't have anything now, in case they come for you. If they're not here later in the day it should be okay. Let's wait until about three o'clock this afternoon and see what's happening.'

Three o'clock came around and by this time I was in a mess, totally dehydrated and feeling terrible. Then the nursing roster changed, and one of the nurses whom I knew well and got on with appeared. I called her over. 'Do you know when I'm going in for the operation today?'

'An operation? Really, you sure?' Off she went and looked at the operation list. 'You're not down on the roster.' Then it dawned on me. Clearly one of the nurses with a warped – in my view, anyway – sense of humour had put the sign up when she'd guessed I'd bunked off down the pub. How I laughed.

Meanwhile, I had been doing some research. Carolyn's sister was a doctor, so she did a little scouting around the doctors'

Who's Who. It turned out that in Oxford there was a guy called Bob Handley, and he was meant to be an orthopaedic genius. As it happened, the hospital was on the same track and I found out that the wheels were already in motion to get me transported to Oxford, to the John Radcliffe where Handley worked. Bob Handley is still considered one of the very best, if not *the* best, orthopaedic surgeons in the country.

The first time I met Bob Handley was one of the most memorable, and arguably most important, encounters of my life. I was stuck in an isolation room because I was being screened for MRSA, which was a big thing in those days, and they were waiting for the test results to come back. My legs were hoisted in the air, attached to all sorts of medieval metal work with bits of rope and pullies, so I was virtually unable to move. All of a sudden this scruffy, tired-looking bloke comes whisking in, sits at the end of my bed, grabs my notes and announces: 'Right, let's have a look.' No introduction, nothing. Suddenly he looks up from the notes, a little concerned.

'You're being screened, aren't you?'

'Er, yes.'

'Oh, bugger it. I should have scrubbed up before coming in.' And then he starts to laugh.

I have no idea who this guy is. 'Sorry, who exactly are you?'

'Oh, I'm Bob Handley, I'm your consultant. We're going to have you in for surgery tomorrow. This screening thing, you probably haven't got the hospital bug, but maybe best we just keep this between the two of us, though. I've never been here, okay?' He laughed again.

'What about my heel?'

'Yes, doesn't look good, does it? What I'm going to do is rebuild it so you can wear a normal shoe, how about that?' By now I'm not sure what I've got sat here at the end of my bed.

'Sorry, but that sounds a bit crap, actually. What about my climbing?'

'Well, that's down to you. Depends how hard you want to work afterwards. My job's to rebuild your foot, after that it's down to you. See you in the morning.' And off he went.

For the first time in weeks there was hope. It was brilliant, absolutely brilliant.

CHAPTER 2
LIVING ON FUMES

My time in the John Radcliffe was bearable, compared to my initial experiences following the accident, thanks to the utter brilliance of the staff. The location helped, as well, because it's not that far – straight up the A40 – from where I grew up, so my parents popped up every few days and Andy Fowkes came up once a week or so.

The Olympics had started, and because of the time lag from Atlanta, I used to watch the Games late at night on a television I'd stuck at the end of my bed. Some of the nurses watched with me when it was quiet, sitting at the end of the bed and following the action. It was curiously domestic and normal, and, if I ignored my feet, really nice. I don't remember any of their names, but I think it would be lovely to tell them how grateful I am for what they did for me.

Bob Handley did as he promised. No fuss. He just got on with it and rebuilt my right heel – the heel that not long before I'd been told was just too smashed to do anything with. By the time the operations he carried out were over, the ends of my legs were like a Meccano box. When they showed me the X-rays you couldn't see any bones, just a cat's cradle of metal. It made me feel a little sick.

They put on these removable fibreglass casts, which were fabulous: one red and one blue. I only had to wear them when I was travelling or going anywhere, so most of the time the plaster casts were off, and I had a back splint on. Suddenly I could get about a little in a wheelchair, which, having not left bed for weeks, I became obsessed with. But what I really wanted was to go home and this became a focused mission. The occupational therapist was not too keen on that plan; she wanted to know what home was like, for obvious reasons – it would make a difference if it was four-storey house or a bungalow.

'It doesn't matter what home is like,' I told her. 'I'll move back in with my parents. I will cope; it's what the Cools do very well. They cope. You don't understand. Just let me out, just get rid of me.'

Most of the time it was simply excruciatingly boring. And things started to get to me. There was a guy in the room next door called Gary, who was suffering from some form of schizophrenia. All day long, he'd be calling the nurse: 'Nurse! Nurse! Nurse! Nurse!' Hour after hour, day after day: 'Nurse! Nurse! Nurse!'

The nurses would come running over. 'What is it, Gary?'

'Nurse, sit me up!'

They would sit him up and two minutes later: 'Nurse! Nurse! Nurse! Lie me down.' They'd go in and lie him down. 'Nurse! Nurse! Nurse! Nurse!'

The nurses were saints. They were so kind to all of us, particularly me it seemed. When the night shift was sending out for pizza or some other takeaway, they'd always ask me if they could get me anything – they were wonderful. It was the small things like that that made me feel normal.

After what felt like a lifetime, my father came to pick me up.

It was such a blessing to be let out; like being born again. Reality set in immediately, however, when we found there were no wheelchairs available that I could take home. Eventually a really old antique wheelchair was found in a cupboard somewhere, the dust was blown off it, and I was wheeled out. We got to the car and I realised that I hadn't the faintest idea how to get from the chair into the car without using my feet – I'd been expressly forbidden from putting any weight on my feet at all.

'How do I get in the car?'

We tried various things until it became clear that I was going to have to hoist myself into place. Inevitably I put pressure on my feet, which hurt. By this stage I was turning into Mr Bean, hanging onto the outside of the car while Dad tried to lift me in. My feet were throbbing with pain. Eventually I got onto the back seat of the car, Dad having moved the front seat as far forward as it would go. The door shut and I found myself lying flat on the back seat of the car while my Dad was threading the wheelchair into the boot. I burst into tears again. I guess it was the relief of finally being out, being allowed home; it was overwhelming.

I often wonder how my parents coped during those weeks; my father was out of work at the time and would sometimes visit during the day on his own. I wish now, as his own health is eaten away by dementia, that I could remember more of the conversations that we had together, just the two of us; sadly I can't. What I can remember is him lifting me into the car that day. Being a father myself now, and having the joy of holding my own children, I'm curious to know how he felt lifting his grown yet helpless son into the car. Personally I remember being enveloped in his arms for the first time in many, many years and feeling a huge sense of security, a feeling that is hard to explain and one that, regretfully, I have never experienced since.

I was non-weight-bearing for three and a half months, but I had my freedom back. I started to crawl around like Guy the gorilla, using a pair of kneepads that floor tilers wear, developing big calluses on my knuckles from pushing myself around everywhere. My parents had a tiny wooden bungalow and I spent all summer outside in the garden, enjoying the sunshine and trying to keep myself busy. I was always pushing it. I didn't listen particularly well to the doctors who told me to take it easy. A couple of days after coming out of hospital, Carolyn drove across and picked me up, and took me to Belgo for mussels and frites, washed down with quality Belgian beer amid a bunch of friends. It was too soon, and I shouldn't have done it. We got back to Carolyn's house and my dressings were covered in blood, my feet throbbing with pain. All the wounds were opening up. I had been an idiot.

Then my left foot got infected. Bob Handley had stitched up my right foot with standard stitches, but my left foot had been done with dissolving stitches – or they were supposed to be dissolving, at any rate. When it was time to take the stitches out of my right foot it was a quick snip, snip, snip, pull, pull, pull and job done. I pointed out to the nurse that there seemed to be something that looked like fishing line sticking out of my left heel.

'Right, well, we'll just pull that bit out. The rest will have dissolved inside.'

She gripped the end with some evil-looking pliers and pulled. All that happened was the skin along the side of my foot rucked up tight. She pulled again and the same thing happened, only this time painfully.

'That's odd,' she said, and yanked it a bit harder – this time it really hurt. 'Well, we'll just leave it a little bit. The stitches probably need a little longer to dissolve. Every now and then, just play with that loose end yourself, and it will dissolve eventually and you can pull the remaining bit out.'

A couple of weeks went by and nothing happened, until I went for my check-up at the Radcliffe. This really big, jolly chap looked at all the X-rays. 'It's all healing very nicely,' he said. 'What's that stitch still doing there? Did the district nurse not take out? Right, let's have you on the bed and we'll sort it out.'

'No, you're not going to be able to pull it out.'

'Don't worry; it will have all dissolved inside.'

'Do you know, I don't think it has,' I said, but he was quite certain he could sort it out. He took some surgical tweezers, big bloody things, gripped the end and pulled.

Sharp intake of breath. 'That kind of hurts,' I said.

'I just need to pull it a bit harder,' he replied.

So he put his knee on my calf and heaved really hard, and nothing came out apart from a howl of pain from me. By now the penny had dropped. 'Ah, it hasn't dissolved.'

I'm biting the pillow with pain, thinking, 'I did tell you that a few minutes ago.'

The long and short of it was that my left foot got badly infected because the stitches hadn't dissolved. It was a bad batch or something. So I had to go back into hospital for Bob Handley to operate again to pull out the infected stitches and chop out some nasty tissue. It was not an easy job as he had to open up my foot again. This time I opted for an epidural rather than a full anaesthetic. Naively, I thought, 'If I have an epidural, I'll be able to watch.' Everything went numb from the waist down, which was quite spooky, and I got carted into surgery, excited at the prospect of seeing them hacking away at my foot. But Bob Handley was having none of that and made the theatre staff put a screen up so I couldn't see what was going on. I was really disappointed. 'Can't I watch?'

'No, because you may go into shock from what you see. It's not pretty and it's your foot.'

There was a junior doctor by my shoulder asking questions, just making sure I was okay, ready to alert Bob Handley and the anaesthetist if I showed any signs of being able to feel what was going on. To keep me distracted, he asked me how I'd bashed up my feet. So I started telling him the story.

'Oh, my son climbs,' said the consultant who was assisting Bob Handley. 'Where were you?' So I explained a little bit.

'What route is that, what grade?'

'An E5.'

At this point, Bob raised an eyebrow, and his right-hand man explained. 'An E5, that's quite hard. You and I wouldn't be able to get off the ground on an E5, Bob.' I could see Bob's mischievous smile, which I had come to love over the weeks – well, I say that, I could see the corners of his mask rise in what I knew to be his mischievous smile. He looked at the junior doctor, and then at me. 'No,' he said, 'but I bet I could fall off one just as well as Kenton!'

I was in a wheelchair all through that long summer of '96, and then, as I could start to put weight on my feet, they tried to give me a Zimmer frame. I was twenty-two years old at this stage – there was no way was I going to hobble around as if I was in my dotage – so I settled for two crutches instead. Yet again my pig-headedness made things harder for me, since crutches don't work particularly well when you've got *two* bad feet. With one bad foot the crutches can take the weight from the bad foot and then you move forward with the other. With two bad feet there is nowhere to put the weight down. However, I figured out a way of moving. I would put the crutches in front of me, then very carefully and very slowly I'd hobble towards them, and, as the crutches would get closer, I'd jump one crutch forward and then the other, before once again hobbling towards them. It was not ideal, but I managed, albeit incredibly slowly and somewhat unsteadily.

Of course, I started climbing again as soon as I could, even when I was still in the wheelchair. I'd started wheeling myself outside to the garden table at home and pushing myself up, with my hands on the tabletop and standing on my feet. Often I would take one hand off, and then both hands, just for a moment, and put them back, and then do it again for a little longer until my feet started to hurt. The first time I did this was strangely scary, because although deep down I knew nothing serious would happen, I still had visions of seriously damaging the bones. I almost certainly shouldn't have been doing this so early in my recovery but I wanted to prove to myself that I could stand.

I wanted to go one step further, though. There is a very good indoor climbing wall under the Westway in London. Now it is covered from the elements, but back in 1996 it was an outdoor concrete ramp, built so that wheelchair users could be hoisted up, while the steep underside was used by climbers – so steep that I hardly had to use my feet at all. I'd be trundled to the bottom in my wheelchair and from there I could pull myself straight onto the wall, hauling myself upwards, occasionally dabbing my feet gingerly onto the wall. It was a huge breakthrough for me, mentally as well as physically.

With the crutches I was determined to push on, even against all the best advice. I wanted to go up to London to see some friends and I persuaded my mother to drop me off at West Ruislip tube station. There's no lift down to the platform at West Ruislip station, so there I was, hanging on to the banister, trying to keep hold of my crutches, and figuring out how to get down the steps. It was a painful process, limping down each step slowly; it took me so long that at least two, possibly three trains left in the time it took me to descend the twenty-five steps. All the way down I had a nagging feeling that I was being watched. Eventually I manage to creep down and throw myself onto a Central Line train but not before glancing up to see my mother walking away from the top of the stairs. She had stayed to make sure that I was okay, yet, knowing my stubbornness, she had allowed me to struggle down on my own. It was incredibly sweet of her.

I had to get off the tube at Notting Hill, and that's when the trouble really started. I managed to get off okay, by treating the gap between the platform and the train like a crevasse. I hobbled along the platform so slowly that another two or three trains came and went while I tried to make my way to the exit. There's no lift at Notting Hill, but there is an escalator.

Ah, the escalator. How the hell do I get on that?

The only way I could move was by putting a crutch in front of me, then the other next to it, so I could start my shuffle, but I could see that as soon as I put a crutch down, it was going to be whisked onto the escalator and moved away from me. I stood there while more trains came and went, disgorging their passengers who beetled onto the escalator and away. No one gave me a second glance. In the end, I plucked up the courage. I waited for the next train to come and go so there was no one around, then I made my way forward. I put one crutch on the escalator, it did exactly what I thought it was going to do: it moved up. But as it moved up, my shoulder rotated around, meaning that I fell over and I found myself lying on the escalator, with my rucksack luckily underneath me. There was still no one around and I began to wonder what would happen when I reach the top. 'It will probably eat me,' I thought, 'and that'll be the end of that.'

When I did get to the top, I bumped around as I was pushed forward. Eventually I crawled off the escalator, but I could not find a way of standing up. I needed a table or a chair to grab, or somebody there to help. Meanwhile, another train had arrived, and people started coming off the escalator with me lying in front of them with two crutches and a rucksack. 'Someone will do something,' I thought, but almost unbelievably they just walked around me. No one offered to help. Not a soul. I didn't have the wit, or possibly I was too embarrassed to ask someone, but then again they could see I needed help without me broadcasting the fact. They could clearly see I was in distress, that I wasn't a drunk or a vagrant; that said, even if I was a drunk or a vagrant it shouldn't have made any difference.

While I was in a wheelchair, or on crutches, I received some of the most generous acts of kindness, with people going out of their way to help me; equally, I was left on the floor of a tube station with not one person even asking if I was okay. And people wonder why I prefer mountains to cities.

Eventually I managed to hoist myself to my feet and finally get where I was going. What should have been a relatively quick and easy journey felt nothing short of an epic struggle that left me exhausted, but I was mobile and this felt fabulous.

I had taken Bob Handley's remark to heart. He had kept his side of the bargain to rebuild my feet, now it was up to me. I threw myself into physiotherapy, particularly hydro sessions. I'd come out of the changing room in a wheelchair and get hoisted up and dumped in the hydro pool, and I'd start walking. Length, after length, after length. In between, against the physio's advice, I would do big weights sessions and parallel bar work.

Mike Austin, a friend of mine who was off to work for the British Antarctic Survey, came to visit when I was working out one day. At the end of the session he called me back to the bars; he'd noticed I was not making much effort. The bars were soul-destroying; I didn't seem to be getting anywhere. 'Walk towards me,' Mike said. I wanted to prove to him that I could do it. I was willing every fibre in my body to move, but I simply couldn't do it, I just couldn't take a step – I was literally having to re-learn to walk. Every bit of my body was tensed up, I tried to take a step and I fell forward, grabbing the bars. But I had an incentive now, someone else pulling for me. So I tried doing it again and again and again. Finally, I took about four steps. Actually, they weren't so much steps as a controlled fall – I literally fell into Mike's arms. But he held me tight in a bear hug and we both burst into tears.

That was my first step on the road to recovery. Nobody in the medical teams – except for one or two like Bob Handley and my first physio, Kathrine Livingston – really got it. I didn't want to walk again. I wanted to climb again.

Bob Handley is still head of orthopaedics at the John Radcliffe. Provided there's some sort of postal system available, I have tried to send him a card from just about every expedition I've been on since that time. I've no idea if he has ever received them. I'd like to think that he has.

CHAPTER 3
ALPINE ADVENTURES

The first real climbing I did after the accident was with my friend Alun Powell, and it was an attempt to complete a climb we'd tried a couple of years before.

Al was at Leeds at the same time as I was, and I'd never met a character like him before. He had this mullet – long hair at the back and short on top – it looked terrible; he made his own clothes; he was a vegan, and had been a hunt saboteur. He was also a really talented climber and a phenomenal fell runner.

We had been on a disastrous trip to the Alps in the winter of '94 or '95, together with Rich Cross and Willy Edwards. We went down to the Ecrin, in the southern part of the French Alps, as Al had spied a very strong, unclimbed line on L'Olan. It needed to be climbed in winter, because the line would be safer with solid ice rather than the rotten rock that the area is famed for.

That whole trip turned into an utter debacle from the start. It was hilarious. We'd got maybe three hours into France when Al's little combi van broke down. The four of us were squeezed in with all the kit, and we'd broken down just off the motorway near Laon. We'd been driving down without using motorways in order to save money on the tolls – mad!

What do you do when you break down? Call the AA. Except we didn't belong to the AA, or to anyone else, for that matter. So we sat there wondering what to do. Eventually, the four jolly climbers came up with the plan: Al would hitch back to the UK, buy some insurance, then hitch back to the van, and then we would call the AA and *voilà*! Brilliant: the brains trust triumphs again.

The plan was for Al to leave first thing in the morning, so we decided to cook a meal in the back of the van using the hanging gas stove we used for climbing and sleep in the car as best we could. Drawing the short straw, I got the two front seats, which no matter how I wedged myself in were deeply uncomfortable. The windows were shut and all steamed up – well, it was winter. Suddenly there was a knock at the window; we could hear dogs growling. 'Oh, God, who's that?' We had visions of it being the gendarmes, and we'd find we'd contravened some obscure French laws about camping at the side of the road, and would all be slung in jail, the van impounded. Being the one in the front I wound down the window as slowly as possible.

It wasn't the gendarmes; it was the guy who lived in the house we'd parked outside. He had these two huge dogs with him, one of which I remember was called Egor, and as soon as the window was wound down far enough he stuck his head right into the car. He was a very Gallic sort, with a big moustache, and he spoke in machine-gun French. We assumed he was asking what the hell we thought we were doing. It didn't help that none of us spoke any French, so it took us a while to realise that he wasn't angry – that he was, in fact, trying to help. In the end we figured out he was saying, 'You English! Come in have a meal and sleep in the house.'

Once we'd twigged what he was saying to us, we objected: 'No, no, no, we're fine here, we've got all sleeping bags.' But he wasn't having it. 'No, no, I insist.' Finally we agreed that we would visit him the next morning for breakfast. Early the next day, before dawn, Al set off on his mission to try to hitch back to Blighty. The rest of us spent the day wandering aimlessly around the town before heading back to the van. Once again we were loitering inside the van, when – once again – there was a knock at the window. This time it *was* a gendarme. The gendarme, we eventually figured out, was asking us, 'What are you doing? You've got to move along.' I took on the translation work: 'It's the car . . . *la voiture* . . . the car's kaput.' Then the owner of the house rushed out and told the gendarme, 'They're with me! Hey, push the car onto the driveway. And come in for dinner.'

The gendarme reluctantly gave up and moved on, we pushed the van onto the man's driveway, and followed him into his house, where he had laid on the most amazing spread – even if we hadn't been hungry and cold it would have been amazing. There were oysters, there was beer, there was wine; his wife was cooking all sorts of dishes, they came flying out of the kitchen, one after the other: local delicacies, French staples, it never stopped. Jean-Yves – for that was the man's name – phoned his mates, telling them about his unexpected house guests, and two of them came along, and what started as a simple dinner spiralled into an evening of utter, drunken debauchery. We told him and his wife and friends stories about the mountains, having attempted to explain that that was the reason we were in the country. They particularly enjoyed the one about the Haggis: that it's got one leg shorter than the other and it runs around the mountain always going clockwise. Willy Edwards got so drunk, he went upstairs to the loo, but he couldn't find his way down the stairs, and passed out in Jean-Yves's six-month-old daughter's bedroom.

I don't think that I've ever drunk so much booze in my life. It was hideous. One of my last images of the night is of one of his friends who had been invited along for the evening: 'Hey, come and meet these stupid *anglais*!' The friend decided to try to drive home. He was last seen heading up the road on his motorbike, his rear lights swaying back and forth across the whole road. To this day I wonder if he made it home.

We ended up sleeping in the van again. Sometime in the middle of the night, Al returned, found us all in the van – we must have reeked of booze – and climbed in too. In the morning, Jean-Yves appeared, somehow bright and breezy, and invited us all in again: 'Come in, we'll do you breakfast.' We all had stinking hangovers, apart from Al, who was fed up that he'd missed the party but now had to contend with the after-effects; but we had now got the insurance, so we made the telephone calls. The AA were very accommodating, and gave us the hire car that we'd been after. The loader arrived, and we dropped off the van, and then, waving goodbye to the wonderful Jean-Yves and his wife, picked up the hire car.

We threw our gear in the car, and raced down to the southern part of the Alps, and attempted the route, but we didn't really get anywhere on it. The weather was abysmal; partway up we had to dig a snow hole. We ended up spending two nights in that snow hole, which was probably worse than being in the broken-down van on the side of the road. It was a calamity, an utter calamity. Everything was soaking wet. Retreating off the route, in a full-on storm proved harrowing, and then, to cap it all, we got avalanched and then the ropes got stuck on one of the abseils. In the face of such conditions we simply cut them and left most behind. Hiking back to the car in the wet snow, our spirits were decidedly low, although Willy managed to brighten things up by jumping into a freezing-cold water trough stark naked to have a much-needed wash. Arriving back at the car was a huge relief, throwing everything in the back and heading north for home. It was four or five hours later, just as our clothes were finally almost dry and things were looking a little less bleak, that the bloody hire car broke down on the flaming autoroute. If you think that sounds like *Groundhog Day*, then imagine how it was for us, living it out for real. Not knowing what to do, Al and I walked across some fields to a nearby village, to find a phonebox; and after some pleading and begging to the AA another low loader was promised. After a long wait in the cold it finally arrived at the car, but of course there wasn't enough room for us all in the cab so Willy and I ended up sitting in the car on the back of the low loader all the way to the nearest major town, which had an office for the hire car company and where it had been arranged that a taxi would take us back to Laon.

It was Sunday evening by the time we, at last, got back to Laon. The van had been repaired but it was in the garage compound. Of course, being a Sunday, we couldn't contact the owners, so we had to break the car out. We snapped the lock and left some money, before rapidly driving away towards the coast and the ferry.

We arrived back at my parents' house at three o'clock on Monday morning. Willy and I were paralytic. We had managed to get hold of a crate of beer somewhere along the way to drown our sorrows and between the two of us had drunk the lot. After waking my parents with our drunken shushes my mother set to work making bacon sandwiches and tea for us all. To this day she sweetly talks about this, saying how Willy and I were slumped against the wall giggling like schoolgirls. Poor Al and Rich now had to carry on driving all the way back to Leeds before starting work as school teachers just a few hours later.

It was quite a week – a week that had been hilarious, and terrific fun, but we hadn't got the route done.

Fast-forward two years. I was recovering from the accident, and Al rang me up out of the blue. After a little bit of small talk he asked, 'What about doing that route?'

I didn't need to ask which route. I hate leaving things undone and it had been on my mind. 'Hey, yes, fine, let's do it.' I was on the mend – in some pain still but it was manageable – all things are relative – and I would be rock climbing again, which was way more than anybody had said I'd be able to do. I was relatively mobile. I could do it . . .

When Al picked me up, he was driving another bloody van, this time a Vauxhall Astra. We drove all the way down to the southern Alps, well, not we – he was the only one who could drive as I hadn't got round to taking my test at this point. After an age we finally arrived at the road head by a tiny mountain hamlet called Desert. We walked to the little hut set under the north face, and spent the night there – in fact, it was Christmas Eve. We started climbing on Christmas Day.

We managed to get relatively high on that first day and dug a snow hole; so we sat out the night and carried on the next day. It was my turn to block lead, which meant going first. It was the first time that I'd led over this sort of terrain since my accident, and I had a mental impasse – I just couldn't commit to what I needed to do, even though it was relatively easy ground. It was not only a little bit of a mental block but it was also something of a physical one, too: I was struggling with my feet and my ankles. I've always been very honest – you have to be on a mountain – so I said to Al, 'I'm struggling with this; it would be much quicker if you took over.' He took over the lead, climbed up a bit higher and fired in a belay. The next pitch proved harder and more time-consuming; by the time I followed the pitch it was obvious that the day was slipping by. Above us loomed some difficult-looking mixed ground, a runnel that lead to what looked like a fierce overhang. It was hard, hard climbing. Al was picking his way slowly upwards, the occasional shout of 'watch me' was uttered, which would jolt me back to attention. Then suddenly, and without warning, Al was airborne, taking a big fall, ripping off a load of crucial ice. Pulling back up to his high point he attempted the overhang again, but despite his best efforts, he was rebuffed. By now it was getting dark and we had to make a decision on what we were going to do.

We decided that if we tied the ropes together we might just be able to reach the previous night's snow hole (an indication of how difficult and therefore slow the climbing had been that day). The only issue that I could see with this plan was this: because we hadn't expected to go back to the snow hole, the last thing we'd done before we left was to relieve ourselves inside it. I say 'we'; actually, I'd dumped in the snow cave.

So we got back down to the cave and Al was pretty adamant that I should go in and 'sort things out' while he organised the ropes and equipment. Because we'd busted our way out of the hole in the morning I had first to rebuild the doorway, then I went in and there, right in the middle of the icy floor, frozen solid, was my turd. I decided I just needed to push it to the door and push it out.' But it had frozen to the floor of the cave. 'Never mind,' I thought to myself. Grabbing my ice axe, I hit it with the hammer . . . the idea being to dislodge it, instead it exploded. There were little flecks of human excrement all over the snow cave – everywhere, all over me, all over my sleeping mat and rucksack. Because it was frozen, it didn't smell, so I scraped it out the best I could before Al came in.

Of course, one of the great things about a snow cave is it

keeps you out of the elements, and once you're in there, it warms up. So slowly, over the next few hours, the frozen pooh thawed out and the place began to reek.

'Can you smell that?' Al said. 'What the hell is that?'

'Sorry, mate, best you don't know.'

The next morning we climbed back up to our high point using the ropes we had left in place for speed, and we found a slightly different variation to avoid the overhang. As we got higher the difficulties eased, and I felt I could swing leads again. Al had done the bulk of the hard climbing, it was his project, it was his plan, but the strain of doing all the leading had tired the poor bastard out. It was nice finally to share some of this burden.

Eventually we got up to the junction with the north ridge that leads more easily up to the summit, which meant that we had essentially completed the new climb we had set out to do.

In those days (nearly twenty years ago now) it wasn't really the done thing to climb routes to junctions or to the end of the difficulties and then abseil off, although it's now common practice. But given our physical state, and the deteriorating weather, we both readily agreed that we should head down sharpish. We abseiled back down the way we had ascended, arriving back at the base just after dark, and trudged wearily back to the little hut. Our celebrations were short lived: a cup of tea and biscuits followed by some much-needed sleep. It was the first significant climb I'd done since the accident: an 800-metre new route in a remote part of the Alps, which was quite a big thing in climbing.

Arriving back at the car about five days after Christmas we found a letter on the windscreen from the local gendarmes, saying: *When you get back down, come and see us. We've noted your car, there's been no movement, we're concerned.* We threw the rucksacks into the back and I found a few bottles of beer behind the seat, which I quickly necked, and which went straight to my head!

Jumping in the front Al turned the ignition. Nothing. The car was dead. We worked out that the gendarme had opened the car to check on it, and left the interior light on, thus draining the battery.

'Don't worry, we're on a hill!' Al said. So I clambered out and went round the back of the car to push start it. I pushed it over a little rise, and then the car accelerated away as gravity took over. Al tried to bump start the car, but it just juddered then died. I thought we would be able to keep it going, but even though the car coasted on – we were in the Alps, so there was nothing but downhill, 18 kilometres in all – nothing happened. We were trying and trying, and nothing. In the end, the road finally flattened out and the car ground to a halt. 'Now what?' I thought. We just couldn't get any life from the engine at all.

Al looked at me. 'Go on then, off you go. Go and knock on someone's door.'

'Why me? I can't speak French.'

'Well, neither can I, but you're drunk. Go on, off you go.'

I must have been drunk enough to think that made sense, so off I went up to the nearest house, and knocked on the door. A guy answered and I struggled out, 'Uh, *monsieur*, uh, *parlez-vous anglais?*'

'*Non.*'

Oh, this was good. I tried again: 'Uh, uh, *l'auto, la voiture*, kaput. Kaput. *Avez-vous le . . . la* lead? Jump?' In time-honoured fashion, I waved wildly at the car. Al had put the bonnet up and I mimed the action of sticking jump leads onto the battery and made the noise I imagined the engine would make. 'Jump lead, jump lead!'

Amazingly, he understood. 'Ah, ah!' He disappeared back inside the house and then a few minutes later the garage door to the right opened and an arm appeared from the darkness with some leads. Taking them from him, I walked back to the car before realising that the leads on their own were useless. I turned around just in time to see a knackered Citroën 2CV burst out of the dusty old garage, revving wildly. Jumping out of the way, I watched as he raced up the road and slammed on the brakes, stopping with the Citroën's rusty bumper mere inches from ours. Leaping out, he yanked open the bonnet and we got all the leads connected. Meanwhile, I had helped myself to another bottle of beer, and passed one to our helpful new French friend. The buzz I got convinced me that, this being right after Christmas, everyone was still in a festive spirit, apart from poor Al who was driving. He didn't really drink, either, at the time, which meant all the more for me. We got the car going, revved it up a little bit, and before the guy took his car back inside, we turned it off and turned it on again. There was nothing; which of course meant our new friend and I had to drink some more beer while we pondered the problem. We – well, Al really – ascertained that it was probably the alternator – not charging up the battery – so we connected everything up again and this time the engine fired. We said goodbye to our helpful friend, and set off.

We still had to go and see the gendarmes, so we drove to the police station and parked up right outside, being careful not to turn off the engine. The guy at the front desk looked up and recognised the car. He leapt to his feet and started shouting to the other officers out back, 'The English! The English are here!'

As soon as we went in the other officers started quizzing us: 'Why didn't you tell us? What were you doing?' And when we explained what we'd been doing, they were all: 'Oh, the Olan. You climbed the Olan in winter?' It was all slaps on the back, everything perfectly fine. The bottles of beer came out, we drank some more, and then we went back and sat in the car.

'What do we do now?'

I had some friends that I'd recently been working with who were spending New Year in Alpe d'Huez. 'Why don't we go there? We've got another week. Let's go there; we'll do some skiing, do some ice climbing.'

So we drove all the way to Alpe d'Huez, which was a couple of hours away, and ended up staying with these two guys I knew from Wales and their mates. They were on a full-on boys' trip. We eventually found them and went into this little apartment that they'd rented – the inside was a thick fog of cigarette smoke, with centrefolds up on the walls. They were big into their dope, and they were having a riot; there were copious amounts of wine, beer, and everything else, but they were not just potheads. They were big into their ice climbing as well.

We slept on the floor of the apartment for a few days, spending New Year there. We were pretty grubbed in. We were exhausted after doing the climb, but these guys were total party animals. 'Come on! Out we go!' They were up for anything and knew every scam known to mankind. Like how to run a big tab up in bar and then run out without paying. New Year's Eve, for instance, we were in this bar drinking champagne, totally bevvied up; of course, the tab was rising and rising. Just before midnight, one of the Welsh lads produced this huge marine flare, and set it off in the bar. Everyone in there went piling out the front door, choking on the thick, orange smoke. Everybody was outside, staff included, and no one was going back in any time soon, so in the confusion we just wandered off, on to the next bar. This sort of thing happened night after night.

One of the days we went ice climbing with them. The day was pretty full-on but we ended up in the bar afterwards as usual. One of the boys started telling me a story about being banged up – he'd spent I don't know how long in prison. I asked casually, thinking it would be for something like fraud or maybe a prank that misfired, 'What did you spend time in prison for?'

'Oh, I kind of tried to chop a guy's leg off.'

'What?' I managed not to spill my beer.

'Yeah, we're in the local pub one night and this guy comes up and starts chatting to my girlfriend. I didn't really warm to him.'

'Jesus. And what did you do?'

'Well, I knew he was going to be in the pub the next night, so I went back. I took an axe with me and when I saw him I jumped him and hacked at his leg with the axe. The bastards did me for GBH with intent.'

And there I was ice climbing with him – and he had not one but two axes.

We had to finish up with these guys and although New Year's Eve was a couple of days behind us, both Al and I hadn't recovered from the climb and were feeling exhausted still, mainly due to the non-stop partying. We simply couldn't maintain the pace of the Welsh boys. Al also had a job to go back to, so we decided it was time we headed back. Of course, the car wouldn't start again, so we called out the Welsh lads and used their jump leads. Al then turned to me, and said, 'You know what this means, don't you?'

'I haven't got a clue.'

'We need to drive back to the ferry without turning the engine off.'

'You're joking.'

'No, we can't stop. If we turn the engine off, we're not going to get it started again. So we need to drive all the way back to the ferry and then once we're back at the ferry we'll sort it out from there, but at least we'd be back on home soil.'

So we – or rather, Al – drove all the back from Alpe d'Huez. At one stage he was so tired, he said, 'I don't care what you talk about, just talk to me. You've got to talk to me, I'm falling asleep. Just talk to me.' I knew he'd studied astrophysics and as I happened to be staring out of the car window looking at the stars, I started quizzing him about the stars. I learned all sorts of amazing things about the nebulae and everything that's up there – Al just downloaded everything he could think to talk about into me.

Somewhere in northern France we needed fuel so we had to pull into a service station. Al said, 'Right, I'm not going to stop the engine. We're going to fill up with the engine running.'

'Really? Is that a good idea?'

'We've got no choice.'

I got out of the car and ran round to the pump, but it was one of those machines that only took a Carte Bleue, and none of our cards worked – we only had UK debit cards. It was about midnight, we couldn't hang about, and we realised we were going to have to drive on to the next station, but we were on fumes. We couldn't give in to despair. The whole Olan epic, from start to finish, was beyond belief: beginning with a van breaking down on the first attempt, through low loaders and breaking vans out of pounds, my accident, and now here we were with a car with a knackered alternator, about to run out of fuel, somewhere in northern France, sometime around midnight. Luckily there was another service station not too far away and we pulled up to the pumps, Al kept the engine ticking over while I filled up with fuel; we must have looked mad. I paid and we raced off to the ferry.

At the ferry we kept the engine running but once loaded on board we had no choice but to turn off, we sat there and worried.

'What are we going to do? Are we going to start it up again?'

'No, let's just leave it. If it doesn't start, it doesn't start.'

There wasn't much point worrying about the car till we needed it again, we decided, so we went upstairs, and headed for the restaurant.

Al and I didn't use the restaurant in the same way as everyone else; we didn't have a penny between us then, so instead we did a minesweep. We went into the restaurant and hung around near the exit area, and when people got up to leave and put their used trays on the tidy rack, we whipped the trays off and ate whatever food was left over. Al is a vegan, so for him this should have been quite tricky. This is one of the things I've never understood about him: if any food – even meat – had been thrown away, he'd eat it, because it had been thrown away and so would be wasted otherwise. I could never quite work out how his constitution could handle that.

So we sat and had a hearty meal before the announcement came over the Tannoy, asking everyone to 'please return to your car'. We went back down to the car deck and got in, chanting, 'Please start! Please start!' Al turned the engine, it chugged and spluttered and stopped. We waited a few seconds; chug, chug, chug, chug, splutter, splutter, and bugger me if it didn't start. Thank the Lord!

I was living in London at the time, so Al kicked me out in east London somewhere just off the M25 and I hitched back while he drove back up north. So, that was L'Olan: two epic trips, bookending my accident.

CHAPTER 4
ALASKA AND THE WORLD

I had to get some money together to keep on climbing, but there was one thing I was clear about at the time: I didn't want a permanent job. For a while I worked in an outdoor-gear shop in Shepherd's Bush, London, but I found it too restrictive. Going to Scotland one winter before my accident, I had said I'd be away for four weeks. Conditions were really good, so I ended up staying an extra ten days, and I lost my job. This was quite an eye-opener to me, a brief glimpse of how restrictive a nine-to-five job could be, although by this stage I had already decided that the nine-to-five way of life wasn't for me. I also knew that I didn't want to have a career in the mountains. I was very concerned that any sort of career in the hills would take away from my enjoyment.

Throughout my twenties I was vocally against becoming a guide. But I had to earn money somehow. So, like many climbers – and cavers, too – I used to work at height, doing something called industrial rope access. That's essentially scaling tall buildings, cleaning windows, fixing things, doing whatever has to be done – at height. What we had to do was throw ropes over the parapet, and climb over the edge, suspended by the ropes, and then abseil down carrying out the work as we went.

It doesn't matter how competent you are at climbing – you might have just climbed Everest or climbed a super-hard sports route – get to the edge of a parapet on a very high building, look straight down, and tell me that is not scary. It takes time for your body and your mind to get used to it. When you climb over a parapet for the first time after an expedition it's always the same. The anchors will be set up on the roof and the rope systems all put in; logically you know it all works but . . . You harness up, grab all the tools and the seat before roping in; then you end up hanging on to the edge with your fingertips with the void beneath you, and before you let go you are checking everything multiple times, but there's always a take-up in the rope, the rope and anchors always have some slack in the system. When you finally fully weight the system you might slump down six inches before the ropes come tight. Six inches doesn't sound much but believe me, for that brief moment your heart is in your mouth and then you breathe out. 'Thank God, it's all worked.' It's always the same.

After my accident, a climbing partner of mine, Dan Donovan, who was working on the ropes, opened some doors for me. I did the training course, passed my level 1 roped access ticket and then I'd pick up work as and when it came in. Abseiling down the side of buildings, fixing glass, inspecting anything at height, removing bricks on tower blocks; I even did four months on the roof of the Millennium Dome (or the O2, as it's known today). I suppose I became a climbing bum, literally working to feed my climbing habit.

For a long period I was working above the roof space, or in the roof space, air-sealing supermarkets, because the big revolving doors they used to have were scaring people away, so they had decided to replace the doors with a large open void. Now if you have a big void in a supermarket, you need a positive air pressure or all the air comes from the outside in. Somebody had worked out that what you need to do is make the store as airtight as possible, and then it works. So that was our job: we had to seal every little hole, in and around all the roof spaces, to make these buildings as airtight as possible. Always working at night, when supermarkets are closed or partially closed, working between the ceiling tiles and the outer ceiling. Somebody had also realised that by air-sealing it you made the building very energy efficient. I understand that in less than a year Tesco saved enough money on their energy bills to pay back the cost at every store.

I started working all around the country. Jobs would take between four and six weeks, working Sunday, Monday, Tuesday and Wednesday nights. On Thursday morning I'd head back to Sheffield, where I was living at the time; I'd climb Thursday, Friday, Saturday, Sunday morning, and then go back to work. It was brilliant. We were on time-and-a-half for working nights, and we were given an overnight allowance, too, so I would stay in cheap B&Bs and save all the money. I'd work for three, four, five months, and then go on an expedition, coming back penniless before starting the process all over again. I did this for six or seven years – it was absolutely fabulous. Admittedly, the work itself was grim but most of the teams I worked with were great, which more than made up for anything else.

At that time, Everest wasn't even on my radar. A lot of climbers skirt it, partly because they can't afford to go. Even if you've put your own expedition together it's phenomenally expensive. I preferred climbing on smaller, more technical peaks, where I got more climbing in, and I wasn't alone in that mindset. Many of the biggest Himalayan mountains are predominantly snow plods, because in terms of technical ability they are relatively easy climbs, at least by the standard routes. Even the south-east ridge of Everest is not technically hard for someone with a reasonable amount of experience.

The achievements of people like Chris Bonington and Doug Scott in 1975, in scaling the south-west face of Everest, was different, and we all wanted to emulate that. But my friends and I didn't have the wherewithal to put together massive expeditions of that kind. It costs a fortune, even in those days the south-west face expedition cost close to £100,000. For less than a tenth of that kind of money four or five of us could go to Pakistan and do a whole expedition for seven or eight weeks. Simply put, we just couldn't put the funding together to go to Everest, so why even consider it, when you could go to the other mountains and do firsts? That's what we were always after: we were looking for first ascents.

My first time in the Himalayas was Pakistan in 1993. It was bloody brilliant, and, including the flights, the whole trip cost me £550 for eight or nine weeks. I can't remember now if the mountain, Shani, was unclimbed at the time, but certainly the north face we went for was unclimbed. Shani is just south of the Hunza Valley in Pakistan, in the Gilgit District.

There were six of us, and we flew to Karachi, then travelled overland by train to Islamabad. We flew there because I'd read, in Andy Fanshawe's book *Coming Through* that it was cheaper to fly to Karachi and travel overland. Andy Fanshawe was the generation before me, and he was one of my idols, so if Andy did it, we would do it.* Karachi is now – in 2015 – on the Foreign Office list of places to avoid; it seems to be a really dangerous place now bordering on total anarchy, with stories of local bandits holding

---

* Andy died in the Cairngorms, on Lochnagar, in 1992 and the UK lost yet another leading light in the climbing world.

up trains with rocket launchers and robbing the entire train. But things were different twenty years ago, and anyway we were in our late teens/early twenties, with the appropriate attitude to life.

When we finally got to Islamabad after twenty-one gruelling hours on the train, we dragged all our kit across town, but we were too early for the bus, so we sat about all morning, stranded, on our mound of kit. We were exhausted, and with nowhere to sleep, and no money, we became a spectacle in the bus station in Islamabad. People looked at us in utter wonderment, these white boys with all this pile of kit. And that's when I got really sick.

When we finally got on the bus and there was an argument about the seats, because we didn't realise that the seat numbers on the back of the seat referred to the one in front. That meant we were all sitting in the wrong places on the public bus, but just before everything got totally out of hand and we got into trouble, I threw up everywhere, and all of a sudden we could have whatever seats we wanted, because all the seats were covered in vomit.

To their credit, the locals were really concerned about me throughout the whole bus ride, and it wasn't a simple trip down to the next town, this was twenty-nine hours up the KKH (the Karakorum Highway), one of the most spectacular and dangerous roads in the world. I had heard some terrible stories about the people of northern Pakistan, but they were so nice. The bus made numerous unscheduled stops just for me, and at one of these one of the passengers dragged me off the bus before virtually carrying me, because I was so weak, to find the local doctor. They mixed Sprite lemonade with salt, and forced it down me. I was so ill that at one stage I ended up unconscious around a toilet in Gilgit; the team just left me there while they went out shopping to get some food. I came round from my semi-conscious state hours later, shivering with a fever, covered in my own vomit and excrement. It was a harsh introduction to travelling in this part of the world.

In the end the expedition itself was a great success. Although we failed on the north face of Shani we did climb two new routes, one to an unclimbed summit, while the other was a second ascent of the peak. With this success I was well and truly hooked. The next year I went to Nepal and did a new variation in the Himalayas, on Kusum Kanguru, on the north face. Following this trip and the subsequent time spent travelling, I had a couple of years climbing in Europe back in the Alps.

The next big trip was scheduled for Pakistan in 1996 . . . Of course, I never made that expedition because I'd smashed up my heels. So along came '97 and there was a change of idea: Al Powell had researched a fjord in Greenland with numerous unclimbed mountains. It would be more of an adventurous rock-climbing trip than big snowy mountains. He had already roped in the Benson twins (Andy and Pete, with whom I would share many an adventure in the future) and he asked me to come along as well. With my smashed heels still in semi-recovery this style of expedition seemed to be a good option, and so it proved to be. The climbing was fantastic, on sublime granite, the Base Camp was warm, sunny and green (a far cry from base camps in the Himalayas) and the general level of fun was off the charts.

Pakistan followed in 1998, which proved to be a hard slog. We didn't get close to summiting the objective, the huge unclimbed west buttress of Sani Pakush, 6,885 metres. I was nearly killed by rock fall at our high point on the third rock tower, which really spooked me, and then, to rub salt in my wounds, I took a huge fall in a crevasse once we had reached the relative safety of the glacier having spent two days descending in a harrowing storm.

Around this time I started to ramp up the amount of time I was spending away on expeditions. For the next few years I would do three or even four trips away each year, following the climbing seasons around the world, seeking out new areas or at least unclimbed peaks. I had the privileged of climbing with some of the UK's – and arguably the world's – best climbers at the time, the likes of Mick Fowler, Steve Sustad, Andy Cave, Simon Nadin . . . The list goes on, and it was a great time.

Meanwhile, slowly, I was building something of a reputation, at first with my contemporaries, and then in the climbing press. This was the pre-Internet days, so those who knew me knew of me, but not many others. My big breakthrough was Alaska, and that came about because I was climbing with Ian Parnell in India. The two of us tried a very hard new route in 2000 on an unclimbed mountain called Arwa Spire in the Uttarakhand State of northern India.

I met Ian because he'd been winter climbing with John Arran, an amazing rock climber, at one of the British Mountaineering Council Scottish international climbing meets in 1997. Every couple of years the British Mountaineering Council put on an international meet, which brings dozens of people together in one spot for a week. It is always full of energy and buzz, with foreign climbers being partnered or hosted with local climbers. The meet is always a bloody brilliant week regardless of what the conditions in the hills are like. I think Ian was meant to be hosting that particular week but for some reason he was climbing with John who was a good buddy of his. I'd gone along to the meet because I wanted to drink some beer, be around some friends, and be part of the banter, even though I could hardly walk because I was still struggling on my recovery. In spite of that I did get the opportunity to go walking one day with the late and great George Band, the youngest member of the '53 Everest team.*

Ian tells the story of how we first met, and I'm pretty convinced it's not entirely true. His version is that he had been climbing for the day and was walking back to his car with John. Climbing in Scotland means long days, walking for many hours, quite often in the rain or snow, with the wind howling. It's often a momentous effort just to get to the climb, let alone do the climb itself. Late in the afternoon, Ian was walking back to get a well-earned cup of tea and probably a beer. In the gathering gloom he says he came around the corner and there was this 'thing' – his term – on all fours. It looked up and apparently this 'thing' was me.

He walked over, looking down at me, and I thrust a hand up. 'Hi, my name's Kenton. If I can just get to the crag today, maybe there's a chance I can climb tomorrow,' I said, giving the idea that I was going to stay overnight.

(In reality I wouldn't have been on all fours, but I would've been struggling, really struggling, to walk, probably with two sticks, maybe still with crutches, which would've been an absolutely ludicrous sight: no one in that physical condition should have been on that path, let alone trying to go climbing.)

'Well, hi. I'm Ian and this is John.' And they quickly scurried on, because they didn't want anything to do with this maniac on all fours, probably covered in bog dirt, because I'd been falling over. I fell over a lot then.

Ian says he went round the corner and turned to John and said, 'What *was* that? There is no way on the planet would I

---

* George went on to partner Joe Brown on the first ascent of Kanchenjunga in 1955, the world's third-highest mountain, and had a long fruitful climbing career despite holding down a high-stress job in the oil industry. In his time he was president of both the Alpine Club and the British Mountaineering Council. Above all else, though, he was a really lovely man.

ever want to team up with somebody like that – what an idiot.' And they walked off to get a beer. That chance meeting was the start of one of the most profitable climbing partnerships I have ever had, although I didn't see Ian again for a number of years.

Ian later wrote about why he liked climbing with me, and how, when I first started climbing again, I refused to let my injury hold me back: 'Kenton had trouble massaging his stumps back to life. Six years previously he'd fallen 10ft and crushed his heels to pulp; he still can't walk properly. After a big climb or a night's clubbing he's forced to crawl for half an hour before circulation returns. He rarely complains and doesn't let it slow him down. While I watch him suffer I think of all the able-bodied climbers I know back home who always find excuses not to do anything. But this is one of the reasons why I'm here with Kenton.'

I forget exactly how he muscled (he would say *I* muscled) in on the first climb we did together but I'm glad he did. Ian had moved up to Sheffield from Bristol and ended up living just down the road from me. In 2000, a group of us intended to go to India; we were going to try the Arwa Spire, a mountain that I'd failed on the year before. There were six of us: the Benson twins, Al Powell, Dave Wills, Ian and me. We always climbed in pairs and my partner was Ian, even though I hardly knew him.

We wanted to climb in capsule style, a style used on extremely technical hard faces. You climb from a fixed camp, normally a hanging ledge called a portaledge, and fix a few hundred metres of rope to the mountainside. You then return each night to the camp before moving the whole camp higher up the mountain and repeating the process. I'd never climbed with Ian before and it was quite a learning curve. Even today he still frustrates me in the way that he approaches everything, but now I look back on it with deep joy. Ian is Ian and he's one of the true characters of the climbing world, he's always got this lovely positive demeanour about him. But he's never fit, he's always got the wrong kit, or it's busted or broken, and he's constantly knocking over cups of tea in a tent. All these things, which should and often do infuriate me so much, I love him for.

In the end we failed to climb the route up the front face of Arwa Spire (there's a lot of failure in my career), although it has been climbed subsequently, and we were trying to get back to Base Camp. The snow was horrendous, we'd been walking for what seemed like days, we were utterly exhausted, it was getting dark, and I was struggling with my feet, constantly falling over. We were walking over the moraine, full of crumbling and unstable blocks of granite, so it was time-consuming, irksome, and a little bit dangerous. Totally beaten, Ian and I sat on a stone together, eating our last chocolate bar, hungry, tired, hurting, and cursing this bloody moraine. It was then that Ian made his throwaway comment: 'We should go to Alaska.' He had been to Alaska the year before with the late Jules Cartwright and done an amazing new climb. 'There's no moraine in Alaska.'

I looked out at the bleak rocks in front of me in astonishment. 'What do you mean, there's no moraine in Alaska?'

'You fly over it all and you land in the heart of the range and you go climbing from there. There's no moraine, there's none of this, it's all snow and ice.'

This was a revelation to me, because moraine was something that I accepted as a price to pay wherever I climbed; it was tedious, and bloody painful.

A mere six months later we both stepped out of the de Havillan Beavor skiplane on the Kahiltna Glacier. And so began our two seasons in Alaska. It was these seasons that really strengthened our partnership and started to put us on the map – partly because of Ian's fabulous photography, which meant he had very good connections with magazines, and partly because what we were climbing was noteworthy.

In 2002 Ian and I climbed a route called Denali Diamond. We planned to do the second ascent, taking food and fuel for three days, which was a bold move considering the first ascent had taken seventeen days.

It essentially boiled down to one thing: we didn't want to carry food for seventeen days, inching our way up it. Instead, we planned to bludgeon the climb into submission: go light-weight, go fast, commit ourselves to it – up and down in three days. Speed is your friend. If you can climb fast, you can catch the weather windows, you can get up and you can get off. In Alaska you have almost twenty-four-hour daylight. You can climb in pushes, that's climbing without planning to bivy; you can do it if you just keep climbing.

This fast approach had been bandying around in other sports at that time. It was all about a different athleticism, about over-coming challenges with speed. In climbing, that meant a move-ment away from big, heavily laden expeditions to fast and light. One of the triggers for it was Mark Twight's books, *Extreme Alpinism: Climbing Light, Fast and High*, published in 1999, and essentially the sequel, *Kiss or Kill*, published in 2001. In the latter he describes a climb that he did with Scott Backes and Steve House. I don't quite know what it was that clicked with the three of them, but they demonstrated what could be done when they repeated a route, the Slovak route (or the Czech Direct, as it was once known), on the south face of Denali. The Czech Direct had its second ascent in 1999 by two young, talented guys, Gilmore and Mahoney, who took five or six days on it, which was considered at the time really impressive. The following year, Twight went in with House and Backes and did the same route in *sixty hours*. They just climbed constantly, doing it in a continuous push, on maybe four hours' sleep. That opened the floodgates. Every one of us young things wanted a piece.

That was the first time that somebody had gone in there with the mentality of single-pushing something, going to the summit while very lightweight. The interesting detail, though, is the total amount of climb time: there was actually very little difference between theirs and that of Gilmore and Mahoney. As House, Twight and Backes got really tired, of course their productivity dropped off, while Gilmore and Mahoney were overnighting, getting up each day fully refreshed, which helped them in the late stages of the climb.

Fast and light hadn't just come from nowhere. It had been bubbling under the surface since the end of the 1970s, and in the early '80s it had started to occur in the Himalayas, when climbers shifted from the big siege-style expeditions to more Alpine-style expeditions with smaller groups, lighter weights, little or no Sherpa support and no fixed ropes. At the end of the '90s, and early 2000s the timeframe was squeezed even more. This came thanks to the introduction of better equipment, lighter materials, better fitness levels. There was a new attitude involved as well. Twight was one of the first guys really to train for specific routes. It was the outcome of a whole different mentality and the results were startling. The training grounds had been originally the Alps and Alaska, and then the likes of Steve House, Marko Prezelj and more recently Ueli Steck took it to the next level in the Himalayas.

It took a while to become accepted universally, because you need a high degree of confidence to be able to climb continuously, without the big-team support around you, and there were still many people using the older techniques. But within a few years pretty much everybody had accepted this new style – the only real exception was the big commercial expeditions to Everest and other 8,000-metre peaks as well as some smaller peaks like Denali.

Commercial expeditions to the big peaks are always going to be heavyweight in comparison, using fixed ropes, with Sherpas, and working from fixed camps, because they're taking paying clients – amateurs – to the summit and need a degree of safety.

That's one of the reasons why there is this split between the guys like Steve House and the big commercial climbing firms. Although Steve understands commercialism, he's very anti it. Like me, he's a commercial guide, an IFMGA guide (International Federation of Mountain Guides Association), but he's very much against the big commercial expeditions in the Himalayas. I see his point; it's diametrically opposed to everything that he's tried to do himself, and when, and if, he guides in the Himalayas, he will just take one client with him and they will climb the exact same mountain Steve would climb for himself. He's fairly unique in that way. And in many ways that's the same model that I've tried to live to.

During our time in Alaska Ian and I were lucky enough to climb a number of new routes as well as bag a couple of first British ascents. One of these was on Mount Hunter, the third highest mountain in Alaska. It's got an amazing wall, the Moonflower Buttress, on the north aspect, which, at the time, had a huge reputation. There were only three routes on the Buttress at the time, and Ian had done a new route on it previously, with Jules Cartwright. Next to the Moonflower was an unclimbed buttress, a little bit smaller, but it emulated the Moonflower in shape, so we named it the Mini Moonflower. We were the first to put up a route on the Mini Moonflower, although we dubbed it as a warm-up route it offered sustained and brilliant climbing. A few days later we went back and climbed the Moonflower by the original route, which today is known as the Stumps Route. The original name however should be White Punks on Dope, after the first team that climbed to the summit. That was the first British ascent of it, and we tried to free it; it had never been climbed free before, and we got really, really close to doing it, which would have been quite a big thing back then. Unfortunately we didn't manage it, but there was another team there, Marko Prezelj and Steven Koch. They saw what we attempted to do, and they did free it about two or three weeks later . . . Buggers.

I felt lucky and privileged to be climbing then, lucky to be a part of that great group of people: Steve House, Mark Twight, Scott Backes, Johnny Blitz aka the Blitz, Roland Gaubotti, Marko Prezelj; a *Who's Who* of climbing. It was brilliant to be a part of the Alaska set, to be trying new techniques, to be climbing fast, to be part of that revolution in my own small way. I guess it was a bit like being part of the music scene in Manchester in the late '80s. I was in was the right place, at the right time, with the right blend of people, with the right attitude. It was going on all over the world, but it seemed to me, at least, that it was centred around Alaska. Perhaps because that's where I was; for all I knew it was going on in Europe as well. There are still opportunities in climbing, that's one of the great things about it, but at the time it seemed like we were all chasing the same goals, one big fraternity. But make no mistake, there was a very competitive side to it.

Let me give an example: there was a route on the Washburn Face on Denali that hadn't been climbed – a glorious-looking line that we'd had our eye on. We had been quietly thinking about it for a while, but Ian had let the cat out of the bag when he'd spoken about it to some American climbers. The little tinkers went and climbed it under our noses, and called it Common Knowledge, as a friendly dig to us. That sort of thing was happening all the time. There was intense but friendly rivalry, but at the end of the day everybody would come together, to chew the fat, drink beer and tell stories. All these years later I'm still friends with Steve House, Bruce Millar, Kevin Mahoney and Ben Gilmore all of whom were part of that scene.

After our time on the Moonflower we headed back onto Denali, and did a huge new route on the Father and Sons Wall. The first person to do a route on the wall was Steve House, calling his route First Born. So I called our route the Second Coming after the second album by the Stone Roses, an album that I was listening to a lot at the time. In light of the name of the wall and Steve's route name it seemed apt. However, at some point Ian renamed the route Extra-Terrestrial Brothers, which stuck, so called because I ended up having a bit of an extra-terrestrial experience up near the top after nearly fifty hours of non-stop climbing. It's a big wall, a massive wall. We didn't take a sleeping bag. We were on it for nearly three full days, climbing continuously, with only one stop of about four hours. I was so exhausted that, by the time we reached the summit ridge, I was hallucinating, convinced there were people on horses on either side of us on the ridge. Ian had to help me down. It was quite a memorable couple of days climbing.

When I did start thinking about climbing in the Alps again, or going further afield, I had to factor in how to pay for it, and that's where guiding came in. But in order to become a guide of repute, you need a reputation to back it up, and that comes about because people learn of the climbs you've done. To do that, when you've completed a new route, you write it up, and log a climb through various sources – it may be as simple as just mentioning it to a magazine – and then it gets logged. In Alaska you log these things with the Park Rangers. Alaska's quite well regimented, which was something of a change after my experiences in Greenland, and in India and Pakistan. There is a sort of 'sign in, sign out' system. You are even expected to carry all your waste out, and that includes human waste.

When we first went there, there was an expectation by the rangers that we crapped into biodegradable bags, and threw them down a crevasse. By the time of our next trip, the rangers had decided this was not environmentally friendly, so they gave us this little container, a mini potty. When I asked what it was for I was told: 'That's what you need to put all your excrement in. When you go to the bathroom you use this and you need to carry it all out.'

'You're joking, aren't you?'

'No, no, this is what we need you guys to do.'

'Well, what happened to chucking the bags down the crevasse?'

'No, you can't do that any more, and we will be weighing it on the way out; we know roughly how much matter you will be producing.' They'd worked out how much faecal matter a human being would produce in the average Denali climb and produced these little pots, waterproof and sealable. 'If you're not within a 10 to 15 per cent range, we're going to fine you.'

We were aghast; we were planning on climbing new routes, going lightweight and fast, keeping all our weight down, and suddenly there's no crapping behind a bush any more. We were not doing the standard west rib on Denali, we were off to do a new route, and we'd just been handed something that was half the weight of all our equipment. In the end, because of that, we got special dispensation.

After India, and then two trips to Alaska, Ian and I made plans to climb Annapurna III in Nepal. When it came to expedition planning, I was almost always the yes-man: people would come up with an idea and I would say yes no matter how stupid or ambitious it may have been. Annapurna III, though, was my baby. It was born out of frustration. In 2003, there was to be a star-studded British team going to Everest, on the fiftieth anniversary of the first ascent, and I wasn't invited. It wasn't just me; a number of us were not invited, including Ian Parnell. We were a bit pissed off by that, so my comeback was simple: what can we do to steal the thunder from that team? Let's go and do our own thing, and that's where Annapurna III was born.

I researched it and Ian, Johnny Varco (this American guy that we pulled in who we had got to know the winter before in Chamonix. John was more akin to a Brit than the average Yank. He also happened to be a shit-hot climber and a good guy) and I went ahead with the expedition in the autumn of 2003. We had a fabulous time, although it pushed me, and probably the others, mentally and physically way beyond anything I'd done before and probably since. Annapurna III's only seen two ascents, the first by the Japanese on the east ridge and the second by us, on the south-west ridge.

The basic plan was to attempt the unclimbed south-west ridge, a route that a big team of strong Slovenians had tried a few years previously. Slovenia is to climbing what Brazil is to football. The success rate of their climbers – people like Tomaz Humar, Silvo Karo and Marco Prezelj – is off the charts. Why is that? I think back in the day it was a way to escape the day-to-day control of their lives under Communism. It helped that they had – and still have – a very good club system. They could all hold down jobs in the army or the police force, and get paid, and then go away climbing. There was a huge amount of national pride when they had success, and the state got behind it. They were unbelievably good and the stuff they were doing was a generation ahead of what anyone else was up to. However, on Annapurna III the Slovenians had failed, even though they were in a ten-man team, fixing rope in a heavyweight siege style. We went about it differently, just the three of us, lightweight Alpine style; it was going to be complete commitment.

79

What we didn't know – and couldn't plan for – was that the mountain was going to push us way beyond what we thought we were capable off. After a couple of days on the route we were under what we thought would be the crux section of the climb: the second rock band that had repelled the Slovenians. Staring up at it from below it was easy to see why: it was a steep, uncompromising band of shattered granite with few if any obvious lines of weakness. I led off on the third day of climbing and got us established on the rock and then John took over with a couple of hard, bold leads into the rock band. Then came the crux, led with a masterful performance by Ian. It was hard straight off the belay with some steep broken mixed ground. As ever, Ian wasn't as well prepared as he might have been: he had one technical climbing axe, which was quite good in ice, and one straight-shafted axe, a super-lightweight thing that was as useful as a chocolate teapot and which we nicknamed 'the time bomb'. The good axe would go in the ice, and then he'd repeatedly bounce this crappy lightweight aluminium thing off the bullet-hard ice before finally getting some poxy insecure hold, and then start to pull on it. Of course, it had no grip, it wasn't designed for this, so his hand would slowly slide down towards the end of the axe. Meanwhile, he had pulled the good axe out, and was furiously trying to get it back into the ice before his hand literally dropped off the end of the other. If it wasn't all so serious it would have been comical.

Slowly – painfully slowly – he picked his way up the pitch, inching skywards. Even from the belay we could see his shoulders heaving as he tried to suck oxygen into his lungs in the rarified atmosphere of 7,000-plus metres. At one point, maybe 35 metres out, he stopped; a blank expressionless face peered down at us, looking for some form of comfort in the isolation that he must have been feeling on the lead. Summoning up some deep internal

drive, he once again swung his axe and moved up. He was teet-
tering with one foot pushed out wide, grasping for purchase
against a granite block, his other foot skating against the ice; his
right arm seemed to be bludgeoning the ice like a murderer
attempting to finish off a resistant victim, time and again, until
the axe stuck.

'Watch me,' he screamed. I looked up and saw the rope hanging
limp from his harness in a huge lazy loop to a sling dropped over
a rock some 10 metres below him.

'God, not from there . . .' I thought. 'Please don't fall from
there.' A fall from there would probably be fatal, if not from the
fall itself then definitely from trying to get him off the mountain
in an injured state. We were totally committed, with no way of
contacting the outside world. Still Ian fought on; retreat was not
an option. Letting out one of his trademark roars, screaming to
the gods above, the wind whipping his words away as quickly as
they were uttered, he threw his body weight from one side to
the other in his upward fight. From below it looked like a jerky
dance he was performing with some unseen partner; many years
later I described it as akin to a dance with the devil.

'Watch me,' he screamed once more, but this time his voice was
telling me so much more: it was a plea for help. He needed a
reply, the words themselves irrelevant, but providing him with the
knowledge that although he was isolated on the lead, he wasn't
alone. Then finally he reached a point where he could stop. John
and I watched helplessly as he desperately tried to construct a
belay before he slumped down, totally exhausted. He had won the
fight, but at what cost? He had led an amazing pitch, hard climbing
at about 7,200 metres, higher than any of us had ever been before.
He had really opened up the route onto the upper reaches of the
mountain and we ended up on steep snow. We'd got through the
rock band but we were absolutely spent and it was getting dark.

So we dug out a crappy ledge from the snow and spent the night there; it was freezing, with nowhere to put the tent up. Then John became really ill. He had developed a terrible hacking cough over the last few days but now he was coughing up gooey blood, and I thought he had pulmonary oedema. Ian and I looked at each other. We didn't have to say a word, we both knew – we all knew – that this was bad . . . this was really bad.

We had to get some food and water in us, but we had problems cooking; the wind kept blowing the stove out. We couldn't even sleep side-by-side, we were just all strung out in a long line, and I was furthest away from John. It pains me to say this, but I wanted to be away from John that night: his constant coughing was a reminder that he was alive, but I was worried that come the morning he might not be with us.

Ian woke me up in the middle of the night – I say middle of the night, it was probably two o'clock in the morning – saying, 'Where's the stove?'

'What? Why?'

'I've got to get a hot drink.' It was so cold that night, and we had spent so much energy that day, we had nothing left in the tank. Ian was literally freezing to death, even inside his sleeping bag. I gave Ian the stove and then tried to fall back to sleep on the little ledge, feeling scared and insecure about life.

Forty minutes or so later, bless him, Ian woke me up again. He had been sitting there all that time with the stove between his legs, melting water to make a hot chocolate. And he gave the hot chocolate to me. 'There you go.' Then he sat there for God knows how much longer making himself one. And that really sums Ian up – what an amazingly selfless thing to do. It was, retrospectively, also an important thing to do, because that hot chocolate, that hot drink, had an essential warming effect that saw us through the night.

That night ranks as one of my worst memories. The darkness was as penetrating as the cold was, and we lay there – three exhausted bodies, three minds lost in their own world of confusion. I was scared, really scared, not just for myself but for us all. I was convinced John was going to die, and worried how Ian and I would cope if that happened. We were such a tight unit, would we struggle on and get back or would we crumble? The minutes felt like hours, the hours lasted for ever. I could feel the wind tugging at my bivy bag, it seemed so unfair that it would come down to this, having fought so hard. 'Just give us a break, please – anything,' I thought. 'Why be so mean? Just let us get through tonight.' My final memory from that night is waiting, simply waiting for a glimmer of dawn. When I finally saw it I succumbed to sleep in the knowledge that I'd made it through the night.

We woke up in the morning to an amazing sunrise. We were miles from anywhere – I don't think I've ever been anywhere quite so remote – and although I felt very out on a limb, realising that nobody knew where we were, I could still appreciate the beauty of it. What about John? There was no coughing coming from John – no sound at all, in fact. I was horrified. 'Oh, God.' I could feel Ian wriggling around, so I knew he was all right. I sat upright – everything was still freezing cold – I wiped the sleep away from my eyes. I could hear Ian trying to raise something from John: 'John? John?' Nothing. 'John?'

'Fuck, shit; what are we going to do?' Think. Then there was a slight rustle, and all that came out of his bag was a hand and a rather shaky thumbs-up. 'Thank Christ, he is alive,' but all he could muster was to wave his arm.

He clearly didn't have pulmonary oedema. In the end we figured he'd picked up a chest infection and maybe the extreme excursions of the day combined with the altitude had affected him, but it didn't matter; what really mattered was that he was alive. That day, I took over leading, and I led every single pitch from there to the summit. Nothing was anywhere near as hard as what we had done, but it was steep exposed ground. That day we topped out on the ridge. We didn't know how far the summit was – we'd seen it from Base Camp and it had looked bloody miles, it had been one of our major concerns – and now here we were traversing the ridge, and that's where there's an iconic photograph taken by myself looking back to Ian and John.

At one point the ridge flattened out in an odd, wave-like snow feature. I was leading out first, when suddenly I fell into a crevasse, disappearing into a hole. 'What the —' I was roped up but it was still a bit of a shock.

But I didn't fall miles. Instead, looking about, it occurred to me that this wasn't really a hole; it was a funny break in the ridge line, covered because of the snow conditions. It also dawned on me that it would be a great place to put up a tent, out of the wind. It would mean a shortish day's climbing; but more importantly it would offer somewhere to rest and recover in safety out of the wind.

Once inside the tent, John tried to get the stove going, because – typical us – we'd mucked everything up and left one of the stoves in Kathmandu, so we'd had to buy this really cheap, 600-rupee stove in Pokhara. It had saved our lives the day before, but like most things on mountains, you never get a good turn twice. John was trying to get it going and all of a sudden it flared up and there were flames everywhere and we nearly got fried at 21,000 feet.

The rest did us all good physically, and mentally our spirits soared – it was as if my silent prayers of the previous night had been answered. John, through some super-human resilience, had rallied to his normal self. That evening we discussed plans for the next day: we had no idea how far we were from the summit, but it was all or nothing. It had to be – we were too far gone to spend any more time up there. The plan was simple, we were going to leave everything there – tent, sleeping bags, food. We pared everything right down; we took a single sleeping mat and a stove, just in case: we really had no idea how long we would be out for.

Actually, the summit turned out to be way closer than we'd envisaged, maybe three or four hours from the tent. The last 100 metres or so were like a dream; I was constantly expecting to find a false summit, but no, this was it. We all huddled against the wind and shot some video before retracing our steps to the tent where we collapsed for a second night of relative comfort in our crevasse.

The next day we started the descent, willing our broken bodies to give us just a little bit more. The first day we made it to the top of the lower rock buttress, which represented safety in my mind: from here we had good rock anchors to abseil off to reach the glacier, and then it would just be a long walk back to Base Camp.

We got all the way down to the glacier and returned to our advance base camp, and then we decided we were going to try to clear out in a single carry back to Base. We loaded up with humungous rucksacks, making up maybe 40 kilos, trying to get everything down in one go. It was a torturous 10 miles to Base Camp, but it felt a lot further, that's for sure. As we staggered down, it began to get dark and one by one we got split up on the glacial moraine. Luckily Ian had his head torch – I was so tired I couldn't be arsed to find mine in the mess inside my rucksack. Then the moon came up and we were all alone, lost in our own worlds, having just pulled off something quite spectacular.

It's hard to describe how tired I was, stumbling about on the glacier, on the moraine – a bloody moraine again – with these huge bags on our backs, which we called pigs because they're pigs to carry, pigs to haul. At one stage I fell down a moraine wall, losing my footing in the darkness, the pig came over my head and I cartwheeled down, stopping two-thirds of the way down the slope, all bashed up. Sitting in the dirt, I burst into tears, not because I'd hurt myself but from the sheer frustration of the descent. Eventually I pulled myself together. Sitting on the moraine wall I gazed out across the broken ground ahead, and there was this movement, and it was John – at least, I think it was John – on the opposite moraine wall. He had watched the whole thing, and he hadn't said a word. He just stood up in the dark and walked away. I don't think John actually knows that I saw him there. I was speechless, I didn't know what to say; to this day I don't really know what to make of it. Retrospectively, what could he do, hold my hand and say, 'There there; it's going to be all right'? I knew it was going to be all right, I just wanted the bloody thing to end. We were each in our own little world of pain – to be honest, it wasn't that little; it was a colossal world of pain. We were so beyond what I had thought a human being was capable of.

We finally made it out from Annapurna III Base Camp a few days later. As the expedition leader on paper, I was in charge of things, especially things like money, and you should never put me in charge of money. I got the money wrong by a factor of ten at the start of the trip so by this stage we had completely run out. We certainly didn't have any money to pay the porters, so it was imperative that we got back to the road head before the porters, so we could get to a bank to try to get some money to pay these guys before they stoned us to death, or worse. I remember being in a tea house about halfway out to the road head and we had to borrow money from people – we didn't have enough to pay the $5 each for the lodging. One girl very kindly bought us a few beers when she found out what we had just done.

At the time the Communist Party Maoists were prevalent in Nepal; essentially Nepal was then very close to civil war. As we passed through one of the villages there was a temporary Maoist checkpoint where a young boy with an AK-47 was asking for money. This was fairly typical at the time in the Annapurna area: the party claimed it was a tourist tax, which we had somehow managed to avoid on the way in. We were supposed to pay $10 or approximately 1,000 rupees, and would be given a piece of paper, signed, to say that we'd paid our tourist tax; if we were stopped again, we could wave the piece of paper and we would be let through. It was quite organised in a chaotic sort of way. Of course, we didn't have a piece of paper and, more than that, we didn't have the bloody money. As we approach the checkpoint, we stopped for a cup of tea, spending time eyeing up the checkpoint, talking through our options. What were we are going to do? The guy had an AK-47, and looked about fifteen, so rational discussion probably wasn't our best option. John being John, a larger-than-life guy who loved guns and all things redneck, came up with the worst idea of us all. 'What we'll do is we'll walk up to him, push him out the way and run.'

'What? What sort of plan is that?'

Since we couldn't think of a better idea, that was the plan we adopted. So we walked up to the kid and he started calling out, 'Tax.' And John literally pushed him out of the path and we started running. The boy pulled himself together, leapt to his feet and started running after us, with the AK-47 in his hand. Of course, we'd just spent ten days on a mountain and we were physically screwed, so I was sure he was going to catch up.

I sprinted up the hillside, following John with Ian behind me.

John and I took the high road and Ian took the low road, and that's when we lost each other. We didn't see one another again for days and had no idea what had happened to each other. Ian made his way back to Pokhara, managed to organise a flight to Kathmandu, securing the last seat on the only available flight for a week, and was back in the UK before we'd even left Pokhara. Meanwhile, John and I got stuck there with all the kit and then we had to get the local bus back to Kathmandu, where we spent a week trying to sort out flights. During this time I became a borderline alcoholic, drinking beer, while John was sick for most of it. The Rugby World Cup was on, so that was great. I spent my afternoons watching rugby with Kit Spencer, an ex-Gurkha officer who ran the Summit Hotel where we were staying. I was normally in a semi-comatose state, because I'd drink beer all morning. Of course, being an ex-pat Kit loved this because it gave him a great excuse to drink beer with me.

I found that week in Kathmandu a difficult time. It wasn't so much that it wasn't fun, more that I was trying to come to terms with what we had done. John and I had had a stupid little bust-up when we'd finally reached the first tea house after leaving Base Camp and this had affected our relationship; it was nothing more than a reflection of the strain we were all under during the expedition, but it didn't help that John was now sick. When we eventually returned to the UK John and I were both due to do a short lecture tour and this went some way to reconciling things, the environment of being together in the UK with others around us made it easier to be close to one another. We never fell out, as such, but that climb turned out to be the last one I did with John, although certainly not through design: he was a fantastic person to climb with and an even better friend to me. I didn't climb with Ian for a very long time either. I stayed very much in touch with him when

Tower Scoop on Ben Nevis, winter 1992. A very early trip to the mighty north face of the Ben with Simon Grayson while we were both at Leeds University. The trip was done in Si's trusty Ford Fiesta, while the jacket was borrowed from a flatmate. Si and I teamed up for a number of weekend hits to Scotland, climbing among other things my first ever Grade V – Vanishing Gully – and the classic Point Five.

The dinosaur roars. An aborted winter '93 attempt on the north face of the Matterhorn saw (*from back left, clockwise*) me, Roger Fowkes, Andy Fowkes and Mike Austin roadtrip it down to the South of France and the rock climbing of Buoux. While fleece salopettes may not have cut it with the local French hotshots, our plastic dinosaur that we stuck to the bonnet of the car served us well.

Ben Moon makes the groundbreaking ascent of Hubble on Raven Tor in the Peak District. In 1990 this was given the grade of Fr 8C+ and represented the world's hardest rock route. Published in a magazine that summer it inspired me to start climbing – it captured everything that was cool about rock climbing.

Train to Islamabad. It's amazing the lengths we went to to save some pennies. Here (*top left, clockwise*) Al Powell, Andy Fowkes, me and Barney Wainwright lounge in a sleeper train through the Pakistan province of Sind, in summer 1993. This 21-hour train journey in 40 degree heat was nothing short of torture, eclipsed only by the 29-hour bus journey that followed.

We were young and carefree. (*Left to right*) Joe Cater, Stu Rose, Chris Locket and I hang out en route to our successful ascent of the north face of Kusum Kanguru in the Khumbu in Nepal in the spring of 1995. Looking back, this expedition was one of total enlightenment, with us all being in way over our heads, yet successful and enjoyable. Note Chris in his cotton hockey club tracksuit bottoms.

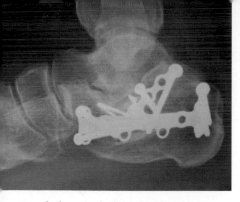

Bionic Man. (*Left*) An image of my right heel bone taken in 2014 after I managed to fracture it again. The initial injury of '96 which was to both heels led to a month in hospital and 18 months rehabilitation. The initial prognosis was that they would have to fuse both my feet and I would never climb again.

I ended up with three operations to rebuild my feet and I'm still in constant pain even today. (*Right*) I threw caution to the wind and was rock climbing again before I was even out of the wheelchair.

The biggest issue was always getting around in the chair, hence the kneepads in my lap for when I resorted to crawling.

Tired but Happy. (*Left to right*) Me, Al Powell and Ian Parnell after our successful ascent of Arwa Spire, seen behind next to the left skyline ridge. Despite its remote nature and height (6,193 m) we found a fat guinea-pig-type animal a few metres down from the summit, happily hanging out. The rodent was obviously better at undertaking the gruelling approach to the mountain than we were. After this trip in October 2000, Ian and I vowed to go to Alaska where it's possible to fly to the base of the mountain.

Feeling happy about life. Alaska is nothing short of designer climbing. It has it all: great mountains, a lifetime of fabulous new routes, and easy access. Here I'm leading yet another pitch of stellar steep ice on the Mini Moonflower off the Kahiltna Glacier during the first ascent in May 2001. Even Parnell trying to break my hand with falling ice didn't dampen spirits that day!

My first Alaskan season was rounded off with the first ascent of Extraterrestrial Brothers on the Father and Sons wall off Denali. This huge wall was dispatched in a 55-hour single push with a pit stop of only four hours. This ascent was part of the early revolution of the light and fast ethos that took hold in Alaska in the early 2000s. Our bid for the north summit was cut short due to my exhaustion and the hallucinations that followed.

Hanging bivy on Denali Diamond. (*Below*) The plan was to make the second ascent of the now-classic route on the mighty south-west face of Denali. This, our second bivy, was made in desperation by hanging the tent vertically from the rock while we perched a bum cheek each on a tiny ledge.

The summit of Denali (May 2002). Utterly exhausted, there was nothing to celebrate. In a white-out with no map we were stupidly ill-prepared. The descent, which took in parts of the Rescue Gully, Orient Express and the West Rib as we tried to pick our way down the mountain, was probably the most dangerous part of the whole route. When we finally made the 14,000 camp we were clapped in by two lines of climbers and rangers who were keen to celebrate our success with us.

Annapurna III (October 2003) tested the team both physically and mentally way beyond our expectations. The only respite on the route was the relatively easy angled snow between the rock bands. Here Ian catches John Varco (in yellow) and myself moving up towards the second crux rock band with the vast view of the Annapurna sanctuary behind.

Down time on expeditions is a high point. John Varco introduced us to his music tastes ('Yeah I like both types... Black Sabbath and Ozzy...)' and a card game known as the Alaskan Way. On Annapurna III there was little boredom. It's worth noting his taste in books.

John Varco serves me his weapons-grade coffee. We kept things low-key on Annapurna III, even down to not having a mess tent so meals were often taken outside. Breakfast is my favourite meal on trips, and on days like this one with the sun out it can stretch to many hours.

Annapurna III. John links a crucial traverse on the second rock buttress. This wildly exposed line was made up of hideously loose flakes that felt like they would peel off at any time. Completing this traverse gave access to the upper reaches of the buttress which held the crux of the route which Ian Parnell bravely battled.

I lived in Sheffield, because he lived down the road, but I didn't do another serious climb with him until I climbed the north face of the Eiger with him and Sir Ranulph Fiennes in 2007, when Ian was the photographer who came along to record the ascent.

For me, though, the Annapurna III expedition was a defining moment in my life. It's one of my proudest moments in the mountains but at the same time I always look back and wonder what happened to the three of us. I think we lost our innocence on that trip, climbing somehow crossed a barrier with us all, certainly it did with me – the seriousness of it all and the mental effect scarred me for a while. Although the trip was so much fun, with huge amounts of laughter and happy times, it also represented a darker side, one that I've never quite been able to explain. Perhaps I stared into the black hole of life a little too deep; perhaps I didn't like what I saw.

I got back from Annapurna late on a Friday and watched England win the World Cup in extra time the following morning – what a crowning way to finish an amazing expedition.

Then in January the following year we heard that the expedition had been nominated for the Piolets d'Or climbing award – the Oscars of the climbing world – one of five expeditions picked out by a jury and the French publication *Montagnes*. We were pipped to the top prize by the Russian team of Valery Babanov and Yuri Koshelenko, but that didn't matter, the mere recognition from our peers meant everything.

It was on the back of the trip that I got invited by Jagged Globe to climb Everest. They wanted somebody who had proved themselves at altitude, reckoning that if you can climb at about 7,000 to 7,500 metres, you can happily climb higher.

From here on, climbing took a different route for me: it became my work. I felt I'd lost my innocence on Annapurna; now the amateur climber Kenton Cool departed the scene. All of a sudden I found myself climbing a lot for other people. I still did my own trips, and I still climbed a lot for myself; in fact, my rock climbing probably reached its pinnacle a few years later, when I was climbing pretty hard rock routes just for myself.

The life I'd been leading up till then was draining me and I wanted to go about things differently – to be able to make plans for my immediate future, never mind the distant future. A few years earlier Jagged Globe had asked me to lead a trip to the Himalayas, to climb Ama Dablam, the 'Matterhorn of the Himalayas'. The mountain stands at nearly 6,800 metres, and in the autumn of 2001 it was the closest I'd been to Everest so far, in terms of both height and distance. At that time it would also have been my highest mountain. I had attempted higher peaks in Pakistan, notably Sani Pakush in 1997, but I hadn't managed to reach the summit on those occasions. This would be my first real foray into high altitudes.

Working with Jagged Globe at that time made a lot of sense. They would find the clients, they would organise pretty much every part of the expedition. My job would be to lead the expeditions on the ground. I'd be the one who called the shots, held it all together. I'd get the satisfaction of doing a job that I really enjoyed doing, and the opportunity to climb a mountain new to me – I'd never climbed Ama Dablam before – and I'd be paid to do it.

Initially I hadn't even factored the money in. I know that may sound naive, but I had decided to guide not to earn money but more because I saw it as an opportunity: if somebody else was paying my air fare, then I'd be able to take some time in the area to do some climbing while at the same time I'd be saving money. I could do a trip, get nicely acclimatised and then do my own climbing off the back of it. Ironically, it never worked out that way, as I was always too tired to do my own thing after a guided expedition.

The first commercial expedition that I led was to the Nepalese Himalayas, climbing some low 6,000-metre peaks in the Khumbu region. For a first-ever guiding trip, it was a great experience and I loved it. Apart from one thing: I had a falling-out with the assistant leader. In her defence she was the perfect person for the job, balancing all my weaknesses and also keeping me somewhat in check, but we just didn't see eye to eye on a number of things. There was one small issue that happened once the expedition was over, however, that I still struggle with to this day. I say 'small' and it was small, but it said big things to me, things that I still see today in certain aspects of our world.

I go about life in a certain way. I understood the reasons why we had risk assessment forms, and why everyone on the trip needed insurance policies, and why there were dos and don'ts, but I honestly believed – and still believe – that a good dollop of common sense goes a long way.

The expedition was essentially over, we were back in the beautiful grounds of the Summit Hotel, which has a very colonial feel to it; the sun was out and we were drinking beer and cocktails in the late-afternoon sun. We'd had a very successful expedition and everybody was feeling very jolly; so, as we're all a little bit tipsy, and to entertain us, I put a slack line up. A slack line is a tensioned piece of climbing tape and all you have to do is balance on it; it's like a tightrope that is no more than two and a bit feet off the ground. My idea was we'd all try to get on it in turn and attempt to balance.

I had a go, even though with my knackered ankles I was in a bit of pain and am generally rubbish at balancing. The trouble with a slack line is if you're as hopeless on it as I was, you get spat off and sometimes you hit the floor with a bump; and sometimes the slack line can slap your leg as you get ejected off and that can hurt. Seeing this, my assistant leader rushed up and said to me, 'I don't think this is a very good idea. It's outside the remit of any insurance policy.'

'Yes, whatever,' I replied. 'Now, come on, your turn, up you get.'

But she carried on: 'No, I don't think it's a very good idea.'

I was incredulous. 'Yes, well, come on, we all fly home tomorrow.'

The next thing I knew, Kit Spencer came over to our group, puffing away on his pipe. He was the face of Jagged Globe in Nepal and he has no choice but to toe the company line, so I wasn't that surprised when he said, 'I'm not entirely sure this is a sensible thing to do, Kenton, my old son. Maybe we'd be best to take it down.'

'Really, Kit?'

'Yes, I can see you're all having fun but it's insurance and all that.' My co-leader had obviously gone across and had a moan to Kit. Now Kit is cut from the same cloth as me in many ways, and he was clearly finding the conversation very uncomfortable, but I had to do what he said.

Climbing Ama Dablam wasn't really harder than any of the climbs I'd done before then; in fact, it was easier than many, because there were fixed lines on the mountain. However, climbing it gave me a depth of experience that one can only achieve from being on mountains like that – things like being at high altitude, and of course the complexity of the experience of expedition life. It was on this expedition that I was exposed for the first time to the core family of Sherpas that I still work alongside today, many of whom I now consider firm friends. I also met Dave Morten there, an American whose career in the mountains and family life have paralleled mine over the last fifteen years; I am proud to call him my friend. I'm convinced such friendships are deeper because of where and how they are forged, the efforts that we put into what we do, the shared things we see and experience. The mountains pull you together; the rest is often up to you.

It was the same way that I felt sat on top of that cliff in Dorset on the first climb I ever did: you're sat there, the sun's going down, and you've tried really hard and you've pulled something off. You're sitting there feeling very content. Now, I got that feeling on the expedition to Ama Dablam, and all of a sudden somebody was paying me to do it. It was like a dream come true. I suddenly realised I loved guiding expeditions!

To some climbers, I appear to have 'sold out', but I don't see it that way.

PART TWO
EVEREST

CHAPTER 5
BASE CAMP

There have been many things written about Everest Base Camp over the years, mainly from those who either have never been or have never spent any significant time there. The more so since the terrible events in the spring of 2015. The earthquake focused the eyes of the world on Nepal and Everest.

I've read that Base Camp is a hellhole, the world's highest cesspit, over-crowded, unsightly, badly organised and a collection of egos. This is not a description I recognise and I've spent, on and off, over two, pushing three, years of my life there. For me Base Camp is a unique place where a wonderful, diverse group of extraordinary souls come together for a few short weeks each year. It's a city of tents 17,000 feet high, half the cruising height of a modern passenger jet, and some 10,000 feet below the summit of Everest. It's vibrant, fun, friendly – well, I think it is – multi-cultured and international. In the past I have seen a coffee tent serving great apple crumble there, a cinema, even a massage facility one year.

It is rare in the world to find a place where people from every nook and cranny of the world come together with a single common goal. Some, of course, are there for work – the Sherpas, cooks, cook boys, yak herders, and the Western expedition guides – but most are there 'just' to climb. Climbing has the ability to cut through any social position: religion, colour, background and gender. The bottom line is that people come to Everest every spring to find something in themselves, and to attempt to stand on the highest point on the planet. It is an endeavour that makes everyone equal. Money, status and ego mean nothing. The great Swiss climber and mountaineer Ueli Steck recently tweeted from his tent at Base Camp: 'If you want adventure, don't come here.' But the fascinating thing is that he returned only the following year, such is the pull of Everest.

When I'm at home in Gloucestershire, all I want is to be on the mountain. I can sense every footstep, every boulder, every twist and turn in the dusty trail that winds its way through the Nepalese foothills, with that great mountain as an astonishing backdrop. Oddly, the final day of the trek to Base Camp has never been one of my favourite parts of the trail, mostly because of the dust, the crowds of people and all the smelly, fly-infested yaks that are constantly around you. It's a hustle of a path that winds its way across a high moraine wall before finally dropping down onto the glacier path covered in boulders, and it's really unpleasant to walk on, especially for me with my decrepit ankles. In recent years a Base Camp cairn has been constructed on the outskirts of what the climbers would call the 'true' BC, the idea being to try to keep trekkers out of Base Camp proper, which can become very crowded on the narrow paths. As far as I'm concerned, all it has done is generate an extra kilometre of trekking. I know it sounds silly but when you pass the cairn you feel you should be at BC but in fact you have another twenty minutes or so to get there. At the end of a long day coming in from

Lobuche when the legs are jaded, it seems like you've been cheated. But there's no use in moaning; it's simply head down and grind it out.

Yet when I'm on the mountain I think of home. Some of my Sherpa friends have spent ten years or even more of their lives at Base Camp. Most live in the Khumbu Valley, so they are just a few days walk from their families and friends. For me it's thousands of miles back to my wife and soulmate, Jazz, and our two children. There's no opportunity for me to pop home during our rest period before a summit push. Strangely, I've only recently started to miss home while there, possibly because Base Camp has felt like a second home for so many years, especially in the early days of my Everest career when there was no other place I would rather have been. I grew very accustomed to life there. It's hard to explain what the feeling is but it's essentially one of total contentment.

Mountaineering is a simple way of life. When you are on a mountain, nothing exists other than the objective of getting to the top. Once I caught a bus in North India after attempting to climb the north face of Klanka. My climbing partner Nick Bullock and I had been cut off from Western life for five weeks with no news from the outside world. As we bumped and ground our way back to civilisation, a young local asked if he could practise his English on us. He launched into the most precise and articulate assessment of the state of European politics, the modern face of Premiership football – particularly with regard to overseas financing – and moved on to ask our views about having Gordon Brown as a new Prime Minister. Nick and I were speechless. We had no idea that Brown had even stepped into power. More to the point, at that moment we had no interest in the fact. Our lives had become stripped back to the few simple things that were important to us.

Base Camp is a very colourful place. Hundreds of red, yellow, blue and green tents are pitched everywhere, with miles of prayer flags cascading down from the puja altars. It's a wonderful tonic for weary eyes, especially after days of walking on the dusty trails. Walking through this tent maze, it's easy to get lost, especially at the start of the season when the paths are not well defined. And it's bigger, much bigger than most people expect. It takes an age to walk from one end to another, especially if you know people. I'm forever being invited into camps to drink tea or chat. Often a cup of tea or coffee and a quick catch-up with an old friend can last all morning.

I know only too well that it takes an age to get from one end to the other because I had to race the length of the camp once in 2013. I was waiting for a chopper to take me down the valley: I had managed to secure a seat through some dubious connections, but it was a very loose arrangement. After sitting on my own on the lower heli pad for thirty minutes, which was beginning to feel a little odd as there would normally always be people milling about when a chopper is due, it suddenly dawned on me that the chopper must be coming in to land on the higher pad. The use of multiple chopper pads came to being in 2012 when the number of flights into Base Camp dramatically increased and those camped near the landing pads were becoming upset with the disturbance, as well as the danger that the low-flying choppers presented. (This is a far cry from my first season in 2004 when choppers came to Base Camp so infrequently that almost everyone would stop what they were doing in order to watch the chopper land.) That day in 2013, as I began to trot back through BC I could make out the distinctive *whomp, whomp, whomp* of a chopper painstakingly making its way up the valley, battling against the low air density. I had to be at the pad before it touched down – my seat on the chopper was flaky at best, and the pilot certainly wouldn't wait for me if I was late. The race was on.

It's hard to sprint across Base Camp at the best of times, but now I had a heavy rucksack on my shoulders. As my legs propelled me across the rocky terrain my lungs started to protest. Despite being well acclimatised, I was struggling to get air, and it began to feel as though someone was pouring burning lava down my throat. The lactic acid started to build in my legs and they too began to scream. By now the chopper was looming large and making a beeline for the helipad; I was losing the battle. Head down, I charged, determined not to be left with a few days walk down the valley. The chopper sped overhead and my shoulders sank, but never one to just lie down I continued my lung-busting run only to see the chopper flair up and abort its landing. The pilot swung the machine round, slowly clawing altitude, its engines screaming at max revs, before making a second approach.

As the skids touched the boulder-edged landing pad I burst through the ring of Sherpas who were standing watching, looking for the load master, who turned out to be a long-time friend, Lhakpa. He saw me and grinned, nonchalantly indicating that I could jump on board. As I approached the door he asked where I had been. Shouting above the roar of the engines, I said, 'The lower pad.' He burst into a terrific toothless grin, which he followed with a huge belly-roar of a laugh that could still be heard above the deafening noise of the chopper.

The general vibe at Base Camp is relaxed and open. Between rotations on the mountain, climbers and Sherpas kick back and enjoy themselves, marvelling in the environment that they are lucky enough to find themselves in. I never get bored of the view from Base Camp, nestled as it is among some mighty peaks, and although one can't see Everest herself, the vista is breathtaking.

A normal day at BC pans out like this. Wake anytime between

6 and 7 a.m., depending on the time in the season. Later in the season the sun will be on the tents by 7 a.m., making them almost unbearably hot, whereas in early season the cold means that people tend to clamber out of their tents somewhat later.

My routine is always to be in the cook tent first. I know I can get some ginger tea from Bhim the cook. It's also a time to check on the Sherpas if they are on the mountain: this means a quick radio call or, better still, I'll ask one of the staff what is happening. I can down a couple of mugs of Bhim's delicious ginger tea before anyone else rises, then I'll wander over to the mess tent and prepare breakfast, which is normally cereal or porridge followed by perhaps pancakes or eggs of some description and bacon on toast, all washed down with tea or coffee. I then supplement things with a protein shake for good measure. On a nice sunny morning, breakfast is taken outside the mess tents, where climbers and Sherpas alike can sit and stare up at the Khumbu Icefall and track the progress of climbers making their way up or down.

The morning has a habit of quickly disappearing if I'm guiding an expedition, chatting, drinking coffee or simply staring at the view. Sometimes there may be a trek down to Gorak Shep, the last village on the trail before Base Camp, for lunch, more for a change of scene rather than the culinary delights on offer; or perhaps a stomp up to Pumori Base Camp for photographs with its magnificent view of Everest – arguably one of the best.

Lunch comes and goes quickly, leaving the afternoon spread out before dinner. I will normally use this time to visit friends in other camps, or, if I'm due to climb onto the mountain the next day, I'll check equipment and make sure that the hard-working Sherpas are all primed and happy with their loads. Occasionally I'll laze in my tent reading, finding a little solitude among the bustle.

Late afternoon, just before dinner, will normally find me playing backgammon against Henry Todd. Henry Todd, or as he is sometimes called 'The Todd-father', is something of a legendary figure on Everest. With a colourful past and a once fierce temper, he has quite the reputation. But he has a heart of gold and over the many years I have known him, he has been nothing short of a confidant, mentor and a great friend.

Or I might spend some time with the New Zealand outfitter Russell Brice and his team if they are in camp. Russ has his now famous guides meetings where his team of guides, combined with a few select others, come together over a glass of whisky, hot water and honey. I'm sure a real whisky lover would baulk at the idea, but with the temperature dropping rapidly outside it has a welcome warming effect on the body. The meeting does occasionally have serious undertones, with the guides catching up on what has been happening on the mountainside and what the next few days may have in store. Russ is famed for his hospitality, and on more than one occasion I've stumbled back into my own camp late at night, often without a head torch, which of course is an immensely stupid thing to do. Others have been known to have to stay the night in a spare tent, even though Russell's camp is a mere fifteen minutes' stroll away.

There is little better than snuggling down in a warm sleeping bag when the temperature is below freezing outside. Early season will see the temperature at Base Camp drop to minus ten or even colder. Almost as soon as the sun dips below the horizon, my breath is clearly visible, billowing out of the small hole in the sleeping bag in the blue-white glow generated by my head torch. Water bottles quickly freeze solid inside the tent. It's an obvious trick, but taking a bottle of hot water to bed, pre-warming the bag before you jump in, is a simple piece of advice I give clients, because it also means that you have a bottle of water to drink from in the night or early morning that isn't frozen solid.

I love being tucked up in my cosy sleeping bag with a book. I vowed years ago I would never use a Kindle. I've always loved physical books: the feel and smell. However, here is a situation where my stubbornness is a real disadvantage. Tucked up tight in a sleeping bag it's hard enough to hold a book, never mind turn a page. Hands have to come out, allowing freezing-cold air to rush in. Meanwhile, my Kindle-reading friends gloat that not only can they happily hold a Kindle through the sleeping bag, but they can turn the page with a simple flick of their nose.

I remember one rather embarrassing Kindle-related episode from 2011. I arrived at Camp Two one hot afternoon and was appalled by the number of duffel bags that were being stored there by clients. It's usual to have some equipment carried to Camp Two by the Sherpa team, but to arrive and see a duffel bag each and for it all to be taking up the seating area at Camp Two was too much. I blame it on the heat of the day and the exertion of the climb from Base Camp, but as the Sherpas looked on laughing I systematically lobbed the bags out of the mess tent and into the surrounding snow. When the owners of the bags arrived I demanded to know what was in them (which to be honest was none of my business), and asked why the hell they had to have so much stuff carried up in the first place.

I saw red when summit boots appeared out of the bags that people were, as far as I was concerned, simply too lazy to wear. Big Everest summit boots aren't the most comfortable things, they are big, bulky and cumbersome, and in recent years people have resorted to having the Sherpas carry their boots up to Camp Two so they don't have the inconvenience of wearing them through the icefall (instead they wear smaller, more supple boots). This practice really annoys me. I understand that most people need the support of the Sherpas in order to summit the mountain, but this behaviour strikes me as really unnecessary.

That particular day the final straw was seeing a Kindle emerge from the depths of a heavily packed duffel bag. Almost screaming at the poor woman who owned it, I demanded to know why she had a Kindle at 6,400 metres. What the hell was wrong with a book? It would be so much lighter to carry and perhaps then she wouldn't have to abuse the Sherpas by asking them to carry so much personal kit. Her reply was quickly delivered: 'Kenton,' she said, 'a Kindle is half the weight of a physical book and mine contains seventy books, so I'll never get bored here . . . How many books have you brought up?' I sheepishly confessed to carrying up two, which comes to four times the weight of a Kindle. I slowly retreated to my tent, tail between my legs, muttering. But, whatever! I stand by my view that having summit boots carried up is criminal, and I carry all my own stuff to top it off!

But when the day comes to make for the summit, everything changes. All the socialising and calm turns into purpose and excitement, anticipation, adrenalin. There is also tension, as everyone starts to plan the summit push. All our experience, training, commitment and mental fight move front and centre. It's the time when I start earning my wage, it all becomes serious. After all, this is why I'm there.

CHAPTER 6
'SHE DIDN'T ROLL OVER'

2006 was my third year on Everest and it turned out to be perhaps the most important ascent in terms of my Everest guiding career, at least on a personal level. I had climbed successfully in 2004 and 2005 in near-perfect conditions, both times for Jagged Globe, and now I was back in 2006 as lead guide for them again. That's not to say that there had not been drama in the previous years: in 2005 I got smacked on the head by a stone. It was a stressful year 2005, the weather windows came really late in the season so many teams packed up and left. At one stage it looked as though there would not be a summit window at all, which is unheard off, but those who waited were eventually rewarded at the very end of May. The weather window was tight but it was stable for a scant couple of days and teams snuck up and down. The climbing conditions were good and temperatures mild for Everest, which made the ascent relatively simple in the end. I say simple I actually got hit on the head by a rock on summit day. I remember it quite vividly: the team was making progress up to the Balcony in the dark, no more than three hours out of the top camp, when all of a sudden something entered the cone of light from my head torch. The next thing I knew, I came to hanging on the fixed line with a splitting headache. My vision was blurred and I quickly worked out that I'd be hit by something, probably a rock. In the darkness it was impossible to see the damage; the only thing I knew for sure was that I was bleeding: I could make that out from the growing red patch in the snow. I waited until John Taylor (aka JT), one of my clients in 2006 and one of three police officers from Victoria in Australia, that I was guiding, caught me up and I asked him to assess the wound. His immediate reaction was 'Shit, you're going down.' But after a few minutes of applying pressure, I pulled myself together and decided to continue up. It was probably a bit foolish, but at the time it seemed totally sensible. When I eventually got back to Camp Two a couple of days later I had to have eight stitches put into a deep gash on my forehead.

That episode taught me how carefully you need to treat social media. I had a great relationship with all of the staff at Jagged Globe, who I was working for that year, but there was one girl in particular who I hung out with a lot. She arrived in her office the morning after my accident, and the first thing she did was check the answerphone. There was a message from a news outlet in the States. They had picked up, through someone's blog that a climbing group's leader had been incapacitated high on Mount Everest, and they had phoned up the office in Sheffield to ask for a comment. Of course, she knew I was the leader so she was understandably panicked. To make matters worse, the batteries in my radio had died so my whereabouts were unclear to those at Base Camp. As a result, everyone was panicking, but the truth was that apart from a serious headache and only partial vision (which was either related to the knock or a side affect of high altitude), I was enjoying myself on the mountain.

I'm always astounded by the way news filters out, and I learned from this incident to control the release of information when things aren't working. It really comes down to the old term: no news is good news. I remember explaining this to my parents years ago, that they shouldn't worry just because they don't hear anything. In this modern era of communications, everyone expects there to be information – blogs, tweets, telephone calls, etc. – and if it dries up for whatever reason panic ensues. Yet the reason for the lack of information may be as simple as a dead battery or no cell signal; after all, we are climbing a bloody mountain. The media love a disaster, latching on to any thread of a story as it unfolds. Everest is a very public place, people can listen to your radio conversations and before you know it it's in a blog or been tweeted, and of course this information is often misinterpreted.

In efforts to combat this, it's not unusual for teams to have a go-to frequency that they use if there are any issues on the hill, a simple password will alert those in the loop to change frequencies to have a 'private conversation'. But in the wake of a big emergency, like the 2014 icefall avalanche or the 2015 earthquake, all teams now use a common frequency to coordinate the rescue efforts, and of course anyone with a radio can listen in.

Come the ascent in 2006, I was well prepared. I had a really great team in place. We were planning a slightly old-style ascent compared to the smaller, bespoke ascents that I lead today. We all trekked as a group, there were six of us in total, and we bonded well, building a strong relationship, which is exactly how it should be. Doing so meant that we were all looking out for each other on the mountain, which makes it safer for everyone. The whole expedition was, essentially, running like clockwork.

Early in the expedition, despite a poor forecast, I felt we could still make a start with an acclimatisation run up to Camp One with the plan to overnight there. We climbed up through the icefall, and just as we got to Camp One, it started to snow – and it snowed and snowed and snowed. I'd expected some, but it continued to snow, metres of it. In the end we were snowed in for four days. We ran out of food, ran out of fuel, and I had to radio down and find someone at Base Camp who might help us. Eventually, Guy Cotter, who owns Adventure Consultants, one of the other guiding companies, came on the radio and I asked him for food, because I knew that they had a stash nearby. He replied, 'Well, I think our food store is about 50 metres away from you.' It was incredibly kind of him.

A 50-metre walk sounded fine, a stroll in the park in normal conditions, but it was still snowing and we were having to dig the tents out on a regular basis. Later that afternoon, during a slight lull in the storm, four of us ventured out and paced out 50 metres from our tent, to roughly where we thought the Adventure Consultants tents should be. It had snowed so much that the tents were buried. Quickly locating the spot we dug down, found their tents, and raided their food. At last we had something to eat, and it made a nice change to eat different food from our own rations.

That was all very well, but we couldn't stay there for ever waiting for the storm to pass. So we decided to make a break for it, to get back down to Base Camp. All we had to do was find the fixed rope at the top of the icefall and follow that. We tried two or three times, all the while worrying about the huge, yawning crevasses that exist all around the top of the icefall and now covered in snow so that they were invisible to the eye, but each time we ventured out we failed to find the ropes. It sounds silly that we couldn't find them, but metres of fresh snow and low cloud had changed everything into a white, featureless environment. Wandering around was relatively safe as we were all roped together, but the chances of finding the ropes were almost zero. Each time we turned back we had to follow our tracks to the tents as they too had disappeared from sight in the cloud and snow. We weren't alone up there. Kari Kobler and his team were also stuck. But Kari, being a little older than us and clearly a lot wiser, didn't try to move from his tent at all. He and his team didn't leave the tent for four days, whereas I tried to get back down to Base Camp every day. On each attempt we would pass by and he would shout a greeting and good luck to us from the warmth of his tent; then a couple of hours later we would sheepishly pass by him again. This episode was the start of a really good relationship with Kari, who is one of the great characters of the Himalayan guiding world.

Eventually, a big, powerful team of Sherpas ploughed their way down from Camp Two, at the same time as a team forced their way up from Base Camp. The two teams met up at our tent and that's how we got out. Everyone agreed that there had been an astonishing amount of snow. There's usually one big storm cycle each year, but this was way beyond what anyone had seen for years.

It was no surprise that during the time we were stuck at camp, one of the biggest avalanches I've ever seen came thundering down on Nuptse. It started high on the north face, probably triggered by a cornice collapse, before rolling down the mountain. It was completely silent from where we were, but clearly visible, even though we were a few hundred meters away: colossal amounts of powder snow. I confess it was quite exciting; it dusted us all at Camp One. I was glad we were nowhere near it. An avalanche of that size can be deadly, as the world saw in 2015.

The acclimatisation phase had gone well, the extra time at Camp meant we all felt well adjusted to the altitude even though it was a bit different from the norm. So now we had to wait for

the teams of Sherpas to be ready. In those days the big commer-
ical groups would get together and send a team of Sherpas to fix
ropes from the South Col of Everest up to the Balcony, which
is at about 8,500 metres, fairly close to the summit. Then which-
ever team went first would fix the rest of the rope. In fact, in
my first year – 2004 – we had fixed the rope. I was quite proud
of that; it makes for hard work, and because of this it causes a
team to be slower (and you have to be very conscious of your
clients). Things changed after 2006 and now the rope gets put
all the way to the summit before any teams even think about
summiting. This came about as a natural evolution to how the
mountain was guided. It was silly to be taking clients up the
same day that teams were attempting to fix rope; it was a recipe
for disaster. It's much better to use a small team of strong Sherpas
to fix to the summit unhindered, and then allow the teams to
follow in their wake.

Anyway, back in 2006, my team made it up to the South Col of
Everest with Kari Kobler's team. But Kari had, in my view, made
a mistake: he had decided to bring up all his clients to the South
Col without supplementary oxygen, and they were all knackered.
My take on things is that if you're going to use oxygen on Everest,
you might as well just use it from the word 'go'; it's obviously
very tough on the body in such thin air, at those low temperatures, no matter how acclimatised you are. Perhaps Kari was
trying to 'give the mountain a chance' and use as little oxygen as
possible. I can respect that concept but I wouldn't ask a client
to do the same. Having climbed to close to 8,300 metres on
Everest without oxygen, I know how hard it is on the body. Kari's
team arrived late in the day at the South Col, and they were too
tired to do much more.

It was pretty evident that the task of putting the rope in place was going to fall on our team. I was leading the team but I had a tail guide, a little Bolivian called Carlos Escobar – no relation to the drug dealer! Carlos was a great guy, often mistaken by Sherpas as one of their own because he had a similar build and dark skin.[*] Along with Carlos was Rhys Jones, who that day became the youngest person to climb the seven summits; Baz Welsh, who was a school teacher; Harry Fathering and Phil Drowling (who through illness wasn't with us on the summit push). We got on really well, more like a bunch of friends climbing together than a guide-led group, which is exactly the sort of bond that I have always tried to build in a team.

We were preparing to leave South Col at the normal time: ten o'clock at night. From the start, nothing went wrong, but everything seemed to be taking an inordinate amount of time. We were a little bit late leaving when one of the guys had a problem with their O_2 cylinders, and the deep snow on our climb up to the Balcony made things take even longer. I was acutely aware that time was ebbing away. Because of the deep snow being blown about by the wind we had to dig the rope out which had been fixed to the Balcony, taking up more time and energy. The Sherpas were out in front, re-breaking the trail, even though the line had only been put in the day before.

If you have ever waded through deep snow, you'll know how physically demanding it is. It's ten times harder than if you're following. Nevertheless, the Sherpas were doing an amazing job busting in the trail. But by the time we got to the Balcony it was already light, when it should have been the middle of the night. When the team got there everyone changed oxygen cylinders. Harry and his Sherpa Mingma had already decided to turn around.

---

[*] Regretably Carlos passed away three years later, succumbing to cancer, which was a terrible shame.

I think Harry was getting a bad vibe about the day, and sensibly he was concerned about timings. Kari Kobler was also there with his team, and he too made the decision at the Balcony that it was too late in the day, that his team were too tired. I took stock and decided that we should carry on. One of Kari's team wanted to stay and climb alongside us, and I was very happy for him to do that as he was a fit, experienced guy. He had a strong Sherpa with him as well, which was good news: we needed all the manpower possible if we were to succeed.

Once we'd all swapped over our cylinders, I gave a pep talk to the guys: 'Right, it's getting very late in the day. [By this, of course, I meant late for our purposes, as it wasn't even 8 a.m.] The Sherpas are really struggling with the amount of snow, and now we've got to fix rope. We're here together as a team – we're not here as guide and clients; this is what mountaineering is about. If you want the glittering prize today, we need to work together. We've got a common goal, because if we turn around now, I'm telling you, we will not have the physical or mental reserves to come back up this season. If we turn around, this expedition is over. So, I'm asking each and every one of you: do you want to go forward? We'll have to carry all our own oxygen now, we can't ask the Sherpas to carry any of our stuff.' Normally on an expedition, each paying client carries a single cylinder of oxygen, which is the oxygen that they're breathing. Their Sherpa support carries two spare for the client, and the Sherpa's two, so the Sherpa's carrying four cylinders to the client's one. With each 4-litre cylinder weighing a little over 4 kilograms when full, it's a huge ask of the Sherpas.

After my little inspirational talk, we readied ourselves for the next stretch. Together with Thindu I left the Balcony. We took turns leading out ahead breaking trail in the deep snow. Thindu's power was immense that day and he took on the lion's share of the work while I carried the rope and fixed the anchor behind him. The whole process was very time-consuming. We were breaking a trail in snow, and behind us we had got our loyal train of Sherpas and support, and then the clients coming up behind. And all the time I could hear a clock in my head: tick, tock, tick, tock. I knew we had to move more quickly if we were to have a chance of reaching the summit.

We were now at 8,500 metres. We were fully in the Death Zone. Even with supplementary oxygen we had limited time here before our bodies gave up, and that time was ebbing away.

The radios were already crackling into life, from people back at Base Camp. First to contact us was Mara Larson who was running Base Camp for Jagged Globe that year. There was also my friend Henry Todd who came online to talk to me. Henry has nearly twenty years' experience on the mountain, and in that time has seen most things. I started to voice my thought processes to him – not so much for feedback, more to say them out loud to someone who would understand the situation. He was pretty clear on what was going on and what the risks were; he never questioned my decisions but he provoked thought with his statement: 'Right, just be aware of what you're doing. You're cutting it really fine; just be very cautious. You're there with clients, Kenton; you're not supposed to be making climbing decisions, you're meant to be making guiding decisions. Remember that.'

There was so much snow that the rock steps, which are normally short, tricky rock climbs, on the way to the South Summit were buried. I decided it would be quicker – and easier – to bypass these obstacles by simply turning them on the right-hand side using the deep snow to our advantage. It was further to climb by skirting to the right but it was by far the best option for the clients. Just as Thindu started breaking trail again, a massive slab avalanche was set off: the crown wall broke where he was walking, and shot across the bowl that was to our right. The whole thing went *brrrrrm*, like a jet engine starting, and he was left standing on the crown wall, with snow disappearing below him. He looked back at me, as if to say, 'What do I do?'

'It's gone,' I called across to him. 'It's not going to avalanche a second time. Carry on.' The whole thing felt very on the edge, but although I questioned every decision, it never felt out of control.

On the mountain there's a thing called 'turnaround time'; the idea of turnaround time is that no matter where you are on the mountain, if you're not on the summit, you turn around and come back down, to ensure you still have enough oxygen, physical reserves, mental reserves and daylight to get down to the top camp. The daylight is crucial: when the sun goes down, everything takes five times longer and things start to go wrong, especially if your energy reserves are running low. So the number-one rule is always: get off the mountain safely and in good time.

Turnaround time is one o'clock at the latest. It doesn't matter where you are, come one o'clock, you turn around. Ideally, you want to summit by seven, eight or nine o'clock in the morning. There's a certain amount of leeway, which is why you usually aim to leave Camp Four at 10 p.m. the day before, and climb right through the night.

On this particular day, we reached the Balcony at 6.30 a.m., when you would expect to be on the South Summit. There we were, grinding our way up. The sun was fully up, and it was getting pretty hot, and when we finally got onto the South Summit it was about midday.

At the South Summit you're normally no more than a couple of hours from the top. I remember looking at the terrain, which of course I had seen before. But now I was looking at it thinking, 'Oh my God, how are we going to get across there?' What was normally a rocky ridge line with some snowy patches was now a hideous-looking snowy ridge without a single rock in sight. Although the climbing would be straightforward, my concern was that I couldn't figure out how we were going to fix anchors for the ropes to safeguard the clients.

At the back of my mind was a picture taken in 1953 by Evans and Bourdillon, who got to the South Summit on Everest a couple of days before Hillary and Tenzing, using a closed-circuit breathing system. Essentially that's a CO_2 scrubber. Nowadays we use an open circuit. The closed circuit was very experimental, and it didn't work quite as well as it was planned, so they were totally exhausted by the time they arrived. Even though they were that close, they took the right decision and turned around. That said, Bourdillon never really got over it. He was so close, close enough to smell the summit, yet he didn't get there.

Here we were, a small group of us, looking across at exactly the same view. It was pristine, just as those guys would have seen it in '53: clean snow, not a single footstep, no fixed lines. We huddled together and discussed what we should do next.

Neither Carlos nor my clients had ever been there before. All I could think was 'If I turn them around now, their opportunity will be gone for ever.' None of them would come back: they wouldn't have the time, the resources, the money. They certainly wouldn't be coming back that expedition. I knew that if I turned the team around they would for ever be thinking, 'What if? What if we had gone second? What if we hadn't had to fix the rope and break trail?' 'What if we had waited an extra day? The trail would be in, we'd just follow the trail.' I asked the Sherpas what they thought. Of course, we knew what the Sherpas would say.

They have a 'yes' culture. They knew that it wasn't going according to plan, but they were working for us and they generally say what they think you want to hear. I knew that no one would or could make the decision other than me.

I spelled out the situation for the team. I had already been up there twice; it didn't really matter to me if we summited that day or not. I wanted a summit as much as the next guy, but I had to make a decision, be positive and decisive. 'We're going to go up, and we're going to lay the line, we're going to open up the highway for everybody else to follow us.'

I had thrown my hand in. We were now committed.

Then I jumped up. 'Right, come on, we've got to try. We've got until one o'clock, we've got another hour and a bit, and that should be enough time.' Deep down I suspected it wouldn't be, but the others didn't need to know that. We climbed down the short step from the South Summit and started to traverse the ridge to the Hillary Step. I've never seen snow that deep at that altitude before or since, and the Sherpas were soon up to their knees again, bulldozing a trail in place, running out rope and anchoring it to anything they could find, digging down, finding old anchors or in other places running multiple ropes together between anchors. They were no longer breaking a trail, they were snow-ploughing a trail. It was a colossal effort, way beyond what I could have asked them to do, and when we got to just underneath the Hillary Step, I looked at my watch. It was, horrifyingly, 1.45 p.m.

It had taken two hours to do something that normally takes thirty minutes. The ridge is generally rocky, and the clients struggle along with their crampons scratching on the rocks. It's a bit awkward, that little stretch. But on that day the rocks were totally buried in the snow. The ridge was totally swamped. It was relatively easy for those following but desperate for those breaking trail.

Then the radio started to crackle. It was Henry Todd again: 'How long are you going to be? Are you aware of the time?'

I tried to sound totally calm in my reply: 'Yes, Henry, I'm fully aware of the time, thank you.'

'Just be aware of your oxygen.' He was saying all the right things, gently reminding me again of all the important things, but he wasn't flapping, he was very matter-of-fact.

Ultimately, when I got down, I got some criticism for what I did that day, especially from my boss at Jagged Globe, Simon Lowe. I understand his point of view; the other teams had turned back. But I was the one with the real-time information; I was the one who saw first hand the snow conditions and the condition of my clients. I knew how much oxygen they were using and how much they had left; I knew what the weather was like on the summit. It was all time-critical decision-making, but we were so close.

In those circumstances, the big danger is blind summit fever. The prize becomes all and you are at risk of becoming irrational. I was working everything through my mind, and I *knew* that we were doing the right thing, despite the time. Then my radio crackled to life again, and it was Carlos, my tail guide. 'Kenton, Kenton, Kenton!'

'Carlos!'

'Kenton, Kenton, Kenton!'

'Yes, Carlos, what is it?'

'Kenton, this is really bad. We make mistake, we make mistake. We should go down, we should go down.'

'Oh my God,' I thought, because everybody was listening. All the clients had a radio and everybody could hear our conversation. Quickly I stepped in, cutting him off.

'Carlos, please! We're going for the summit. We're going to summit, it's fine. We're going to summit, it's all in hand.'

We climbed to the base of the Hillary Step, which is steep but is only 12 or 15 feet high, from bottom to top. To get to it climbers traverse the ridge and end up in this little alcove at the bottom of the step, and it feels very exposed, because you're on a ridge line with a beautiful snow cornice, which, on the right side, goes thousands of metres, down into Tibet. It's very steep on that side, so you have to stay away from the edge. If you're not careful, you stand on the wrong side of the cornice line and it will collapse into the abyss.

You have to judge your position carefully on this tightrope. On your left-hand side is an uninterrupted 2,000-metre drop down the south-west face to Camp Two in the Western Cwm. As we got to the step I spotted the rope from a couple of years ago, which I had fixed in 2004. It was still there, the yellow one. I yelled to the guys beside me, 'The yellow one! The yellow one's the newest one – climb the yellow one!' No one could hear me, it was so windy. I could see the wind whipping snow off the top. And all the time, it was tick, tock, tick, tock, tick, tock, and I was thinking, 'Please climb quickly, guys.'

By now, the clients were way out of their comfort zone, and I was trying to instil in them a sense of normality. 'This is okay, guys; don't worry . . . it's all in hand, you're doing brilliantly.'

Next we had to climb up this steep rock. And I mean steep. Well done, Hillary, 1953, well bloody done! It was a lot snowier then, and I think he climbed up the snow on the right-hand side. Certainly, the famous picture of Dougal Haston in '75 shows that it was snowy all around him; whereas nowadays, you end up with one foot in the snow and one foot on the rock, where there's a rope in place. I've climbed without the rope, but it's quite hard. Today, with the ropes fixed, it still presents a problem for many. With a jumar on the rope you pull and haul yourself up, one foot planted in the snow to the right-hand side and the other picking out small ledges for the front points of the crampons to rest on. You find a balance point for your body, grab a handful of rope, then slide the jumar upwards again, repeating the process. It should only take a few minutes but some climbers are so inexperienced that this can take them twenty minutes or so, causing a huge bottleneck and making many people, myself included, wonder what on earth they think they are doing there in the first place. Anyway, once you get up there, and you've surmounted the steep part, you step back and left slightly onto a steep slab, you clamber up that, to be presented with a big crack, about six inches wide in the corner, where you jam your foot in. Then it steepens up and you have to make this manoeuvre around the corner, it's *à cheval*, so one leg one side and one leg the other side, and you shuffle, as if you're riding a horse, around the corner. When you see pictures of the crowd on Everest, it is often because they're stuck here, at the bottleneck. People coming up meet people coming down and one person will be shuffling around the rock, and there's no other way around, so it can become crowded, especially if someone is struggling.

So, back in 2006, I was talking to Henry on the radio, letting him know what stage we were at. I was midway through talking to him when my voice went. I choked a bit, gasping for breath and unsure what the hell was happening to me, then realised I had run out of oxygen. I had to swap my bottle over quickly.

Then Thindu dropped the bombshell that we'd run out of rope to fix. 'I've got the spare one,' I told him, and I've been mocked ever since for what happened next. I whipped out 200 metres of rope. Now 200 metres of standard rope is really heavy, and Thindu was astonished as I unpacked. It was 4-millimetre – really tiny, thin rope. I had thrown it in my bag as a last-minute addition, just in case.

'We're going to fix this.' By now all the Sherpas were looking at me as if I was mad.

I knew that from here onwards, the slopes above got easier but we still needed to lay a hand-rail for the clients, for my peace of mind as well as theirs. Four millimetres, even though it's really thin, has still got a breaking strain of around half a ton, so I was certain it would arrest a slip. It wouldn't resist a big-impact fall, but it would do the job. It also provided a big psychological boost to the clients, even if its physical benefits weren't the greatest.

I started unravelling it, but it had got tangled, and 200 metres of 4-millimetre rope is horrendous when it gets tangled. All the Sherpas were waiting for me, so I gave them the end bit and told them to go ahead without me, so off they went while I battled with the tangle. In the end I could only untangle about 80 metres, so that's how much we used.

At this point the clients had no idea how far it was to the top. You couldn't see it from where we were standing – it's only when you come around the corner from there that the view actually opens up, and you realise that you're practically there. On a good day, from where we were to the top is about twenty minutes.

Meanwhile, the radio was going off in my ear almost continually, with people asking me, 'How much further? How much further?' The whole of Base Camp was listening, everybody tuned in to our frequency, and there was even a BBC film crew following our progress and recording it all (they were filming the Himalayan Rescue Association for a documentary that was much acclaimed when broadcast). Of course, I was totally oblivious to all of this at the time. I was locked in to what we were doing, and it felt fabulous. What I was doing could be regarded as reckless. But

I was absolutely on it. I was so in my element. We were on top of the world and we were gunning for the summit.

As soon as I saw the summit, I let out a sigh of relief. We were going to make it, and that's a feeling like no other. I know that getting to the top is only halfway there – you've got to get back down – but I knew that these guys were going to make it. I had a strong team and that made the difference – that was the reason I knew we could press on for the summit. Understanding a team and its strengths and weaknesses is critical to success

As we got closer, Carlos calmed down. We were all in line, and there's a picture of us all snaking our way towards the goal. It was Rhys's twentieth birthday and he really wanted to radio first from the summit, though I didn't know this at the time. But I inadvertently gazumped him. We were about 30 or 40 metres from the top, and I announced it over the radio. My plan was for us to get there and get us off: taking photographs can take twenty minutes or even half an hour. This time I was having none of that. A quick pic and then down.

It was snowing again and the pictures of us up there show our hoods up, everybody hunched down against the winds that were whipping across the top. The clouds were building up down the valley, and we could see in the distance more big cloud formations billowing up. I was now concerned about us getting down before the weather closed in again. The last two years I had been up there, there were blue skies and very low winds, but this felt different, dangerous. I got the radio out, and announced, 'We're on the summit.'

'Congratulations,' said Henry tartly. 'Now just get down. Just get down.' I heard the cheers echoing around, through the radio, before I quickly turned it off. When you're at Base Camp on a summit day, you can hear the cheers go up in the morning as teams summit.

Everyone made it to the top and my words of wisdom were: 'Right, get your photographs, and let's just get the hell out of here.' I knew that I had to keep the team together and motivated for the descent. In my clients' minds they had done what they had come here to do. But the job was only half done. There were no celebrations, no hugging, we probably spent three minutes on the top – that's all the time we had, no slacking – and then we started heading back down.

It was 14.45, way after the time we should have been heading down. I had not just torn the guidelines up, I'd drop-kicked them into Tibet. There I was, in my third year on Everest, this young gun flouting the rules that have been laid down for ten years since the disaster of 1996 when a series of poor decisions lead to the death of eight people in a storm high on the mountain and a rule book of best practice was drawn up. It was after those terrible times that everybody had a really hard look at the industry and a shake up ensued. The situation I had created was not ideal.

Anyway, we started to make our way down, and I was at the back, playing sweeper. The snow made the descent fast, there are none of the awkward rocks that need to be traversed or skirted around on the traverse back to the South Summit; you can beeline your way down, almost running some sections.

When I reached the south Summit I found Thindu sitting down, hunched over. This guy had done so much trail breaking in the dark, but now he was utterly exhausted. I sat next to him, head to head, with our hoods up against the snow. I leaned right in to speak to him: 'Come on', I said to my friend 'we've got to keep moving, we can't stop.' I knew that this was the exact spot where Rob Hall had died with his client in 1996. So I repeated, 'We can't stop. Thindu, come on buddy.' And he sat there, in his big Royal Navy down suit from some previous expedition, and he just breathed out a great puff of weariness. That's how far the Sherpas go for their clients. They sacrifice everything. Sometimes the clients don't realise how much physical effort these boys are putting in on their behalf.

The clients were quickly up and over the South Summit, and on the descent. Once you get over the South Summit you are on your way home, it's all downhill. Although the South Summit is only a little rise, it's steep. It feels like climbing the whole of Mount Everest again, because you are that exhausted. I helped poor Thindu to his feet and, holding on to him, we wearily clambered over the top, and then we started zipping down the lines.

We made good time down to the Balcony, and I knew there would be some hot tea flasks there as we had left a couple there on the way up. I was so thirsty by then, and I realised that I hadn't had anything to drink since leaving camp at ten o'clock the night before – I don't think anybody had. My water bottle had frozen on the ascent and I had thrown it off from the South Summit, because it was just a solid lump of ice and represented nothing more than extra weight. Upon arriving at the Balcony I could see a couple of flasks standing up in the snow, like someone stranded in the desert, we literally pounced on these things. We couldn't get the tops off, they were frozen on tight. I started crying with frustration. 'Fucking hell, let's leave it,' I said and we carried on down with our tongues sticking to the roof of our dry mouths.

I walked into camp at the South Col at 19.15. I was the last one in, and Gyalgen, the Sherpa who had stayed at the Col that day in support, handed me a pan of hot tang (a sugary powdered drink that is common in South-East Asia). I'd had nothing to drink for nearly twenty-four hours by this time. He handed over the pan, now lukewarm, full of grit and bits, and I tipped it back immediately. Then he handed me a pan of Rara Noodles, the local equivalent of Super Noodles, and I just buried my face in them. When the food hit my stomach, it stayed there for about five seconds before I threw up all over the tent. Gyalgen simply said, 'Oh.'

I look back on it many years later, and that was the moment that I realised something about Everest. On both occasions in the two years before, when I had been guiding, reaching the summit had come relatively easily; this time had been a fight. Not a fight in a nasty way, but Everest had played her cards close. This trip represented the start of my real love affair with Everest.

It was the difficulty that excited me. Every single one of my eleven ascents has been different and exciting, but 2006 was the year that I felt I earned my spurs on Everest, my leadership credentials validated.

I think what makes that expedition stand out for me is that it was my show up there. I was calling the shots, and I found I liked the responsibility, I liked being in charge. I got back to Base Camp and I got my knuckles severely rapped. I do listen to criticism, but that doesn't mean I have to agree with it. When I saw Henry, he summed it up well: 'You weren't making guiding decisions, you were making climbing decisions, and as much as I respect that in you, Kenton, you can't do that on this mountain. Not with clients in your charge.' Then his face widened with his huge grin, he wrapped a big arm across my shoulders and said, 'Bloody well done though . . . that was something special, not many others could have done that.' From Henry that meant a lot.

Would I do what I did in 2006 again? The honest answer is I hope so. I did it once and, I have to admit, I got away with it. I knew I was making the right decisions for the team, in the conditions we faced on that particular day

I look back on that summit with a deep sense of pride, despite the fact I get the mickey taken out of me about that top bit of rope. The very next day people were trotting up in less than half the time that we did, with clients who were much weaker than my clients standing on the top by five o' clock in the morning. But this was only possible because of the work that we did that day; we had forged the way for them. We had put in that track. We laid the path for everybody else.

2006 is doubly special to me because we experienced something few people ever experience. In 1953, Hillary and Tenzing, as well as Evans and Bourdillon, would have had that pristine view in front of them, knowing that no one else had ever stepped there before. When we were near the summit in 2006 we saw as close to the scene as they saw, not just because we were there first, but because normally there's the sight of ropes from previous years. The heavy snowfall that preceded the climbing season meant there was nothing visable up there, and that's what made it so amazing to me.

Now, over three hundred people a year reach the summit. Maybe forty people made it on the day after we had been there in 2006 alone. So to have an experience like we did is now rare. Personally I bettered it only in 2011 when I summited in a small team of only four. No one else was even higher than Camp Three at the time. That was unique.

I've been first of the year to the top twice, once in 2004 and then again in 2006. I've been up there early season, I've been up there in the dark, I've been up there with clients, I've been up there on my own, I've been so lucky to experience a mountain so many times in so many different ways, so perhaps it's easy for me to say 'That is what it should be like.' It's not enough to be part of a conveyor belt of people; it's not right that there are queues to summit, most notably in 2012. That's not mountaineering, that's not an achievement. Well, perhaps that's not quite fair. It is an achievement still, but it is not the experience that it should be. The climbers who put time and effort in deserve to experience what I have been lucky enough to experience over my time on the mountain.

On that particular day, I was sat at Base Camp, looking upwards. I was concerned about the weather, in particular the fact that the wind that had shifted direction. I knew that there were many people on a summit push and I feared for their safety. There is an infamous picture of the queues at the Hillary Step that day, queues that perhaps directly led to the deaths of four people. In May 2012 the first summit window was late coming, many teams were hoping to summit on the first day of the window. As far as I'm concerned, those deaths were avoidable, they represented bad project management. There was such a jam that people spent hours there, waiting, eating into their physical reserves, getting colder, even frostbitten. That's not mountaineering, that's something gone wrong. That's not people listening to their inner sixth sense, when the braver thing, the more sensible thing, would be to turn around and come back another time; but people had got summit fever, and they were blinded by what was calling to them.

Some people would look at that and say 'Why didn't the guides stop them? Why didn't they turn them around?' Well, this brings me to a contentious, difficult point. None of the big teams – IMG, Alpine Ascents, and the others – were involved in climbing that day. We have a term for the different sorts of teams on the mountain: some of them are called 'friendlies' and others are not. The 'friendlies' are the commercial teams, and we call them that because I, and the other guides on the mountain, know what their moves will be, and, if there's a hiccup of some sort, we know they have the logistics to get themselves out of it, or they can be relied on to help out in a situation. The others, the lone operators (even if there's more than one of them), are what might be called the 'unfriendlies'. They could be the friendliest people in the world, but the 'unfriendlies' are the unknowns. We don't know what moves they're going to make, and we don't know how they'll deal with any problems that might occur. Do they have the depth of experience to deal with real problems? I think not, in most cases. They are the loose cannons, in that if things go wrong they have to rely on some of us to help them out. One thing's for sure: on that particular day, the unfriendlies' clients weren't being particularly well led.

I summited about four or five days after this, and there were no more than a quarter of the number of people attempting to summit, so much so we had the top to ourselves. It comes down to having the courage and confidence to make ones own decisions, not be one of the herd. It's such an important thing to do, not just in the mountains but in life. In 2012, people followed the decisions of others thinking that this would be for the best. Well, more fool them for not being brave enough to make their own decisions.

CHAPTER 7
TEARS WILL FALL

Death on Everest is not something new to me. One never gets used to it but it is an unfortunate fact of life for mountaineers. We live a selfish life. We pursue our passion and those around us wait and hope.

Back in 2004, in my first year working there – my very first time on an 8,000-metre peak, in fact – I couldn't have been more excited to be at the base of the world's most famous mountain. Perhaps I was naive, or maybe simply too keen. I have heard some people say I was reckless but it never felt like that to me. If anything I was simply confident. For me, personally, confidence is everything; when it's high I feel invincible, which clearly shows in my climbing – there is an extra element to the way I approach the hills. So to me it's never reckless, it's always very well thought through; risks are mitigated and calculated but there are actions I carry out that many see as being . . . well, let me call them bold – but in many ways that is what has set me apart from the rest.

So, on this day in 2004, I made a bold decision. Clive Jones and I decided to climb up to touch Camp Three. 'Touch' refers to when a team will ascend to a given camp but not spend the night there. The weather forecast was so-so, but I thought that we would simply bail back down the fixed ropes if things got nasty, so I wasn't concerned at all.

As we ascended, the cloud billowed up the valley, engulfing the Cwm in a grey swirling blanket. The snow fell lightly as the sun was gradually blocked from view, and Clive and I methodically climbed up towards the tiny specks of tents that began to play hide-and-seek as the cloud obscured them from sight.

As time went on, I grew increasingly aware of the amount of snow falling. The Lhoste face is a huge sweep of snow and ice that tumbles down from the fourth-highest mountain in the world and Everest's neighbour; it is enormous. The angle of the face is steep enough that snow doesn't really stick, it simply sheds off as it falls, tumbling down and gathering more and more fresh snow as it goes. It's not an avalanche, as such, because it's never really big enough. Climbers and skiers call them sluffs.

I punished my body on the last 200 metres of the climb, pushing myself as hard as I could, step after step, my lungs heaving, clawing at the thin air in an attempt to draw in the precious oxygen. I was racing, not so much myself (which is what I normally do), but the weather. I was trying to reach the first tents as fast as possible so I could turn around and we could head down. Below me I could just make out the labouring figure of Clive as he continued to make his way towards Camp Three; he had put in a sterling effort to climb this far so quickly.

The weather was deteriorating really fast and it was the first time this trip that either of us had been to this altitude. I turned back as soon as I reached the first tent, descending quickly to Clive; we exchanged a few words and decided to make our way down together. We were both almost running down the face in an attempt to get out of the maelstrom of snow that was being unleashed on us.

The descent down the 750 metres of fixed lines was painless until the very bottom of the face where the ice angled down at nearly 90 degrees, just above the bergschrund (essentially a crevasse that forms where the glacier meets the bottom of the mountain). Here there was an abseil over the steep, almost overhanging face followed by an awkward traverse to get to the more mellow-angled slopes that led to the flat of the Cwm.

The snow was now cascading down the face in constant waves, never too large but still very alarming. We were the only people on the whole of the Lhoste face; it felt serious and lonely, even with the security of the fixed ropes in place. I bounced down the steep wall and quickly scuttled across the traverse to safety, making it just as a large sluff crashed down over the lip behind me. For a moment the world was nothing but swirling, pummelling snow; it was everywhere and escape was impossible, even on the edge of the sluff. I was hunched over, trying to keep the snow at bay as it penetrated any open zip, cuff or collar. Worse still, it invaded my nose and mouth, making it hard to breath.

As it abated, I screamed to Clive who was still exposed on the face above. I could see his figure in the gloom coming slowly down. He jumped over the lip and came towards me just as more snow tumbled from above and I lost him in a sea of white. I screamed but the only noise that I could hear was the *whoomfh, whoomfh* of the sluff as it poured over us.

Clive was knocked from his feet, his cow's tails or lanyards, which connect him to the fixed rope, jarred tight on the traverse line. He tried get back on his feet but it was hopeless. I saw him for a moment, his eyes boring into mine, his stare one of total horror, and then he was gone again, lost under the white waterfall. I reached out my arms and grabbed nothing but air and snow. Even on the edge of the cascading snow I could feel the life being sucked out of me by the relentless buffeting that pounded our bodies.

A momentary easing in the cascade allowed me to see Clive. He was slumped on the rope, lifeless.

I scrambled back along the traverse as he disappeared from view again and reached out, my gloved fingers clawing around the haul loop of his rucksack. Blindly, I pulled; I pulled with all my might, screaming to Clive to stand up. I saw his arm appear first and then, like a cork out of a bottle, we simply popped out of the snow and away from the runnel that had become a torrent of torture. Clive gasped air in relief.

We staggered down the easier slopes, covered in white from head to toe, looking like snowmen, and collapsed on the ground, away from the face. Even a mere few metres away, the difference was staggering: the snow fell gently around us from the grey clouds; there was silence, none of the roar or crushing weight of snow on our heads and shoulders. We were able to breath: lying on our backs, we both gasped huge lungfuls of air, like open-mouthed fish on the deck of the trawler.

By the time we returned to Camp Two, we were both joking about the whole incident, but there's no doubt being caught in the maelstrom that cascaded from the Lhoste face was serious. Luckily, both of us were uninjured, apart from some superficial frostbite that Clive picked up while we were high on the face.

Three years later, standing in almost exactly the same spot, the team I was leading readied itself for the next stage of our acclimatisation programme. It was a beautiful day, with not a breath of wind in the Western Cwm, and the sun had finally begun to penetrate the numbing cold that comes with the early mornings.

The small party I was guiding had left Camp Two on a regular acclimatisation rotation to Camp Three, the idea being to spend the night at just over 7,000 metres and descend the Lhoste face the following day. Then we would drop back to Base Camp to prepare for the summit weather window and the push that would bring.

On our way towards the bottom of the Lhoste face, I had noticed an object on the bottom of the fixed lines: from a distance it was impossible to make out exactly what it was, but it didn't sit at all well with me. As we got closer, I could see a Sherpa moving towards us at a pace. As he neared the team he began speaking rapidly in Nepali, making no sense until we calmed him down a little. Almost at once I pieced together what was going on. Instructing the team to put on warm clothes, eat some food, take on fluid and stay put, I walked to the base of the fixed ropes with the Sherpa.

Hanging in a grotesque manner on the bottom of the fixed lines was the body of a Sherpa. There had been no movement since I had first spotted it some ten minutes previously, so I assumed the worse. I guessed there had been some sort of a fall: one of his legs was hideously contorted around the back of his body, clearly badly broken.

I radioed the situation back to Base Camp and the HRA (Himalayan Rescue Association), asking for assistance, as clearly the body would have to be removed.

I squatted next to the body, and couldn't see any obvious signs of death. There was the broken leg but that was all; there was no blood on the snow, no ripped clothing, no puncture wounds. I was a little baffled and started to feel slightly shocked. I'd never been this close to a body before and I was struggling to deal with what this meant. It didn't seem real.

Both the Sherpa and I agreed that we should move the body

off the ropes and down from the path, thus giving both the dead Sherpa and the climbers a little distance from each other.

Trying to lift the dead weight of the body was harder than I'd expected: even with the two of us, we could hardly move it. It struck me that the limbs still readily moved, with no sign of any rigor mortis. But then I had absolutely no idea how quickly rigor mortis set in, so why was it a surprise? The thoughts running through my mind seemed totally random and, although connected with what we were doing, they seemed detached at the same time. That is to say, they seemed to bear no relevance to what I was physically doing.

I released the rucksack and let it slide down the slope away from the body. Then, with an immense effort, I raised the body by the armpits. As I heaved, the head moved and – to my horror – a large portion of the skull moved away from the head, and quantities of thick dark blood flooded over the pristine white of the snow, spreading like some hideous red growth. I pulled away in shock and in doing so, dropped the body back down, coating my leg and arm in the blood.

Everything I was now experiencing was happening in a dream-like trance, nothing felt real; yet somehow it was all very, very clear, as though my senses had somehow been enhanced.

It was never a boast, but for a number of years I used to say how lucky I was that death, or at least death on my watch, had never happened. There has been a very long list of funerals of friends and colleagues. A number of years back it was so bad that, when someone rang out of the blue, my immediate reaction was to start to prepare for the worst. I used to dread hearing the phone ring at odd times of the day, which is a funny reaction from someone who likes to think that he is one of the most optimistic people on the planet. Yet, despite losing so many friends, I had never come close to death in its raw state.

So on this glorious morning, high on Everest, this was some-thing new for me; and unlike normal times when I learn about someone having an accident or dying in the hills, when tears would be streaming down my face and I would experience an overwhelming feeling of unjust loss, this time for the moment I felt nothing. The thing was, the body, the dead Sherpa, wasn't even registering with me as a human being. Perhaps because I'd never known him in life, I couldn't feel the loss – or maybe I was just focusing on the unpleasant tasks I had to undertake.

Eventually the two of us managed to get the body off the fixed lines; we dragged and partially lifted the poor dead Sherpa some 30 or 40 metres from the path, and away from the fall line of any debris that may have tumbled down the face. While moving the body, we had inadvertently left a huge red streak across the snow. The stark contrast between the white and the red would have been rather beautiful if it hadn't been so macabre.

We climbed the short distance back to the path, and only then did we realise, perhaps irrationally, that it would be unacceptable to leave the evidence of our efforts in such an undignified way. Trying to clear up the bloodied mess was difficult: the blood had seeped into the frozen ground, and every time we tried to kick the offending snow away we did nothing more than spread the area yet further. In the end we had to dig out untouched snow from above the scene and bury the areas that have been tainted by the blood. The whole act seem to take a few minutes, but in fact it was way over an hour from the moment I first reached the body until we slowly and sorrowfully walked away.

It was at this point that my own emotional dam crumbled.

I can only assume that I had simply been going through the motions, ticking the boxes that I thought had to been ticked in a situation like this. It was only on the walk back to the gathered team, after we had pulled the body off the fixed ropes and laid it carefully on the ground, away from the scene, that I was engulfed by a wave of emotion. No longer a body, somehow he was now a human being, like me, with a life that had just been lost. An hour before he was alive and now he was not.

The tears rolled down my cheeks as I walked back to the growing gaggle of people who stood battling against the cold at the bottom of the Lhoste face. The party was beginning to swell in number as Western climbers and Sherpas arrived to climb the face. I could taste the salt on my lips as the tears left their tell-tale lines on my face, dripping from my chin. My footsteps seemed leaden, despite the downhill nature of the trail, and my whole body felt numbed. I understood then that I was in shock.

The team were all now sitting in the sun, some on their ruck-sacks to keep their bums off the snow and the cold. As I approached, I took some deep breaths; in attempting to wipe my tear-stained face, I had only managed to wipe my blood-stained fingers across my cheeks. I had clear feelings on what I person-ally wanted to do, but it wasn't just about me: I had four people whose dreams, aspirations – and, ultimately, welfare – hung on my next decision.

The questions came at me rapidly, not just from my own group but from the others who were now also there. I struggled to understand what was being said, the words melting into one long drone, the bombardment was too much; trying to make sense of what was being asked, my reply was simply more tears. I could feel their warmth trickling down my nose; using the back of my hand, I wiped them away, only for more to replace them.

It was Tori's (one of the team) voice asking if I was okay that finally cut through the numbing sensation that had overcome my body, bringing me back from the darkness that was closing in all around. I looked down the Cwm, drinking in the crisp beauty, the stark contrast between the snowy environment and the blue sky, and all I could think of was what a wonderful day it was, so serene, so quiet . . . What a wonderful day, what a wonderful day . . . What a wonderful day to die . . . And then the tears flowed uncontrollably again.

Ben offered me some warm juice. I pulled myself together and simply said, 'We need to make a decision.' It was such a bland statement but it offered some distance from the events that had occurred.

I couldn't stop my mind straying back to 2005, the year after Clive and I had experienced the sluff at the bottom of the face. I had found myself at Camp Two early in the season, and on that particular day there weren't many people in camp. One team that was there was a French Canadian team, made up of only three members; they were camped at Base Camp next to a NASA research team from Brown University – a team that I knew. One of the Canadian team, Shaun, had been feeling unwell, so he had decided to lose some altitude in an attempt to recover. He had hiked down valley, but while at rest in Dughla (a tiny gaggle of tea houses) he had collapsed. Despite being on board a chopper in a little more than forty minutes (in 2005, the only choppers capable of reaching such heights were the old Russian Mil Mi-7s, huge machines used extensively in Afghanistan by the Soviet Union in the '70s, and the tiny Lamas), he was pronounced dead by the time the chopper landed in Kathmandu.

This clearly rocked the Canadian team, not just the fact that Shaun had passed away but also the suddenness of it all. Literally, he was there one morning over breakfast, then dead by late afternoon.

That evening, the girls of the NASA research team asked if I would mind accompanying one of the Canadian team, Gabriel Filippi, back to Base Camp early the following morning. Until that point, I had never met Gabriel (I now consider him a friend and relish the too-few opportunities we have to meet up, normally in a tea house in the Khumbu somewhere), but it was a request I had no trouble agreeing to.

Early-morning light in the Western Cwm is something very special and it is hard to describe. It's a weak white colour, with just the smallest hints of blue, yet it is crystal clear at the same time. I sat clutching a metal mug of hot sweet tea, warming my numbed fingers in the cook tent. Pasang Temba*, our loyal hard-working cook, looked sad: he knew the reason why I was heading down to BC. Sitting next to the door, I kept glancing at the trail snaking down from the higher tents at Camp Two. A solitary figure in red caught my eye – it could only be Gabriel at this early hour. Gulping down the tea and shouldering my rucksack, I said goodbye to Pasang Temba, who was furiously trying to press some chocolate into my hands for the trip down. I intercepted Gabriel in the weak gully that runs parallel to the camp, introduced myself, and together we set off down the Cwm.

I'm often asked what my most vivid memory of Everest is. People normally expect me to say my first summit, or maybe the time I was filmed phoning my wife from the summit, when I burst into tears, but it's not; it is the forty minutes it took to descend to Camp One that day with Gabriel.

The two of us talked very little, just exchanging a few words from time to time. I could sense that he wasn't keen to chat, no doubt trying to assimilate what had happened the day before. The trek down the wide expanse of the Cwm was magical. There was not the slightest breath of wind, and there was just a hint of snow crystals hanging in the air, like fairies playing, occasionally catching the light – glistening pinpricks of light that seemed

---

* Pasang Temba tragically passed away in the earthquake and subsequent avalanche of 25 April 2015.

to explode before us. There wasn't a soul around apart from Gabriel and me, while all around us there wasn't so much as a cloud, just a thin veil of mist, enough to make the Cwm utterly devoid of sound. We were both totally lost in our own worlds: mine was one full of the beauty and wonderment of the location I found myself in, this path I had trodden many, many times – yet here I was experiencing something so special; while I can only think that Gabriel had a very different world, one tinged with immense sadness and loss. To this day I hope that the sheer beauty did make it through and that that is what he remembers of his friend that day, and not the darkness. Life is so much more vivid when it is at its most fragile.

I was explaining only recently to my wife Jazz about something I had heard on Radio 4's *Desert Island Discs*, when Professor Hugh Montgomery – also an Everest summiteer – was interviewed by Kirsty Young. The professor was recounting what he told a patient who was unconscious yet clinging on to life by a slender, stubborn thread: that she could die, that she didn't have to hang on to life for him; and after he did so, the old lady suddenly stopped breathing and passed away. As I was recounting the interview I found myself weeping.

CHAPTER 8
SIR RANULPH FIENNES

The first time I saw Sir Ranulph Fiennes, in the summer of 2004, it took me a while to recognise him. Well, why would I expect to see Britain's foremost explorer – a man renowned for his extraordinary feats of endurance, including running seven marathons in seven consecutive days on seven continents only the year before, and one of my personal heroes – why would I expect to see him sat on the edge of an 'intermediate mountaineer' group, listening to the guide explain the course they'd be taking part in over the next few days near the Swiss resort of Saas-Fee?

I arrived for the briefing in Saas-Grund in my customary style – which is to say last-minute – having driven over from the small apartment I was renting in Chamonix. The group of fifteen clients was listening intently as the head guide droned on; the other four guides and I stood at the back. That's when I noticed the older white-haired gentleman with unfeasibly large eyebrows. I recognised him, but I couldn't place him.

'Who's that, Marty?' I asked one of the other guides.

'Dunno, mate,' said Marty, a Kiwi, so he can be excused his

ignorance of British heroes – just. 'Some Brit dude, Ran something or other.' And that's when the penny dropped who he was.

Back then, I was only an aspirant guide. Although I had already been guiding in Nepal, the UK, Alaska and on Everest for many years, as the full guiding qualifications are not required in these places. But I still needed to get full guiding qualification for the Alps. That meant I had to listen to what the course director said, and act accordingly. Naturally I found this almost impossible, and during this particular course I disagreed with the director on more than a few occasions. The first time was when he split the group up for the following day's climbing; I was hoping to be asked to guide Sir Ranulph, but instead was given the two Js – Jen and Jan.

The next day we were all going to climb the Jägerhorn. Once at the top, the teams would descend before trekking up to a nearby mountain hut. We would spend the night there and climb the Weissmies by its standard route on the Monday. Once all this was done we would return to our valley base.

The Jägerhorn is a great mountain to warm up on. At a little over 3,200 metres, it's perfect to help the body get used to the altitude, before moving on to the Weissmies, one of the classic 4,000-metre peaks of the western Alps. The south face of the Jägerhorn is a huge sweep of imposing rock, and technically quite demanding; at the very top of the mountain, a huge wooden cross adorns the summit. Meanwhile, on the right flank is a popular *via ferrata*, or 'metal path', which allows the mountain to be climbed by mere mortals such as those in our group. The concept of *via ferrata* dates from the First World War (although there are some instances of them being older), when Italian soldiers built supply routes over the mountains, drilling and banging metal cableways to safeguard the passage of their troops. After the war, these cableways remained; today, more and more are being built all over the Alps, allowing people to experience mountains that they would otherwise not be able to, in a safe manner. That said, they can still be very scary sometimes.

The *via ferrata* that we were going to use was of moderate difficulty; each team could expect to take around three hours to summit. Slowly our team of three made our way skywards, using the metal stanchions for our feet and hands. In places there are ladders to climb up, and while occasionally there is only the rock to climb, you are always protected by the cable that snakes its way alongside. We summited the east peak and descended round the back for a bit of lunch, to find the course director already there, with Sir Ranulph – Ran, I'd now learned he was to be called. I sat down as close as I could to him and tried to join their conversation, but my team kept asking all sorts of questions: 'What mountain is that? Can we see the Matterhorn? Can we see tomorrow's climb? Have you really climbed Everest?' All very good, but couldn't they see that I was a little star-struck?

The final summit bastion is great fun; unlike the lower half of the climb, we used the rock more than the metal stanchions. I shouted encouragement to my team as they climbed behind me, and when we reached the top I insisted on a team summit shot, and proceeded to show off by climbing up the old wooden cross marking the summit, much to the delight of the two girls as well as Ran's group who were alongside us now. As we sat for a drink and a chocolate bar, I finally got to speak to my hero. Like a small boy I rather nervously asked if he had enjoyed the route. 'Yes, very much so, great fun; can't wait for the next bit,' was Ran's reply. With the ice broken, I wittered on to him about all sorts of nonsense; looking back on it, I think he must have been rather relieved when it was time to move on.

The descent is quite straightforward and the rope between the team members quickly comes off. Once at the bottom of the

Jägerhorn there is a forty-minute hike up the hillside to the Weissmies hut. This beautifully situated hut, right in the middle of the Saas-Grund skiing area, makes for a good launching point for an ascent of the mountain that bears its name. Most evenings spent in mountain huts are quite jovial, especially if they aren't too busy, like the Weissmies hut was that night. Sitting outside in the evening sun after dinner, sipping a cold beer and chatting with clients is a lovely experience.

I'm not sure if it was my clients' fault or mine, but I always seemed to be the last to leave a hut in the morning when I was an aspirant. By the time the two Js were ready, there was a string of headlamps bobbing their way up the hillside, which, I pointed out to my impatient group, is always useful, as it's a clear path to follow. Our initial climb followed a summer walking path before moving on to the glacier. At this point the teams had to put on climbing harnesses and rope up together to protect anyone in case they fell into any of the deep crevasses.

The normal route on the Weissmies is quite straightforward, being graded F (*facile*, or 'easy' on the Alpine grading scale). The only really awkward part is just down from the summit, where there is a slightly steeper exposed section. Across this part of the climb, the slope is often scoured of snow by the wind, leaving the slopes bare blue ice. When we reached this spot, I came across Ran and his friends; the course director had left them there while he went ahead with the rope, placing ice screws in order to lead each of the clients individually. It's a style of climbing that we employ when climbing harder terrain and, although very safe, it's time-consuming. Ran and the others were huddled against the cold wind and I decided, after considering the levels of skill my team had shown so far, and weighing that against the terrain, that I would spare the two of them the same shivering fate. We stayed short-roped together, secure in the knowledge that this method was more than safe in the situation. By keeping my clients moving, I was keeping them warmer. Ran looked up; 'Hey, why aren't we doing that?' I wasn't going to try to justify another guide's decision, so I kept moving.

The summit was only a further ten minutes away, so soon all the various teams were celebrating on the top. The Weissmies has fabulous views of the Valais Alp area of Switzerland. While the cameras were clicking away, Ran came up to me and asked again why he and his friends had been asked to stand still in the cold while I simply short-roped past. I decided to tell the truth about the terrain being within my team's capability of short-roping, and that I didn't want my clients getting cold. He gave me a long, hard stare, a stare that I would soon become familiar with, and nodded strenly.

Back in the valley that afternoon, I decided to drive to the hotel from the campsite where I was staying and have a drink with the clients in the afternoon sun. As I sat down with Jen and a few others, I casually asked where Ran was (he was, after all, my main reason for coming over). 'Oh, the stupid bugger has gone for a run.'

My reaction was to cough up my beer. 'He's done what?'

It turned out that every time we returned to the valley after a day's climbing, Ran would disappear for a two-hour run. I couldn't believe it; as if the day's climbing wasn't taxing enough. We had started at 4 a.m. and hadn't finished until about 2 p.m. This was my introduction to the dedication that Ran shows in everything he does.

Later that week, as the course continued, I finally got to ask Ran why he was there. It was a very rude question to put so bluntly to him, but I was taken aback by his reply: 'I want to climb Everest, but when I approached Jagged Globe I was told

I didn't have the experience, and needed to complete a number of courses beforehand, to prove my ability.'

I said I was somewhat surprised by this – Ran wasn't someone straight out of an office job with aspirations of adventure – but I had to commend Jagged Globe's due diligence. However, I felt he could manage the climb easily enough, and went on to say: 'I tell you right now, Ran, for a man like you, climbing Everest won't be a problem. Let's face it, it's just a big snow plod, just like your polar stuff but uphill.'

This may sound a little arrogant but I had recently returned from successfully leading a Jagged Globe Everest expedition. Not only had all the team members and myself summited, I had also been to over 8,000 metres without using oxygen. I hadn't found the whole affair easy by any stretch of the imagination, but I came away thinking that Everest wasn't quite the ogre that everyone said. There followed a good hour of in-depth questions from around the table about Everest and what it all involved. Finally came a crunch question from Ran himself: 'So, Kenton, if you're saying that Everest isn't that hard, and that the climbing community don't really see the mountain as the challenge it once was, which mountains do still command respect?'

That was an easy one. 'There's a mountain in Switzerland called the Eiger. It has an infamous north face that has had climbers spellbound since the first attempts on the mountain way back in the thirties. That's a challenge.'

At the end of the week the course finished, I went back home on the Friday evening to Chamonix. Saturday is the only day off in the week for most guides in the summer, and it normally disappears in a whirlwind of admin, washing and some rock climbing with friends. In the evening I drove back to Zermatt for another evening of meeting clients, in preparation for the next course, known as the Zermatt Blitz. This involves climbing, over four days, some of the harder 4,000-metre peaks of the area.

One of those clients was Ran. He'd decided that now he was fit and acclimatised, he wanted to hone his skills. Among the other four clients was Jeremy Ashcroft, from *Trail* magazine, and an old friend of mine, photographer Martin Hartley, both of whom were there to do a piece for the magazine. We started off on Sunday morning and, after riding the cable car up to the Klein Matterhorn, we traversed the Breithorn. It wasn't a tough climb and it took us only two hours to summit. Martin was busy taking pictures all the way up, not just of the mountain but also as many of Ran as possible for a piece in *Trail* magazine. From the top the ridge gets rather presipitous and what with Martin peering through the view-finder I thought at one stage he was going to disappear down the side toward Zermatt. A few stern words soon put paid to that and the camera was safely stowed away. Once on the glacier we still had to keep our wits about us, as it was heavily cravassed and the route was so convoluted it was hard to find the hut.

The Ayas hut served (and still does to this day) all its food and drinks in plastic or paper cups and bowls, because they burnt all the items after use, rather than washing them up, in the belief that this was more environmentally conscious. I'm not sure I agree, but when one considers all the hot water and detergent needed to wash everything they may have a point. After our dinner and a night's rest, we were up in the early hours to climb Castor and Pollux, two mountains nearby named after the twin brothers from Roman mythology.

The early-morning darkness felt suffocating as we wound our way up the glacier on the way to the top. Behind me were Jeremy and Martin; I could hear their laboured breathing in the crisp air, and their crampons crunching against the hard glacier ice. We moved as one long snake towards the huge outline of Castor, slow and steady, as if we were trying not to wake her. As the sun rose, we turned off our torches. Ran moved alongside us with his guide; he still had his torch on. Martin pointed this out. Watching Ran fumble with his lack of fingers on one hand (he famously cut them off himself in his shed after contracting severe frostbite on one of his polar expeditions) was vaguely amusing, as he cursed under his breath, the words vaporising into clouds of steam that danced, taunting him, in the very torchlight he struggled to extinguish. Finally victory was won by Ran and he aggressively shoved the torch into a jacket pocket. He then methodically blew into his cupped hands to warm them, an action that I would grow accustomed to in future years.

The ascent of Castor was straightforward, but while on the summit I looked along the ridge towards Ran, making his way towards us with his guide. I marvelled at what drove him, at the age of sixty; he seemed consumed still by an inner fire to seek out adventure in whatever form it presented itself. As he reached the summit, there was back-slapping and congratulations, and Ran shook my hand for the first time. It was a firm, concise handshake, one that inspired confidence and trust. I'm certain I saw a small wink; a smile split his face before he turned to his guide to offer his thanks.

When our day was finished, we all headed out for dinner together. I arrived at the hotel where the clients were staying (us guides were crammed into one room together in a much cheaper hotel) to see a concerned-looking Ran hanging on the end of a telephone. He had received bad news from home and was going to have to cut short the course, and return to Britain the next day. With only four clients on the course, I offered to drop out, as they wouldn't need as many guides. The course director was grateful for my offer, but he hadn't spotted my cunning plan. I then took Ran aside and said I would drive him to the airport the next morning so he wouldn't have to rely on trains to reach his flight on time. A few hours alone with Ran, listening to his tales – what an opportunity.

Ran was grateful for my offer, though slightly less so when, the following morning, we reached the car park in Randa (cars are not allowed in Zermatt so everyone parks in a massive car park in the village below and catches a train to Zermatt) only to find I couldn't recall where I'd parked my car. I ran up and down the rows of cars, trying not to panic, leaving my eminent passenger on the roadside with our bags, until – a mere twenty yards from where he stood – I came across it. Typical.

I didn't realise then, but that journey and the conversation we had probably prompted what came next in my relationship with the great man.

Five months later, I was contacted by Jan, one of the two Js from the first climbing course. We'd stayed in vague contact, and she wanted to ask me about some climbing opportunity. We agreed to meet in Chamonix for dinner, at a restaurant called Munchie. She told me she'd be bringing a mutual friend, and that they had a 'business proposition' for me. Munchie is a great little place, tucked away down a small cobbled street called Rue des Moulins. The staff are all beautiful Swedish girls, the atmosphere is nice, and they serve the best starter in Chamonix: a basket of Greenlandic grilled shrimp. As it was the off season, the restaurant wasn't too busy; I arrived early and my hosts weren't there yet. I was shown upstairs (always the best place to eat in Munchie, unless it's summer and you can eat outside) and ordered a drink while I waited. Then I saw a tall gentleman bounding up the stairs toward me: 'Ah, Baron von Cool,' he boomed. It was Ran, with Jan in tow behind him.

We all ordered and, while we waited for our food, caught up with each other. It turned out that the following evening, Jan and Ran were to take part in a road running race around the streets of Chamonix. It wasn't until we were halfway through the main course that the conversion finally came round to the mystery business.

Ran opened proceedings by reminding me of what I'd said about Everest and the Eiger; how I had said that Everest didn't hold any glamour for real climbers but the Eiger did. At the time I couldn't really recall the conversion that we had had, but I kept nodding, wondering where this was taking us. Ran explained that he'd been impressed with how my team seemed to be having more fun all the time we'd been on the course together in Switzerland, and that led to his point: 'So will you guide me up the north face of the Eiger?'

I would have loved to have seen the reaction on my own face. The prospect of working with Ran was very tempting but there were a number of obstacles in our way, one of them huge.

Unlike in the UK, where anyone can call themselves a mountain guide and start operating, the Alpine nations – France, Switzerland, Italy, Germany and Austria – take a very dim view of guiding, unless one is full mountain guide. The penalties can be vast fines and time behind bars.

I laid out what it would it take in terms of time and training, and that being guided on the north face of the Eiger wasn't an average guiding job and as such there would be a premium charge. Then I broached the big problem: 'The thing is, Ran, I'm still an aspirant guide, meaning that I can't yet work with you on my own. I have to be in what is called "proximity" of a fully qualified guide at all times.' I explained that I was about a year short of being a full guide; all my training had been done, and I was just waiting for my ski test and a single day's reassessment on Alpine terrain in the summer.

Ran said he was confident that I could guide him safely towards his end goal of the Eiger, and we discussed that it would most likely be a minimum of two, or possibly three years of training, by which time I would be fully qualified. In the meantime, we agreed to keep a low profile; if approached by someone and asked what we were doing, we were simply friends climbing together. In theory, all would be fine.

Ran then decided to drop the second bombshell of the evening: he confessed to being a sufferer of vertigo. I nearly fell off my seat laughing at this point until I realised he was being serious. I struggled to see how the world's greatest living explorer could suffer acute vertigo – it hadn't been obvious in Switzerland, but then I hadn't been his guide then. I decided at least for now that we wouldn't be overly concerned; rather we would play each climb by ear.

No time like the present, so we started the following day. Jan came too, and we climbed at a little spot near Chamonix called La Crémerie, a great place offering four or five different ice climbs of various difficulties. Neither Jan nor Ran had ever climbed steep ice before and the huge wall of ice, extending up to three pitches skywards, would offer a great introduction to the world of vertical ice climbing.

Being so early in the season there was no one else around, so we could leisurely walk to the climbs and take our time selecting which one to do without fear of another team bagging our route for the day. In the middle of the season this area can be very popular and there is sometimes difficulty getting onto a preferred route. It's not always sensible to climb under another party when climbing ice: the team above can easily knock off pieces, which can hit the party climbing below. A client of mine was once unfortunately hit square in the face by the only block of ice that fell that day. Poor Sue ended up with six stitches at the top of her nose. Luckily her good looks weren't permanently damaged, although she had a couple of corking black eyes for a week or so.

Once geared up and ready to climb, I set off up the first pitch of ice on our chosen route. Although not terribly steep, it provides a great warm-up of about 35 metres to an *in situ* anchor. It's a pitch that also allows me as the guide to look down at the people climbing up, and offer advice on technique. Once I was safely secured to the anchor, I shouted down for Jan to start climbing.

Although ice climbing isn't rocket science – to a certain extent, brute force will overcome most obstacles – there is nearly always a glaring difference between men and women when they first start ice climbing. Men, due to their better upper-body strength, will normally pull themselves up on their arms, leaving their feet, adorned with crampon spikes, to skate on the ice. Women, however, often show good technique from the word 'go', making up for their weaker arms by using their feet to good effect. It's often amusing when a dainty girl picks her way up a steep water-fall successfully, while the big strong man runs out of steam halfway up and falls off.

Jan quickly and efficiently climbed her way up to me and, once she was tied to the anchor, Ran started up. I could see him confidently burying his axes into the ice but his feet were not doing a great deal. Each time he kicked with his feet, his crampon points hit the ice at an angle that made them simply shoot off to the side. It was hard not to laugh at one point when Ran ended up lying on the ice, prevented only from slipping off by holding on with his ice axes, while his feet whirled like windmills, trying to get some form of grip.

If there is one thing that Ran has in bundles it's determination, and a small thing like technique was never going to stop him getting to the belay. It was a panting and slightly sweaty Ran that arrived at the belay, but there was a huge grin across his face, which I took for a good sign. 'Great,' was his verdict. 'Although those damned crampons are tricky!'

After a brief tutorial about how to angle the toes in order to successfully use the front points of the crampons, we all made it up the next two pitches, before abseiling back down. Stripping off harnesses and stowing away ice axes, we all trotted off back. A successful first mission on the ice, celebrated with a sneaky hot chocolate *avec Cognac* on the way to the car.

Ran and I didn't do any more ice climbing until the late summer of 2005, when he flew out to join me climbing in and around the Mont Blanc massif. Our first climb that trip went well, although Ran dropped one of my new trekking poles down a crevasse, which hugely irritated me, especially because he can't to this day recall doing such a thing. The following day we drove through the Mont Blanc tunnel to climb on the Italian side of the massif because the forecast there was better. Ran wasn't looking forward to this day, because he would be expected to use his hands rather than the ice axes because we were planning on rock climbing, and one has to remember that on his left hand he is missing joints to his fingers. Rock climbing isn't high on the list of activities that Ran enjoys, mainly because of this handicap. From my perspective, though, it was a great way of getting him more used to moving in a multi-pitch environment. I had asked my friend Andy Houseman to come with us for the day, the idea being that we would climb as a three in much the same manner that we would on the Eiger when the time came.

The place I wanted to climb was made up of a huge sweep of rock thirteen pitches high called Machaby. It's quite slabby, so technique would be of more use than strength. The route that the three of us had chosen was one of the easier routes but also one of the longest, that would take us right to the top of the rock formation.

I knew that the first couple of pitches were by far the hardest, so if Ran could climb up those then the rest would easily follow. Sitting at a ledge at the top of the first pitch, I watched him as he tried to force his cut-off finger ends to grip a tiny rock edge without much joy. 'Try using your feet as much as possible,' I shouted, only to receive an ear full of blueness telling me what I could do with my advice. I could see the frustration building in Ran as he tried in vain to pull on the rock hold. Finally he ran his feet up against the rock, a technique known as smearing, and, trusting his feet, managed to stand and reach a much better hold with his hands. I realised Ran would keep trying until somehow he overcame the problem, but determination alone wouldn't achieve success on this climb, so on each of the hard sections Andy or myself would talk Ran through the sequence of moves that would unlock the puzzle for him.

We reached the top, only to find it a little disappointing, just an indistinct dome of rock with a few small trees attempting to grow in the poor soil. Still, it was a summit and that pleased Ran. The descent proved to be rather exciting that day as we lost our way and ended up bushwacking down some hideous terrain, eventually resorting to abseiling from a tree branch. When we finally reached the road, Ran came close to death. Stepping out into the road he looked the wrong way. A typical silly Brit abroad thing to do. A small Fiat Panda very nearly hit him.

Over the next eighteen months or so, Ran flew out to the Alps regularly and we climbed together, always building towards our end goal of the Eiger. On one such visit we returned to La Crémerie, on what should have been a stress free day but when we got there I was surprised to see to what extent the ice had been affected by the sun as it was late in the winter. The main area, normally a huge sheet of ice, was patchy and rotten-looking. The first route we did wasn't too bad; we climbed three pitches of ice and, although in places it sounded hollow, there wasn't too much to be concerned about.

After a quick bite to eat, we moved on to the next route, a much steeper pitch of climbing. The first section was like the first route, insomuch as it sounded a little hollow but felt safe. I think that this probably lured me into a false sense of security and before I knew it I was climbing up some ice that felt totally unsafe. My ice tools were punching straight through the ice, and I could see the bare rock behind. What really scared me was that there was about a foot of air between the ice and the rock.

What had happened was that the ice forms each year on a steep slab of rock. It generates an icefall maybe 15 or 20 metres wide, with bare rock at the edges. As the season progresses, the sun changes position so that it spends some time each day heating up the rock (as well as the ice, although this has less of an effect). This in turn melts the ice so that the amount that is climbable becomes less and less, until – as on this day – there is only a thin sliver of ice. While this is happening the ice also melts from the inside out, as the bond between the rock and the ice is broken by the heating of the rock. In the end the ice is a free-standing sheet that is only attached at the top and bottom, a sheet that is just waiting for the right moment to fall down. Adding my extra weight to it, and bashing it with my ice tools was probably the worse thing that I could have been doing.

As I was halfway up I weighed up the options and thought it would be just as safe to continue to the top rather than to gingerly climb down to the belay where Ran was waiting. For the next 30 feet I didn't swing my axes once or kick my feet into the ice, but instead very, *very* cautiously I picked and hooked my way up the ice, being extremely careful to try to gradually move my weight from one position to the next. The relief when I pulled onto thicker ice and then finally to the belay was immense. I sat in the snow before I called to Ran; I wondered if I should allow him to climb the pitch at all. I thought it through and decided that if I kept Ran super-tight on the rope, then – if the ice did collapse – he would simply hang on the end, safely. Of course Ran was not aware of the danger and, when he pulled over the top of the icefall as happy as can be, I breathed a huge sign of relief that I hadn't killed one of the UK's most famous people.

After that somewhat harrowing experience, I decided that I would play things safe for the next few days, so instead of climbing valley ice we went high. The Chèré Couloir is a route that Ran and I had done a couple of times before; it always provides a great day out but with a relatively safe feel about it. It also has easy access from the Aiguille du Midi cable car. The climb went without a hitch, and, when we returned to our rucksacks, Ran proclaimed it one of our best days out and couldn't understand why we hadn't climbed the route before. He was somewhat surprised then when I told him it was in fact the third time we had climbed the route together. I politely told him it was the altitude affecting his brain rather than age, to which he just gave me one of those looks.

It took nearly two years to get Ran to the point where I thought he could climb the Eiger. Over that time we climbed many of the classic routes in the Chamonix area, often in the quieter inter-season months. It was a magical time for me and represents some of my more memorable days guiding. To climb the Eiger, I knew we would need the help of an experienced pair of hands, and so I invited my old friend Ian Parnell along with us. Because Ran had had, three years before, a double heart bypass operation, we knew he wouldn't be able to go too quickly, so, although Ueli Steck had recently climbed it in an amazing three hours and fifty-four minutes (he's since done it in under three hours), we planned to take five days to make the climb. This was partly to make allowances for Ran's condition, but it was also because we would be doing so much filming, involving live broadcasts from the mountain itself – ITN had a team out in Grindelwald to cover the climb, and Ian and I would be filming on the climb itself. Ran was planning to raise money for the Marie Curie Cancer Care Foundation, and it was a marvellous and unmissable opportunity to get the kind of media exposure this climb would offer, and the hoped-for contributions that would follow.

As it happened, at the time no Brit had ever successfully guided a client up the north face, and this was something that appealed to my competitive nature. We all congregated in March in Grindelwald beneath the face, with a great week of weather forecasted. Everyone was ready and we knew the face was in good condition due to reports from those who had climbed it a week before. We spent the night at the Eigergletscher station which sits right next to the face before a pre-dawn start the next day. There was a good track across to the start of the route and, despite the depth of the snow, we made good time in the morning darkness. We had decided that Ian would solo next to Ran and myself on the easy lower sections to try to get film footage. This worked well and, as the lights of Grindelwald below us disappeared with the arrival of the morning sun, Ian started to shoot the first of some amazing footage.

The Difficult Crack, the first hard pitch of the route, is half a lie. It is relatively difficult but it's not really a crack, more of a groove. Ran surprised me for the first time on the climb (there were many more surprises to come) as, with little more than a tight rope, his grinning face loomed into sight. As Ian got to the belay I sped off towards the Hinterstoisser Traverse; with Ran's vertigo, the alarmingly exposed traverses were going to be a tough challenge. Ian hauled his way across the Hinterstoisser first so he could film the veteran explorer as he struggled with his demons.

The look on Ran's face as he arrived at the belay said it all. The poor guy was petrified yet he had successfully negotiated his way across the traverse. A little way beyond the Hinterstoisser is the spot we had decided would be our first bivy, a small alcove called the Swallow's Nest. It proved not to be the biggest spot for three, but a little excavation of snow made it bearable for all of us.

The morning of the second day broke cold and clear and we all made quick work of the first ice field before we reached the huge second ice field that dominates the face. Here we moved together over easy ground, with just enough gear to make things safe. At the end of the ice field a tricky snowy pitch led onto the Flatiron and so up to Death Bivy, which, despite its name, is one of the best sites on the route. Although we got to the bivy early in the afternoon, just after 1 p.m. we decided to stop there, knowing there wasn't another good site for quite a way above us. After it got dark we set the camera gear up to do a live broadcast for ITN. Ian struggled in the cold to make it work but before we knew it Ran was talking live on *News at Ten*.

On day three we faced the nasty Waterfall Pitch, set high in the ramp, which is the hardest climbing on the route. Ran had a right struggle, but yet again pulled out all the stops, amazing both Ian and myself by fighting his way to the belay. We were making good upward progress and after months of worry about the climb things seemed to be panning out exactly how Ran and I had wanted them to.

We had a slight setback above The Ramp when Ran dropped one of his mitts and his bad hand got very cold; thankfully, though, the old fox had a spare pair tucked away. We squirmed up the Brittle Crack to the bivy at the Traverse of the Gods. We had to dig this one out and it was here that we learned that Ran was a former Army hole-digging champion, although because of his vertigo he had to dig his 'bed' in such a manner that he was left with a wall of snow on the outside so he couldn't see the drop next to him.

On our penultimate day, we had to cross the Traverse of the Gods. Ran knew all about this pitch and he had built it up in his mind. For a climber this traverse is amazing: with one step the climber goes from a happy comfortable stance to the jaw-dropping situation of being able to stare 1,000 metres between his feet to the ground. The climbing is pretty easy but the exposure is awesome; there is no 'bulge' in the rock to stop your clear line of sight to the ground, thousands of feet below. Somehow Ran plucked up the courage to face this, and in doing so pulled off what I can only say is one of the most incredible climbing moves I've ever seen, not for any form of difficulty but the sheer power of his mind – quite literally mind over matter, which aptly happens to be a name of one of his books.

We spent our last night in the cold perched on the summit ridge so the ITN boys could film the 'summit push' the following day in daylight rather than twilight. Ian, ever the professional, was trying to film a live broadcast again despite the failing light and sub-zero temperatures; finally after what seemed like an age he gave up trying to get the live link to work. As he climbed back to the bivy spot he dropped the video camera, losing the last day's filming. He howled like a lost dog as it disappeared into the darkness. Looking back I often wonder what amazing footage we lost that day.

Day five, and we reached the summit. Climbing the last few hundred metres, the ITN chopper buzzed us left and right, getting some of the best mountain footage I've ever seen. At the summit we hugged and screamed at the cameras in sheer joy; Ran can be seen clearly pointing to the Marie Curie badge on his jacket, conscious as ever of getting exposure for the charity. For myself and Ian, I felt that we had pulled off something special; for Ran, it was another chapter in a rather full book.

After that, what more could Ran possibly ask of me? 'Kenton, I want you to guide me up Everest.' Of course; it had to be. So a year later we made our attempt; only Ran couldn't make it to the top of the mountain. That first year on summit day as we climbed methodically towards the Balcony, Ran decided that if he were to continue he would, most likely, be too exhausted to safely come down. When one considered the media pressure that was on us all, it was a very brave and sensible call. That said, to this day I'm still a little troubled by it. So it was the following year, in May 2009, that Ran was finally able to stand there, at the summit; he and his Sherpa left top camp at 8 p.m., an hour and a half before the rest of the team, so that he wouldn't hold anyone back; the camera equipment froze and the only summit shot taken by Tindu was into the early-morning sun so Ran is little more than a silhouette, but there were no other setbacks. Ran was able to stand, as he put it, 'the closest you can get to the Moon by walking' at last.

That was the culmination of five years of climbing with one of the most remarkable men I've ever had the privilege of meeting. Our paths have crossed many time since those days and it's always a joy to see him. Only a couple of months ago we found ourselves on stage together in Edinburgh for a sponsor we both have. After the event we found a late pizza bar, and the two of us drank beer and ate cheap pizza into the early hours. It felt like being with a very old friend. We haven't climbed together since Everest in 2009; perhaps the experience with vertigo was all a little too much, but if I know Ran like I do, I have a sneaky feeling there may be a few more mountains left in him yet.

PART THREE
THE TRIPLE CROWN

CHAPTER 9
NUPTSE

The mountains that sit alongside Everest frame a hidden valley known as the Western Cwm. At its widest point the valley floor is about 1 kilometre across, and maybe 2 or 3 kilometres in length. The valley is completely hidden from view as you trek toward Base Camp. Even an hour out from Camp, it seems inconceivable that such a valley exists. Once at Base Camp the wonders of this magical Cwm are still hidden; you have to navigate your way past the Khumbu Icefall before the true beauty is revealed. The Cwm is bounded with Everest to the left side; then at the back is Mount Lhotse, the fourth highest mountain in the world, and then on the right-hand side is Mount Nuptse, the nineteenth, first climbed back in 1961 by the Brits, with a very young Chris Bonington on the expedition team.

The first person to look into the valley was George Mallory in 1921. He had climbed up to Nup La, a col between Tibet and

Nepal that sits between Pumori and Lingtren.* From the Nup La he had a direct line of sight straight into the Western Cwm. As he stood there he dismissed the southern route to the summit as utterly impossible, partly due to the hideous-looking Khumbu Icefall, and also the Lhoste face, which he was staring straight onto. In the 1920s climbing what looked like a sheer 2,500-metre wall of ice was way beyond anybody's capabilities. Mallory took a number of photographs, but he was notoriously incompetent when it came to photography and on this occasion he managed to put all the plates in back to front, so that none of them were properly exposed. Apparently he was furious with himself; but the valley, although it was now known to exist, remained wrapped in mystery. It was only properly mapped out in 1951, when Eric Shipton, on the Everest reconnaissance expedition that first formally established where the Cwm was.

The wonderful thing about the Western Cwm for the modern-day climber or trekker – or pretty much anyone who's been there since the 1950s – is its isolation, because it is so well hidden. You can't see into it easily, ringed as it is by these three enormous mountains. For many years, tackling the complete Horseshoe – that is to say, reaching all three peaks by traversing along the top of the ridges between the mountains – has been one of the holy grails of high-altitude climbing. The ridge line between Nuptse and Lhotse is very complex (Lhotse to Everest is easy in comparison): running over Lhoste Middle (8,414 metres) and Lhotse Shar (8,400 metres), it is double-corniced, knife-edged, convoluted, steep and extremely difficult. I don't believe it can be done – it's not impossible, perhaps, but it certainly

---

* On 25 April 2015 a huge avalanche was released from the Nup La, triggered by the earthquake that devastated much of Nepal. The avalanche swept into Base Camp, killing a total of eighteen people in Everest's worst ever single disaster.

won't be done in our generation. Not in a pure mountaineering style. I know that history has a way of proving those sorts of statements wrong – people said the four-minute mile was impossible after all – but I think it would require the development of new fitness levels, some spectacular technical advances and huge logistical support.

However, in 2008 I came up with the idea that it would be possible to climb the peaks that make up the main bowl structure of the valley – not via the ridge lines running in between each one, but as a relatively straightforward climb of each mountain. I say straightforward, but of course it couldn't be that, because we're talking about one of the most inhospitable places on earth. Up Nuptse, then down; up Everest, then down; up Lhotse for the final one, and down again, all without coming back down to Base Camp. We could establish a base in the Western Cwm, and that would make a launch spot for each peak. The Triple Crown, as it became known, could be done.

I needed to find someone to help me finance the attempt, so I drafted a proposal and managed to get quite a long way with it. Vicks, part of Proctor & Gamble, took it very seriously until somebody in America, in a boardroom meeting when they were apparently about to say yes, asked, 'Well, what happens if he dies? How would that reflect on us?' Unsurprisingly, no one really had an answer to that, so the whole proposal got kicked into touch. We couldn't source the funding from anyone else, so the project was mothballed, although I always hoped it might resurface some day.

The Triple Crown was the last thing on my mind in late January 2012, when I was on a train heading for Paddington. My mobile rang; I didn't recognise the number, and I don't like talking for long on the train anyway, but I picked up the call. On the other end was a very voluble lady, talking very quickly at me. Frustratingly, I lost the signal just as the train came into the station, but by that time I had got the gist of what she was calling about. Her client believed that he would be climbing Everest with me in a couple of months. Now, this was impossible because that season I was due to depart on an expedition to take an Olympic medal, awarded in 1924 to the British team who had attempted Everest in '22, as part of the London 2012 celebrations. It was a really big deal, not just for me and the British Olympic movement, but internationally too. I had no plans to take anyone else up there with me – what on earth was this woman talking about?

As soon as I got off the train, I rang her back: 'Right, who are you? Please start again, from the beginning, and explain what it is that you want.' Banke introduced herself properly, telling me that she worked as the UK-based fixer for a Nigerian businessman, Kola Abiola, a very well-connected man whose father had been a well-known figure in Nigerian politics. He had sent an email, or rather Banke had sent one on his behalf, and had assumed – as neither of them had received a reply – that we had agreed to their proposal. Why anyone would think that, I don't know. I spoke to the office about the email and eventually figured out what had happened: the email Banke had sent to my company, Dream Guides, had been received by the office, where it had been taken to be a variant on the usual Nigerian spam email. It had been shunted into a spam folder by the filter and forgotten about, which was a bit embarrassing, considering who Kola is.

There had been no correspondence since, but Kola had meanwhile assumed that he was climbing Everest with me. He had been on a strict fitness regime, and now he was in London and wanted a meeting to discuss when and how we were going to

Everest summit number 1. For me it was never in doubt. After Annapurna III I was riding the crest of a wave, leading my first expedition to an 8,000er. I had total confidence we would be successful, and indeed we were, with all three team members and Sherpas safely summiting on 15 May 2004.

The summit ridge, Everest.
It wouldn't be out of place in the Swiss Alps, which is famed for its sensational ridge climbing. Here seen under heavy snow. To the right is 3,000 m straight down to Tibet, while to the left a mere 2,000 m down to Camp Two.

Breaking the rules.
All leaders need to validate their credentials; for me, on Everest, this occurred in 2006. Breaking all the rules, taking the ascent totally to the wire, we – and I mean we because we were a great team – pulled off something very special, and in doing so opened the floodgates for others that year. In the final 100 m the team fell into line and pushed for glory.

First love. If I was cast away on a desert island with only one form of climbing, it would be trad rock climbing. It's how I started, and my love for it is undiminished, even if family time pressures don't allow me to partake so much these days. Wee Doris at Stoney Middleton classic E4 has everything you could wish for in a route: bouldery start, steep pumpy finish, with a touch of boldness to get the heart fluttering…and the Moon Inn is about ten minutes walk away for a celebratory pint.

That man Fiennes. We climbed all over the Alps in the build-up to the north face of the Eiger, mainly in winter. I love this photo mostly because I tricked Ran into standing in a hole so I could tower over him. Not an original idea: the great Reinhold Messner did the same to Ed Hillary. Messner is somewhat shorter than Hillary's 6 foot 4 or so.

Eiger north face (March 2007). After foolishly telling Sir Ran that Everest wasn't really a technical climbing challenge, he decided that the Eiger north face was the route for him, and together we embarked on a three-year journey to train him up to make the ascent. The steep, uncompromising ground was a far cry from Ran's more comfortable arena of the Poles. His vertigo was also an extra problem. Here I traverse into the start of the difficult crack, the first really hard climbing on the face.

Grandad. Nick Bullock, the old man of climbing. Together we spent three fabulous winter seasons living in Chamonix with Andy Houseman and then Matt Helliker. The house was never short of enthusiasm for any sort of climbing. Here we are after (I think) the second full ascent of Slave to the Rhythm on the east face of Mount Maudit and then a near-death climb back up the mundane slopes to the cable car due to a raging storm. Nick graciously accepted the role of being my best man in 2008, the only time I've ever seen him in a shirt and suit.

Everest summit number 4 (May 2007) With hardly a breath of wind, we could have been on an Alpine summit rather than in the Death Zone. My fifth summit came less than a week later, making me the first Briton ever to double-summit in a season. It was also Stripy Mouse's fourth summit, confirming his status as the world's foremost mountaineering mouse.

The team behind the success. Andrew Carnegie once said that his epitaph should read: 'Here lies a man who was able to surround himself with men far cleverer than himself.' That's exactly what I have attempted to do with Everest. The core of my Sherpa team – close friends I've worked with for close to a decade, their unwavering commitment, power and humour have been the reason why I have such a great record on Everest. I owe them so much. Left to right: Dorje Gyalgen, Lhakpa Wongchu, Jabu, me and Padawa. Between us we have 49 summits of Everest.

Ski 8,000. My appetite for 8,000 m peaks spread from Everest in 2006. Cho Oyu in Tibet was my first in 2010, but with skis to add a little spice. I was the only member of the team who skied from the top, which made for a stressful descent but yet another British first. Repeating the mission a few years later on Manaslu, with Andrew Eggleston and a small team, is without doubt the favourite of my 8,000 m peak expeditions to date.

In my role as ambassador for various brands, including Sherpa Adventure Gear, Bremont Watches and Land Rover, I get to do some pretty cool things. In 2014 Land Rover engaged with the British Exploring Society to find the next generation of adventurers. Morzine in France was the setting in a chilly January for a two-day competition. The teams here are furiously digging snow holes to spend the night in by the headlights of Land Rovers.

The Geneva Spur. (*Above*) For me this is *the* Everest photo in my library, but it's actually a screen grab from a video that Keith Partridge shot. In the background is the magnificent North Ridge of Nuptse, and beyond the lower peaks of the Khumbu are just poking out. It captures the feeling of elation and wonderment that I feel at high altitude, the feeling of being out on a limb, when one's senses become heightened by the location.

Higher, faster, stronger. (*Left*) In 1924 a pledge was made between Great Britain and Baron Pierre de Coubertin to take one of 13 Olympic gold medals to the top of the world. Uncovering the story, tracking down the families and medals, and then fulfilling this 88-year-old promise was a fabulous journey. The highlight was engaging with so many families that have Everest history from the '20s, and being thanked personally by Lord Coe for kick-starting a summer of Olympic sport in 2012 was also a little special.

Dorje Gyalgen, my number-one Sherpa, my colleague, but above all my friend.

Ice climbing has become something of a passion over the years. In 2014 I, along with fellow Sherpa Athlete, Neil Gresham, Ian Parnell and Mark Garthwaite, travelled to Norway to sniff out some unclimbed ice. It turned into a feast of beautiful lines, memorable banter and wonderful Northern Lights. As climbing trips go this had all the ingredients required. Here I'm doing the second ascent of one of Neil's routes on the roadside crag – which was a joke as it was actually a rough fifty minute hike from the road.

climb the mountain. I didn't quite know what to do, so I suggested we meet to discuss our options; as he was just about to fly out to the economic forum in Davos, we arranged to meet in the Arts Club the next day.

When I got there, I said, 'I'm here to meet one of your members, Mr Abiola.' 'Oh, yes,' the receptionist said. 'He's upstairs – you can't miss him.' And she was absolutely right: you can't miss Kola, he is this larger-than-life Nigerian guy with the most infectious, booming laugh, which cut through the conversations at all other tables at the Arts Club – and he didn't give a monkey's. I loved meeting him; I loved his carefree attitude to things, and his indifference to the tutting and head-turning that went on at the tables around us.

Finally we agreed that he would have to defer his aim of climbing Everest that year – it was just not a possibility for me – but that we would look at making the climb in 2013.

The following year, everything had been prepared for our climb. I flew to Kathmandu, based on the assumption that I would be meeting Kola there in mid-April, but as my plane touched down at the airport, I got an email to say that he was going to be delayed.

The email added that the situation in Nigeria had kicked off, both business-wise and politically, partly because of Boko Haram in the north-east of the country, and Kola, who planned to run in the 2015 presidential elections, had to deal with a few things before he came to Nepal.

I'll be coming in about ten days' time, he told me, which was cutting it tight, in terms of readying him for the conditions on the mountain; but I was confident that we could manage a successful ascent and stated as much in my reply.

I decided that, instead of staying in the fleshpots of Kathmandu, I would make my way to Base Camp, to set everything up and prepare for the initial phase of the expedition, ensuring that the Sherpa team were fully kitted out and that all the equipment we would need was ready. I also started acclimatising, but everything was once again turned upside down one afternoon about ten days later when I got another message from Kola, saying, *I'm going to be on the Emirates flight, landing tomorrow at five o'clock in the afternoon.*

Panic. I knew I needed to be there to meet Kola off the plane – that's part of my job as a guide – so I rushed off to bum a lift on a chopper to Lukla, where I waited all through the middle of the day for a fixed-wing flight, and finally managed to get to the airport in Kathmandu just as Kola's plane touched down. Only he wasn't on it.

I bribed an official so that I could see a passenger list, but Kola's name wasn't on the list. He hadn't just missed the flight, I realised, he wasn't going to be on it. I tried to call him but there was no answer, which wasn't too unusual: I'd always found him difficult to contact. By then I was financially up to my eyeballs, because I'd paid everything upfront, out of my own pocket; and now I had a no-show for a client. All terms and conditions between us had been signed, but I was feeling pretty exposed, because I was down six figures, and I didn't know quite what to do about it. My in-country agent, Iswari, who is a great guy, said, 'Well, what are you going to do?'

'I don't know,' I said. I was stumped, to be honest, knocked sideways by this development.

But Iswari, bless him, said, 'Right, I'll shut up the office. Let's go for a beer and discuss this.'

Eventually I managed to have a brief conversation with Kola. He told me he had to be in Lagos for another fourteen days as the situation had gone from bad to terrible. He still wanted to come on the expedition, but unfortunately there just wasn't enough time – the climbing season would be over by the time he arrived and got suitably acclimatised.

Iswari had dragged me to a bar, by the swimming pool in the Shanker Hotel. It was a lovely evening in Kathmandu, and there was a really nice mellow atmosphere, with a wedding reception going on in the grounds of the hotel. Everything was divine, apart from the fact that I had got this big black financial cloud hanging over me. But a couple of beers down, with the edge taken off, an idea came to me.

'I always find the solution is at the bottom of a glass,' as Guy Willett, my partner in Dream Guides, famously said once in Chamonix. 'But it's just a question of finding which glass it's at the bottom of.' As Iswari was ordering our third round of beers (my mood – and my confidence – slowly improving with each one), I had my brainwave. This was a great opportunity to try to rekindle the Triple Crown challenge. Kola wasn't going to show up in time, but I was here, my equipment was here and I was acclimatised. For the first time ever on Everest, I had got an opportunity to do this. I had no client of any description, no sponsor to please, no timetable to follow. I had the permits for Everest ($10,000 each and that's just to get the paperwork to climb. Sherpa fees and Base Camp costs are on top of that). I'd paid for two of the Everest permits, for myself and Kola. I quickly rattled through in my mind what else I would need in order to complete the Triple Crown. After a moment I turned to Iswari. 'Can you get me a Nuptse permit and a Lhotse permit?'

He thought about it for a moment, and said, 'Well, maybe, Kenton, yes, maybe. When for? Do you want it for 2014?'

'No,' I said. 'I need them now, if you can. Can you organise it for tomorrow?'

There was a pause and he scratched his chin and looked at

me and then he grinned. 'Yes, of course I can. I'm a very well-connected man.'

So that was the start of it. The very next day, I was back on a plane, back into the Khumbu, where I managed to clamber into the back of a chopper for the price of a crate of beer. I was flown to Pheriche, and then I trekked back to Base Camp on my own, moving quite quickly because I'd got the bit between my teeth.

In my head I was running over what I needed to do, because everything hinged on the next couple of days, and things needed to happen that I had little control over. I remember vividly coming around the corner, just past the climbers' memorial, heading out in the direction of Lobuche, when my mobile rang. It's amazing, I can get a better signal in the wilds of Nepal than I sometimes get on the train into Paddington. I could hear Iswari as clear as a bell, and the only thing he said was, 'I've got you the permits.' It was game on.

I wandered into Base Camp, and everybody was looking over my shoulder because they were expecting me to have this larger-than-life Nigerian guy they'd heard all about in tow. But here I was, on my own.

My old friend Henry Todd, the Todd-father of Everest appeared, and he looked puzzled. 'What's going on?'

'Right, Henry, let's go and sit down. I've got some stuff to talk to you about.' I didn't want everyone to know what I was planning, so I thought I'd better take Henry off somewhere private for us to have a chat. There were probably a couple of people capable of doing this challenge at Base Camp, but I wanted to be the one to have a go at it first. Ueli Steck was in town with Simone Moro and John Griffith, working on a big project together, although it turned out that I didn't need to worry about them muscling in on my plans: they were about to become involved in something that had – and still has – huge repercussions for all of us climbing on Everest.

Henry and I grabbed a cup of tea, and went to sit in his tent. When I'd finished explaining my plan – and I did worry that Henry would think I was mad – he leaned across in the very dramatic way that Henry does, and said, 'Dear boy, I think that's a magnificent idea.' All of a sudden, somebody was backing me on it, and what had, during my journey up, seemed like a mad fancy was suddenly a pretty concrete reality.

He asked how I intended to go about it, and I explained my idea. I wanted to start with Nuptse, as it's the lowest of the three mountains, at some 7,800-odd metres. Doug Scott went up the north ridge of Nuptse in 1979, along with Georges Bettembourg, Brian Hall and Alan Rouse and in doing so produced an outstanding Himalayan classic.

Henry smiled at me and filled me in on some information that would really galvanise the attempt. He knew that New Zealander Russell Brice had a commercial team climbing Nuptse, which had never happened before, and probably wouldn't happen again for a very long time. Russ was rope fixing on it, or at least planned to do so. That was another box ticked: the ropes would already be in place. I could climb Nuptse in a very short space of time, leaving me with enough energy to tackle the two other mountains in quick succession. Obviously this was a great boost for me, but at the same time it was a shame, because I'd wanted to confront the challenge of Nuptse Alpine style, in the same way Doug and co had in '79. However, the great thing about opportunity, and why you should never miss one when it arises, is that it brings its own luck with it. And having the ropes already in place was a huge stroke of luck.

My next step was to trot straight down the valley and have a word with Russ. I thought I should explain to him why I wanted to use his ropes. I could have just used them, probably, but that's not the way I do things; it's just polite to go and say, 'Hey, Russ, this is my idea, will you help me out by letting me use your ropes?' Some people might not bother with such etiquette but to me it was important.

I made my way down to Russ's tent and asked to speak to him, again in private. Having explained my plan, I went on: 'I could pay some money to use the ropes, or perhaps I could help fix the ropes with your Sherpa team.' I wanted to make it clear that I wasn't just using him as a resource, that as I was a free agent could offer him my help too. Russ, like Henry, was fully behind me, adding, 'I appreciate you coming to ask me first, Kenton, so, yes, we'll support you.'

I found it really liberating, just being on Everest, doing my own thing, and on my own timetable – it was wonderful. I wandered between Camp One and Camp Two as and when I wanted to, meeting all sorts of people as I did so, because I didn't have to worry about looking after any clients. I had met a great guy called Paul Keleher in 2012 and he was back in '13 to climb Lhotse, and we buddied up in order to do the acclimatisation runs together. My good friend Bill Crouse was in town again too, sharing Base Camp, so it was a great vibe.

Unfortunately, Kola's absence still created a bit of a dark cloud. I worried about the money; after all, he had told me he'd be here and I'd spent a lot of money preparing for him, so I would need to get that back one day.

After a few more days I was getting to the stage where I felt that I was physically right. I felt that I was fully acclimatised and could start thinking about the weather and wondering if we might get the right window of opportunity.

But then something happened that had never happened on Everest before: there was a confrontation between a small group of climbers and some Sherpas, and although the Sherpas didn't formally go on strike, there were a couple of days when there was no rope fixing. This was unprecedented.

The punch-up that caused this situation was one of those really disappointing things that will go down in Everest history. I don't think we will ever get to the bottom of why there was, literally, a fist fight, but nobody came out of it smelling of roses. I knew the climbers involved really well; they were the Italian Simone Moro, Ueli Steck from Switzerland, and the Brit Jonathan Griffith, who happened to be one of the photographers at my wedding. They were looking to undertake a very audacious project on Everest – to film an attempt on the west ridge – and they were acclimatising by going up to the South Col of Everest.

There's something of an unwritten rule on Everest, which is that if the Sherpa teams are fixing the rope on the mountain, climbers stay out of their way and let them get on with their own thing. But, like so much of what governs our behaviour on Everest, it's an unwritten rule that nobody enforces. It's just a little bit of a custom on the mountain. Simone knew that, and Ueli probably knew it too; but, hey, as I've always said, if you want to go and climb on Everest, it's entirely up to you. That's one of the great things about our sport: there are very few rules – it's not like the golf club or the tennis club, where there are rules and regulations about things like a dress code. This it's mountaineering, and mostly we do as we please as long as it doesn't endanger anyone else.

The fixing team were working their way up to Camp Three, and Simone, Ueli and Jonathan were also climbing up the Lhotse face, and something happened. It appears that some ice may have accidentally got knocked off onto some of the fixing team. It was an accident, but plainly it caused offence.

There was a little bit of argy-bargy, then Ueli suggested that he and the other two climbers could do some of the rope fixing. Knowing Ueli as I do I suspect he was just trying to help, but the Sherpas took the offer as an attack on their own ability. Everybody then came down off the face and went back down to Camp Two, where a group of Sherpas went around to voice their concerns over what had happened. Allegedly, one of the climbers had uttered some derogatory words and a punch-up ensued. The story goes that knives were pulled, rocks were thrown, blood was spilt. Various Western guides stepped in to eventually calm the situation down but tensions were still running extremely high.

Simone, John and Ueli decided that they had to get back to Base Camp. Normally they would have gone out of the bottom end of Camp Two down the Western Cwm, but such was the bad atmosphere there that they were worried they would be ambushed on the way if they went that way. In the end they left by climbing over the moraine wall, crawling on their hands and knees to the far side of the Cwm to avoid being spotted, and running down the far side of the Cwm in near-darkness to get back down to Base Camp. The very next day, Ueli arranged a chopper and flew out, wanted nothing more to do with it. He has not been back to Everest since.

Things blew over pretty quickly at Base Camp. People started saying, 'You should just kiss and make up; shake hands and let it go.' But a couple of days after it all happened, Jonathan Griffith said to me, 'There's no fucking way I'm shaking hands with somebody who, two days ago, wanted to kill me. I am simply not doing it. I'm not going to shake hands with somebody who's taken a knife out to me and threatened to stab me.'

I was at Base Camp when it all blew up, so I can only go by what I saw afterwards. Both Ueli and John were visibly shaken. Simone, who is characteristically Italian, said, 'Oh, it will be fine,' and in the end he was the only one who stayed. A few weeks later, he was back flying rescue missions in his helicopter, rescuing a hurt Sherpa off the mountainside.

Of course this was all going on while I was making my preparations for the Triple Crown, and I was as ready as I was ever going to be, but I was still waiting on the weather. However, the team who had been fixing the ropes decided that there needed to be a couple of days to sort out the relationships between the various Sherpas, foreign guides and climbers, so there was a little bit of a hiccup in their rope fixing, which meant that the early weather window had been missed. It wasn't the end of the world, I knew the next opportunity wouldn't be far off.

It was about mid-May that the forecast came in. We get very accurate forecasts these days. They come in from various parts of the world but, personally, I put a lot of faith in those from Switzerland, in particular Meteotest out of Bern. The Meteotest team indicated that there was going to be a six- or seven-day window of really good weather and all of a sudden, after a few days of waiting, it was hectic. You don't often get a long period of clear weather like that in the Himalayas so I had to scramble myself and my gear. I was still at Base Camp, and I needed to be up at Camp Two in something of a rush. I went to see Russ, because his team would be putting the ropes in Nuptse, and I wanted to check on their progress after the delays.

Russ said, 'Right, my guys are fixing the rope; they're fixing it today, and they're taking it to the top. We move up tomorrow, to Camp Three on Nuptse, with a view to climbing it the day after, and as soon as they have climbed, I'm stripping the rope out.'

I was surprised. 'You're stripping the rope out?'

Russ said, 'Yes, I've heard people are buying Nuptse permits to jump on my lines. You were the only person who was polite enough to come and ask if you could use them.' He smiled at me. 'Screw them; I'm going to strip the ropes out so they can't use them.'

I was very glad I'd had the wits to ask Russ first. But all of a sudden, my opportunity to climb Nuptse was shrinking. If I wanted to climb it on his lines, I had to go very soon. I went back to my tent, thinking, 'Christ, tomorrow I've got to climb from here all the way up to Camp Three on Nuptse to be in a position to climb it the following day.' After a period of relative inactivity, I was suddenly in a last-minute rush.

I woke at 5 a.m. the following morning, and after a swift breakfast I shouldered my rucksack, and climbed through the icefall on my own, all the way up to Camp Two. I had some lunch at Camp Two and persuaded the helpful cook boy there to carry some of my equipment around to Camp Three, which was at about 6,800 metres. He put in a sterling effort; I think he relished the opportunity to put on his boots, and actually loved the climb. He was a typical Sherpa and despite being just a cook boy he left me for dead over the three-and-a-half-hour climb. We made it to Camp Three by about four o'clock, and there was Russell's team. Camped next to them was someone I recognised: Alex Txikon from Catalonia. 'That's handy,' I thought, because I didn't have a tent with me.

I didn't really know Alex, but I knew by reputation that he's a strong climber. He's climbed eight of the world's fourteen 8,000-metre peaks, all without oxygen. Without a fuss I told him I had no lodgings and he invited me to share his tent. He made great food – way better than my food – and I ended up eating most of his home-made *saucissons*. There was a really jovial atmosphere at Camp Three, because as well as Alex there were Russell's clients, whom I'd come to know pretty well during my stay at Base Camp when I was acclimatising. We had a great evening as a group, it just felt really cool, a good preamble for the climb ahead. Alex and I loosely agreed to climb together the next day.

Our alarms went off about midnight, and I started the laborious task of melting snow to make water, and getting all the flasks ready, which normally takes a good hour or so. Finally I put on my down suit, and Alex and I both switched on our head torches and stepped out into the dark, cold night. Once we were ready, we started the climb up the fixed ropes. We made a great start and very quickly pulled away from the others. The sun came up around four thirty; it was a beautiful day. We found the climbing comfortable; the rope fixers had made a superb line, which made me feel a bit sad in many ways, as it felt a bit like cheating on such a wonderful climb. That said, had the lines not been in I may have struggled to have the energy for the next two climbs, so I was grateful for the work Russ's team had put in.

We carried on climbing up until we came out onto the ridge line, then we kept steadily going up that, getting higher and higher. We stopped at one point for some hot lemon that we had readied in a flask, and some more of Alex's beautiful *saucissons*, and then, just as we approached the summit ridge, the rope ran out.

The fixed rope just stopped. When the Sherpas stop fixing, normally they leave a coil of rope and then some equipment, but they had clearly just run out of rope. Presumably they thought the team climbing up would bring some more rope with them. Maybe they had – but we were way ahead of them. And this was a big problem.

We had deliberately kept our packs light because we had been told that the line went all the way up to the top, and so we had only got one ice axe each, with no ice screws and no rope. How foolish we looked. What to do now? We had to improvise. Alex

179

went down about 30 or 40 metres and chopped some rope off the fixed lines, while I found an old, mangled snow stake that we might be able to use as some protection. We agreed that we should carry on up in Alpine style, roped together as partners. I suggested that I lead by climbing up ahead, to make it up to the edge of the ridge, from where we could launch ourselves to the summit. There was a small rocky part and we decided we'd aim for that as our first stop.

I made it to the top of the ridge and peered down over the other side. The view was amazing; I was looking straight down the south face of Nuptse, one of the biggest, baddest, steepest faces in the world. It felt pretty exposed. Alex joined me and we hunkered down there, and agreed that I should go to the summit first. Alex got the length of rope he'd cut out, and prepared to belay me, to protect me if I fell off, and grabbing an ice axe so that I had two, off I went.

The summit ridge is quite convoluted, it rises in and out, getting pretty steep in places, and as we'd been climbing up, the sun had risen high in the sky. It was now about midday, so the snow had softened considerably. This felt very disconcerting, as climbing on steep soft snow gives you little sense of security. I had no protection if I fell, because, other than Alex on the end of the rope, all I had was this one slightly bent old snow stake. As I got closer and closer to the summit, I lost sight of Alex due to the way that the route curves round. Then once again the bloody rope ran out.

There was no more rope, and I couldn't see Alex, so I got the snow stake out and banged it into the snow. My plan was to tie myself to the snow stake and then scream to Alex that he could climb to me, but the stake never felt firm. The snow was steep, it felt very precarious, and all I'd got to put in as protection was one poxy snow stake that was wobbling around. I thought, 'I am not prepared to belay to this; this is ludicrous.' I wasn't going to risk my life, let alone Alex's. We were in a serious position, and I was struggling to come up with a decent solution.

'We're so close to the summit,' I thought. 'Shit.' And I reached down and untied myself from the rope. To non-climbers, this is going to sound totally bizarre, the most insane thing I could possibly do, but at the time it seemed not only the most sensible but also the safest option. I decided to solo, with no rope, to the summit, which was only maybe 40 metres away.

I started punching through the snow, leaving a bizarre trail across the pristine white surface, as if a crab had scuttled across it. When you reach the summit of Nuptse, it's not as if you climb up steep slopes and, all of a sudden, arrive at the top. You have to do a big traverse to get to it, so I was going sideways for what felt like for ever. The peak is multi-pinnacled, too, so once you're up there it's quite difficult to ascertain which one is the actual summit; I decided one peak seemed higher than the others, so I made for it doing my funny sideways climb until I was under-neath it.

The snow was now really deep and soft, and I was fighting not to slip. Suddenly I was concerned. For the first time ever on a mountain, I had a battle with myself. What I was doing began to feel unjustifiable. I thought of my daughter Saffron, back home. She became the little angel on one shoulder, saying, 'Don't do it Daddy.' On the other shoulder there was the devil (probably my ego), urging me on: 'Do it, do it! Look, you're so close, just do it!' It was the first time I'd ever experienced this, a real physical sensation of being in two minds.

In the end, the devil was stronger than the angel, and I decided as I'd come this far, I needed to complete my journey. I was very much aware that a fall from here would be fatal. 3,000 metres straight. There was no margin for error; one slip, and it would all be over. That really sharpens the mind. I reached up, and all of a sudden, I could see over the summit, and there was Everest, the beautiful vast bulk of Everest, my next objective for the Triple Crown, and my mind filled with thoughts of Saffron, of Jazz, of family, of home. And this time I didn't have the kahunas to stand on the top. I was suddenly scared – very, very scared.

Punching my arms deep into the soft snow just below the summit, I brought my feet up as far as I could and stood up, learning over from my waist. I almost belly-flopped onto the top and touched the summit with my nose, and that was good enough. I'd reached the top, I'd seen it, I'd touched it. I very gingerly inched myself back down, and as I did so it felt as though the steps that I'd made deep in the snow on the way up were crumbling away underneath me. I got back to the rope, tied myself on again, and felt a wave of relief. Then I shot back down to Alex.

'What was it like?' he asked. I could barely speak, so I muttered 'Good' or something like that. 'Give me that – my turn,' he said, grabbing the ice axe, and off he went. I watched him disappear up and over the ridge, but although I couldn't see him, I could feel him on the rope. I felt him go forward, and then the rope stopped. I thought, 'Oh, he must be at the snow stake; this is where he needs to untie it.' There were a few minutes of nothingness, and all of a sudden, I felt movement in the rope again. I sensed Alex was coming back, and, sure enough, after a few minutes, I saw him appear over the edge of the ridge. He made his way carefully down to me and said, 'I can't believe you untied and solo-ed. I saw your footsteps going around the flutings, and then disappearing out of view. How far did you go?'

'I went to what I think is the top,' I told him. 'Did you not want to try?'

'No way. I wasn't untying, that was . . .' He paused, reluctant to tell me I was mad, which I was. 'No, I didn't,' he said emphatically.

I hadn't been bold enough to get onto the true summit, and that kind of upset me once I was safe and sound. I'd seen an amazing photograph of one of the Benegas brothers on the ridge just down from the summit, and the devil on my shoulder started again: he wanted a similar photograph. But who would take it, because I was just up there on my own? I didn't know, but I really wanted that picture.

Without a shadow of a doubt, if we had been fully prepared, with three or four ice screws and 50 metres of decent rope, then it would have been a no-brainer, we could have danced a jig on the summit if we'd wanted, but we didn't have it.

We knew that some of Russell's clients weren't that far behind us, that they would be alongside us in a while, so I said, 'What are we going to do? You know, we could try to find another method of getting you up there.' And I think that for a few moments Alex was pretty keen to try to work some other way of enabling him to summit, but then he sat back and said, 'It has been such a magical day, you know; the summit is nothing.'

In some ways, I envy Alex's attitude. It had been a magical day, and that should have been enough. But I was concerned about that silly word 'failure'. Perhaps I wasn't prepared to hiccup at the first hurdle and that's why I pushed on in spite of the risk: it would have made the next two parts of my challenge rather pointless. But, actually, what he said was right and I admire him for being able to see it like that.

We started our descent, and we were fast going down, using the ropes, once we had got over the small section where we'd cut a little out. When we reached Camp Three, in the late afternoon, we explained to Russ what we'd had to do. He was completely cool with it, and the next day he did what he had said he would do, which was to strip out the first 200 metres of rope making it much harder for anyone else to climb. I was pretty wasted but was keen to get back to Camp Two, so I said cheerio to Alex at the High Camp. I wanted to make use of the good weather window, to realise my opportunity to climb the Triple Crown in one go.

Having quickly packed up my belongings, I left Nuptse Camp Three. My Sherpa friend Dorje Gyalgen had left Camp Two to come and help me back down. Normally when someone thinks you are tired and kindly offers to carry your sack the answer is no, but after nearly sixteen hours on the go I had no issues when Dorje offered to help carry my load. He also had a rope with him, which we tied in with. This is because the top end of the Western Cwm, which we had to traverse around, is quite broken up with crevasses, some of them quite deep. When I had been across with the cook boy, I'd felt we were a bit exposed, so it was nice to have an experienced companion to go back with across that broken ground.

I was still trying to absorb the rush of excitement from the day's activities, while trying not to dwell on the risks I'd taken, but the game was on.

CHAPTER 10
EVEREST

It was getting dark by the time I got into Camp Two. It had been a long day, so I had a cup of tea, a bite to eat, and went straight to bed. I was asleep as soon as my head hit the pillow; the next thing I knew my alarm was going off. It was time to get up – I had Everest to climb!

A cup of tea, and then, after I'd packed, we – Dorje and I – left at about 6.30 a.m. We crossed the upper part of the Western Cwm, and then made our way up the Lhotse face. It was light enough for us to see clearly by then, and, as it was fairly standard climbing, it was no surprise that the two of us to made it to Camp Three in quick time. We probably could have climbed all the face in one go, but I was conscious not only of how much the climb up Nuptse had taken out of me, but also of how much I might need in reserve for my final push up Lhotse in a couple of days' time.

There had been a summit push on Everest earlier that morning, so a lot of people had gone up the Lhotse face the day before in the first weather window, so the trail was now relatively empty, which made for a pleasant change. Considering how crowded Everest had become over the last few years, it was a pleasure to climb in relative peace and quiet.

Dorje and I made it to Camp Three in the mid-morning. We spent the rest of the day lounging in the sun, recovering from the exertions of the day before, and hydrating; it's always wise to take on liquids when you can – you don't always have the chance at high altitudes.

In the early hours of the next day, I clambered back into my down suit, and we set off, this time using oxygen. We made our way up Everest to the South Col, heading over the Yellow Band – the sweep of yellowish rock that comes through high on the Lhotse face. It was a slog. This is one of those stretches on the mountainside without much reward; it's monotonous, and hard work, and not a part of the mountain that I particularly like. It doesn't help that it's really cold to start with, but then, when the sun does come up, it quickly becomes an inferno. I had my down suit on, so I started sweating like I was in a sauna, and, with my oxygen mask on for the first time as well, everything felt really uncomfortable. It was such a grind to get up to the Yellow Band, but once we were over that, it felt as though we were making progress and I began to relax.

We went across the Geneva Spur, so-called because the Swiss very nearly gazumped the Brits in 1952, as they were the first to climb up to that point. As we traversed this broken ground I was surprised to hear and then finally see a chopper labouring its way up the Western Cwm, slowly gaining height. We both stopped to watch it for a few minutes. What caught our attention was the fact that it had a long line underneath – the thin wire cable that is used for pulling casualties out from tricky situations. It made a few passes across the upper reaches of the Lhotse face before heading away. Neither of use dwelt on this and continued heading across the Spur and then we came around the corner to the South Col. It's a mesmerising and beautiful campsite, perched on the Col between Lhotse and Everest. I love it. It's always wind-swept – a hostile place to be, with the wind always tugging at your tent – but to me, being there is simply brilliant.

Dorje and I arrived about midday, we put up our tent, crawled into it, and spent the next eight hours melting water, hydrating, chatting, and trying to snatch some sleep. It's difficult, though, to sleep in the day: you're pumped up, because you know what's coming up. Every now and again I'd take a whiff of oxygen, because I find it's very hard to sleep with an oxygen mask actually on my face. It's constrictive, and because all my saliva builds up inside it, it's really quite unpleasant.

Trying to snatch small bouts of sleep is hard; it seems that just as you are about to drop off, you wake yourself up with a start. What happens, if you're not familiar with the effects of altitude, is that you suffer from something called Cheyne–Stokes respiration, which is a very odd breathing pattern. At ground level, normal breathing is maintained by the build-up of carbon dioxide, not a lack of oxygen. When you are at altitude the body gets tricked. The carbon dioxide build-up is the same, but because the air is so much thinner, you're not getting anything like the same amount of oxygen in. So you take a massive inhalation – as if you're going to hold your breath – and if you're asleep it often wakes you up. Then you switch to very rapid breathing, which then slows, and slows down even further, and then you stop; you stop breathing for what feels like for ever – or at least it does when you're observing somebody going through these stages. The only times that human beings exhibit this type of breathing pattern is at high altitude or on their deathbed. I think it's essentially the body beginning to shut down. Despite the altitude, we managed to get a little rest and, at about eight o'clock in the evening, Dorje and I started preparing, readying ourselves for a ten-o'clock departure. For the clients, being at the South Col must be hugely stressful. Not only are you there, slap-bang in the Death Zone, fighting for your very existence, but you are preparing to climb up into the unknown. For most this is the culmination of many years of dreams and aspirations, and there in front of them is their goal. There's a lot of pride on the line, as well as money and time – the tension can be almost over-whelming. I have a huge amount of respect for those that venture up there, for those brave enough to leave the relative comfort of the Col in pursuit of their dream. The media often slams these wannabe climbers, citing that they pay their way to the top. Well, perhaps they do; but they still have to step out and do it – no amount of money will help you make that physiological move.

Dorje and I left just after ten o'clock at night; Bill Crouse (with his client Hemant Sachev) and Jon Gupta were on their way up, so we were loosely climbing as a little group. There were probably forty or so people climbing that morning, which isn't that many for Everest these days. As we weren't the first to leave, we could see a small snake of head torches bobbing along into the distance. But we were moving faster than them and by the time we had crossed the ice shelf and started going up towards the Balcony, we had caught up with the main group. Since there were just the two of us, being confident and experienced, we unclipped from the rope and climbed past people, feeling very at one with the environment. We got to the Balcony, which is normally the point at which people change over their oxygen bottles, and I said to Dorje, 'Hey, Dorje, just check the oxygen?'

He looked at the oxygen. 'Oh, it's okay, it's okay; let's go, let's go.'

We tried to catch up with the two bobbing lights in front of us. We were getting close, but we couldn't quite reel them in.

It turned out it was Mike Roberts, a buddy of mine, whose client had gone home. Echoing my response to Kola's no-show, he'd said, 'Well, sod it; I'll climb anyway.' So he was climbing with his Sherpa, Mingma, which was why we didn't catch them up, until the summit. It was brilliant to find someone else I knew up there, someone else climbing the way we were and being able to enjoy the moment.

Dorje and I dropped down from the South Summit, across the traverse, and up the Hillary Step, and, *boof*, we're there, we're on the summit.

I checked my watch: it was two o'clock in the morning. We had just done the whole climb in four hours. It was great, one of those times when every aspect of our climb worked perfectly.

The only drawback was that it was, of course, still dark. Normally, standing on the summit, you get some magnificent views. I always tell my clients that they've got to be ready for that, it's amazing. Dorje – and this sums him up – said, 'Do you want to wait until daybreak to get the summit photograph?'

'Dorje,' I laughed, 'that's two hours away. No, we'll freeze; it's minus twenty, we'll freeze to death! Let's just get out of here!'

He smiled back at me. 'I was just checking . . .'

Later, I summed up the moment on my Facebook page: *Disappointment of being early and not seeing sun rise made good with the privilege of sitting alone in absolute silence with my friend just as I've always thought Hillary and Tenzing did. Dorje and I laughed at the stupidity of our small head torches beaming into nothing.*

We made our way back down the ropes quickly, and walked – or stumbled – back into the High Camp on South Col while it was still mostly dark. We arrived just as the sky was starting to turn grey, making it about four thirty in the morning. It had taken us a little over six hours to climb up, reach the summit of Everest, and return back to our tent. Most people probably wouldn't even be at the South Summit on the way up by that stage. It had just gone so well; climbing without a client meant I could tackle the route much more quickly and efficiently, and, having a fellow climber as experienced as my friend Dorje beside me meant I didn't have to keep stopping and checking on someone else.

So there we were. It was 4.30 a.m., and we were back down at the High Camp. Sat in the tent Dorje and I grinned at each other, he made us both a cup of tea, and then I said, 'Let's get some rest.'

We had a few hours in our sleeping bags, but once the sun came fully up, the tent grew too light, so I gave up. There was too much noise anyway, from people moving around, talking, clinking as they put on and took off gear.

I didn't know if anyone at the South Col was aware of what I was attempting to do. I hadn't said much to anyone in Base Camp, or to any of the other climbers we'd met. Dorje knew, of course, and Henry Todd, as well as Russell, and one or two others; but I hoped no one had said anything back at Base Camp, at least not yet. I still had one more peak to climb: Lhoste.

CHAPTER 11
THE DEATH ZONE

Once we were awake and up, it was on to the final part of my attempt.

The plan was to drop down over the Geneva Spur, back down partway across to the Yellow Band, and then climb back up to the High Camp on Lhotse. We wanted to be there by mid-morning so that we would have time to put up a tent, rest, recover and hydrate, and then leave later, about midnight, to climb Lhotse. The route to the summit is a beautiful thin couloir line; it was first climbed by the Swiss as a consolation prize for not being the first to summit Everest in 1954. Just as with Nuptse and Everest, the idea was to go up and down, only this time we would go all the way back down to Base Camp for tea and medals, and then get the hell out and go home.

So off we went. Dorje and I dropped down the Spur, crossed the traverse, and then climbed back up to nearly 8,000 metres and Camp Four of Lhotse. We pitched a tent, and then spent most of the afternoon lounging around trying to snatch some much needed sleep. The last few days were starting to catch up with me. The place seemed deserted. I saw some movement in one of the tents nearby but that was about it; It was only later in the day that a couple of other guys turned up – two Australians who were looking to summit Lhotse without oxygen. They were lovely, but they were two unknowns, the proverbial 'unfriendlies' (even though they were actually very friendly), whose capabilities could have been good enough – but might not have been. Dorje and I carried on with our routines, trying to rest, drinking a lot, eating when we felt we could.

At about four thirty in the afternoon the radio beside me crackled into life. It was the Himalaya Rescue Association, or HRA, asking for somebody to help with a casualty who they believed was in a tent at our camp. The details were very vague: an American, with one of the US guiding companies, had been tending to a stricken climber, but the American, who had just climbed Everest and Lhotse as part of a double-header, was knackered. The HRA wanted somebody to take over the care of the sick person.

My immediate reaction was '*Oh no.*' I know it sounds callous but I try to stay away from this sort of thing on Everest, because of the possible repercussions. I've always somehow avoided being drawn into these situations, more by luck than design. I try to keep a low profile, because you never quite know where it will end up.

The two Australians were still there, but I felt there was no option but for me to go and see what I could do to help. Dorje and I left our tent and went to see where this casualty might be, and what could be wrong with him. There were three tents all in a group together where we were, and there was one other about 40 metres beneath us. By the time we got down there, the American climber had already gone, leaving the casualty alone in the tent with a Sherpa. I wasn't surprised that the American

had left; the first rule of climbing on the mountains – any mountain, not just Everest – is don't put yourself in personal danger.
He had stayed with the casualty all day, and helped the best he
could; but then he had to make the judgement call. He wasn't
on his way up the mountain, fit and full of energy; he was on
his way down, he'd spent considerable time already in the Death
Zone, and he had to consider his own condition. What use would
he be to someone dying if he wasn't well enough to help him?
What use would he be to a rescue party if he ended up needing
to be rescued himself?

A very different scenario played out in 2007, when the English
climber David Sharp died on the north side of Everest. Then,
people were climbing over the body of this dying climber to get
to the summit; nobody stopped to help him. There was a lot of
media coverage of the incident at the time, and Simon Lowe, a
lovely guy and MD of Jagged Globe, took part in a radio debate.
It was put to him that 'climbers no longer have basic moral
values', and he really put the whole thing in context. 'Well, think
about it. You are in the Death Zone, you are struggling to survive
yourself, let alone stop and help somebody else. Your capacity to
help somebody in that environment is very small, and you are
clinging on to life yourself, so how long do you wait with somebody?'

Simon Lowe was quite rightly affronted by the line of questioning he faced on that radio programme, and said that he didn't
appreciate being lectured about the moral values of climbers,
when, only the day before, he'd been listening to the very radio
station he was now talking on and heard about a schoolgirl who
had being knocked down by a hit-and-run driver in Milton Keynes.
Shockingly, passers-by didn't help, and instead just left her in
the road. 'That was in Milton Keynes,' Simon commented, 'where

there's no threat to your own life if you go and help her. Now elevate that to 8,500 metres, where your very own existence is hanging by a slender thread, and reassess it; who has lost their moral values?'

Someone else said that people should have sat with David Sharp while he died, just to give him some comfort. That's all well and good, I wanted to point out, but how long do you sit with somebody at that altitude? Do you wait until you run out of oxygen? Rob Hall had done exactly that in 1996. He had refused to leave a dying client at the South Summit of Everest, and he ended up dying himself. Where do you draw the line? I don't think anyone should risk their own life because someone else has chosen to do just that with theirs. David Sharp was a fairly accomplished climber and one can only assume he knew and accepted the risks.

It's a moral and ethical conundrum. Of course, I have huge problems with David Sharp's death. People were stepping over him on the way *to* the summit, for goodness' sake. Reaching the summit had become more important than saving someone's life. That's just plain wrong. But that's part of the way things happen now on Everest. For some it's become an item to tick off on a bucket list. The purpose of being there – to witness the most remarkable view on earth, to be a part of that beauty, to feel a sense of personal achievement for making it to the highest point on earth, and to share that with your companions and fellow climbers – seems not to be that important for some.

The person who drew the most criticism over David Sharp's death – unfairly, in my opinion – was Russell Brice. Russ was taking part in a Discovery Channel programme at the time, and David Sharp was caught on film, on the head cams worn by his team, when Russ's Sherpas were moving up towards the top. Russ caught a lot of flak; yet, interestingly, he was the person that actually established who David Sharp was and which team he was on. It was Russ who took all of David's personal effects back to the UK; he even met David's family and explained what had gone on even though he had nothing to do with him – David Sharp wasn't even a member of Russ's team.

Why did David Sharp die? Aside from the medical causes, what happened to him on the slopes of Everest that day? When an Everest climbing expedition goes well, there is very little difference, on paper, between an expensive Everest expedition and a cheap Everest expedition. It's only when there's a hiccup that you notice the difference, because the 'friendlies' – the Adventure Consultants, the Himalayan Experiences, IMG, the big commercial groups of that kind – have the depth of experience to guide at that level: they hire Sherpas who know what they're doing, they have a large logistics team backing them up, and, importantly, they pay huge amounts of money to have back-up plans. Some teams – the 'unfriendlies' that I've spoken about – don't always have that, and when things go wrong, more often than not the bigger teams get called in to pull the smaller teams out of the shit. Of course, they do it to the very best of their ability, but there is a dilemma for them, too. The bigger teams, the ones with all the logistics in place, have a duty of care to their own clients. So who should they look after: their own clients or an unfriendly's client who is in difficulty? Do they leave their clients, do they send their clients down, do they send him or her back without a guide? As an Everest leader, I have a duty of care to my clients, so when one of the 'unfriendly' curveballs comes in from the side, and I've got to deal with it, I have a real moral dilemma. Who am I meant to be looking after? I can't leave my client up there alone and at risk.

For a paying client, you can go with 'Fred' for £X, or you can go with me for, say four times £X. We both offer, on paper at least, essentially the same thing. 'Fred' is going to say all the same things that I am saying, namely, 'We're going to climb Everest together and fulfill a life-long dream, and it's going to be a wonderful adventure.' But this is where the similarities stop. Do you want the level of care and the service that I provide, the one-to-one guidance through such a hostile environment, being coached through everything that might happen on an expedition? Do you believe that I'll take you from where you are now to fulfilment of your goal in a safe, meaningful manner? Or do you want to rock up in Kathmandu and pay 'Fred', having never met him before, to join a team where you don't know who your team-mates are, where there's no relationship-building? Without that vital ingredient, you have no vested interest in looking after those other people when the shit hits the fan, and, crucially, they have no interest in looking after you. Do you want a shaky infrastructure on the mountain and Sherpas who are being paid rock-bottom wages.

If you have worked as a team in the build-up to the climb, then you have a vested interest to start pulling that guy out. He's your friend, your buddy, your teammate, whatever you want to call him. That's what commercialism has removed.

When we're guiding on Everest, we're working in arguably the most dangerous work environment in the world, other than maybe the bottom of the ocean or space. Climbing in the Himalayas, I know I'm putting myself at risk, and that my clients are also putting themselves at risk. That's why I believe there should be standards to adhere to. I've mentioned the guidelines that came into being, and the '96 disaster. They came under the umbrella of the IGO 8000. Interestingly I bet no one has ever heard of the IGO 8000, let alone have an understanding of what is considered best practice.

But mountaineering is open to anybody, and so anyone of a

reasonable level of fitness and with no experience in the world can go to Mount Everest. And to me that's a beautiful thing about the sport. You can climb Mont Blanc in your brogues, your jeans and your jumper – if you are stupid enough. Okay, the French guides will raise more than an eyebrow. But if that's what you want to do, that's what you can do. The paradox is that the moment that sense of sporting endeavour is lost, mountaineering will lose its real spirit, which is why there's always this ambivalence about commercialism and regulation within mountaineering.

But here I was, heading into a tent, and I didn't know what I was going to find.

Inside there was a Sherpa, and a man lying unconscious on the ground. He was a big guy, probably 6 foot plus, and bulky with it. His name was Lee Hsiao-shih. The Sherpa was very inexperienced; he may have been a great guy, but he was not like Dorje. Someone with Dorje's experience would have known how to handle the situation, whereas this poor guy was totally out of his depth. He had been put into this difficult situation by his boss, down at Base Camp, who was paying very little attention to what was going on, and he had been up there for a day and a half with this guy. I quickly realised that the Sherpa was exhausted and totally dehydrated. So the first thing I did was to get him out, packing him off back down the ropes. I radioed ahead to a team that I knew was at Camp Three: 'A Sherpa is coming down, be ready for him, make sure you've got some hot drinks. Look after him, make sure he's okay.' Then I told Dorje to go back up to our tent; like a lot of Sherpas, he is very superstitious about death, and I felt it wasn't the place for him. Besides, there was really no point in him being there too. One of us needed to rest and remain alert.

Next I had to turn my attention to Mr Lee. Luckily, one of the Australians has come down to see what was going on: they'd heard the call over the radio and then saw me reacting to it. I don't think he was a paramedic, but he had a great deal more medical experience than I had, and it was useful to have another pair of hands, as I was busy on the radio, finding out what we should be trying to do.

Rachel, the HRA doctor on the other end, back at Base Camp, told me that we had to inject him with dexamethasone, a steroid-based drug. It's designed to work on cerebral oedema, and pulmonary oedema; one of the main problems that come with high-altitude sickness is that you can develop swelling in your brain and fluid in your lungs. The dexamethasone works on those oedemas. I'd administered it once before, to an incoherent Sherpa, who in his delirious state was taking his boot off at 8,700 metres. On that occasion I crushed up a load of oral dex, and gave it to him in a drink. Within twenty minutes I had put his boot back on and was short-roping him down to safety. The effects of dex, when it works, are dramatic. It's a bit of a wonder drug for high-altitude incidents.

However, this time I was instructed to inject Mr Lee, and I'd never administered an injection of dex before. In fact, I'd never injected anyone with anything before – I'd only ever practised on an orange. Fortunately for me, the Australian guy said he would do it as he had experience of administering inter-muscular drugs. So away he went injecting Mr Lee; he also took the time to take me through the procedure step by steep. Then we waited, but there was no visible effect. The sun was now setting, it was getting really cold. I relayed to HRA what we'd done, what had happened – which was nothing – and asked what we should do next. 'One of you has got to stay with him,' was the response.

The first thing that went through my mind was 'Hang on a

second – I'm two-thirds through the Triple Crown here. How long do I stay with him for?' The selfish, egotistical, arrogant – whatever you want to call it – part of me thought, 'I'm really close to doing something quite special.' Now I was stuck in a tent with Mr Lee, and I became quite cross that I had been put into this situation.

The Australian decided to head back to his tent leaving me with the casualty. Although I was happy with this I couldn't help but feel deep down that somehow I had been unfairly lumbered with the situation. Of course, I couldn't leave. I felt I had a moral obligation to stay. I'd taken over Mr Lee's care, and I was damned if I was going to leave him now. I had got the stove going, and as well as putting an oxygen mask on the man's face, I'd opened an oxygen cylinder in the tent to pump it full of oxygen, partly for him, partly to help me, because I needed it as well. I set an alarm to wake me every half-hour because I found that I was struggling to stay awake, no matter how hard I tried. Unsurprisingly the exertions of the last few days were catching up with me. The alarm would ring, I'd wake up, check on Mr Lee, record his stats and then slump back down. I was rapidly becoming exhausted – that is why it is difficult to ask people to stay for any prolonged period in the Death Zone. I found the situation incredibly lonely, sat there helpless with a man fighting with his life. I thought of home, of Saffron and Willoughby. Looking at Mr Lee I vowed I would never be him. I made a silent promise to my children that night that I would never leave them in this manner.

As the night wore on, the tent became like something out of a war movie: there were pools of urine and vomit all over the floor, empty O_2 cylinders, various wrappers and empty food packages; it was really quite unpleasant. There was also down everywhere as Mr Lee had been ripping at his down sleeping bag. I am not sure how many times my alarm had gone off, when for some reason I checked his feet, only to find they were like ice blocks, even with his socks on. I pulled off the socks and I could see his toes were becoming frostbitten, already a ghoulish grey with some nasty blisters forming as well as being totally wooden, so I started trying to rub them warm for him. Whenever I moved about I sent down flying everywhere, and I'd end up spitting out small feathers, like something from a comedy film.

Come midnight, I injected Mr Lee again, only this time I gave him a double dose of dex, and it had an effect. All of a sudden, he was back, not quite like Uma Thurman in *Pulp Fiction*, but his eyes were open, and he was moving around a bit, clutching my hand, and murmuring things that I couldn't quite catch.

It was amazing, the effect that that double dose had on him. 'Wow, he's going to make it!' At least, I was hoping he was going to make it, and I was really clinging on to that. I thought, 'God, we're going to pull off the unthinkable here.' By 'we', I meant the three climbers involved – myself, the Australian and the American – and also Rachel, the HRA doctor on the other end of the radio. I don't think I've ever hoped for something quite so much in my life.

At that point – it must have been about 12.30 a.m., maybe 1 a.m. – I was sure he was going to make it, I went back to the alarm-driven routine, trying to stay awake before succumbing to exhaustion only to be woken a few minutes later by the alarm to check on him again. He was fine for the next three hours or so but when I woke up at about 4 a.m., he was not breathing. 'Oh my God, he's stopped breathing, he's fucking stopped breathing.' I grabbed the radio, but I'd made a mistake. In my sleep-deprived state, I'd accidentally left the radio outside. Of course, it had got cold and the batteries had died as a result. Now, more than ever, I needed that link with Rachel, who, bless her, was up all night long beside her radio, and I couldn't reach her. I didn't know quite what to do; I was angry with myself. I knew that if I did something about the cold I could get the radio going again, so I ripped the batteries out and slid them down my underpants, to warm them up. Once they'd warmed up I could ask for Rachel's advice.

But what to do in the meantime? All of a sudden, I'm twelve, or maybe eleven years old, and I'm at Chalfont Heights Scout Camp, getting my First Aid badge. One of the things we were taught was that if we came across somebody who was not breathing, we should use CPR. I dredged out of my mind what I could remember of those Scouting days, and started doing CPR. God, I had no idea how tiring CPR is. I pumped his chest, probably for little more than five or maybe even ten minutes, but it felt like for ever. I slumped back down, thinking, 'I can't keep this up, I'm knackered.' But then: 'No, I'll do it a little bit more, because, if I give up, he's definitely going to die.' And the responsibility for this man's life made me determined. I kept going, pushing his chest over and over, chanting, 'Keep going, keep going, keep going.'

I didn't know what else to do, because the only other thing I remembered from that first-aid course was that you keep doing CPR until somebody more experienced than you turns up to tell you that you don't need to do it any more. Finally I just couldn't do any more, so I stopped, pulled the now-warm batteries out of my pants and push them back into the radio. I don't know what time it was, but I got through to Rachel, who immediately said, 'Oh, God, where have you been? What's going on?'

'The batteries died. He's not breathing!'

'How long has this been? What have you been doing?'

So I explained what I'd been doing. 'How long for?' she asked.

'I don't know, and hour and a half, maybe two hours.' I was kind of guessing here; I'd not been writing any doctor's notes.

She said, 'Well, it's your call.'

I knew exactly what she meant but I couldn't bring myself to make it. It was just beginning to get light, and I was struggling to make any kind of decision. Then Dorje arrived. He unzipped the tent, stuck his head in, with a big grin on his face and a flask of tea in his hand. He looked down at Mr Lee and said, matter-of-factly: 'Hey, Kenton, he's dead.'

That really hit it home for me.

My small guiding company, Dream Guides, lost a client on Ama Dablam a few years ago. I went to break the news to the family in north London. It was horrendous enough for me, devastating of course for them, but I thought it was the correct thing to do, because word gets out through the Internet fast. I thought I had a duty of care to the client and the family. I didn't quite know how to do it, so I phoned a police liaison officer, a friend of Jazz's, and asked for some advice. She explained it had to be done in person. 'Write down these points,' she said. 'This is what you do. When you arrive at the home and knock on the door, the first thing you do is get into the house, get the wife back into the house with you.'

I said, 'Well, what if she's not there?'

'You wait. Then, once you get through that door, you're inside, then you tell them that their loved one – in this case their husband and father – is dead, and use that word, "dead", because there's no ambiguity about it. He's not deceased, he has not passed away, or anything like that. You say, "He's dead."'

That's just what Dorje said – 'He's dead' – and those words were so final they snapped me back to reality. Mr Lee's head was still in my lap but, truth be told, life had flown out of him hours before.

I had to pass this news on to Base Camp. I was aware that anybody could be listening to the radio, so I was careful about what I said over the channel. By then Henry was on the radio, and I said to him, 'I need to speak to Russell,' which was the code for us to switch channels. Then I explained the situation. Just saying the words out loud was very difficult, very emotional, and I burst into tears.

Henry asked, 'How are you feeling? What do you want to do? You know, we've got a team of Sherpas coming up, we'll support you down.'

I was literally on my knees, and I said, 'Henry, I'm coming down. This isn't what it's all about; this has gone way beyond what I climbed for.'

'Really?' was all he said in reply.

'Try and organise me a seat on one of the choppers into BC,' I added. 'I want to go home.'

We finished the conversation, and then Dorje and I sat there, in the doorway of the tent, drinking tea, with Mr Lee lying dead next to us. The impact of Henry's one-word response slowly sank in. I looked at Dorje, and he looked at me, and the doubts started to creep in. 'Do I really want to go down?' We'd come there with a set objective; we were there to do something. It didn't matter if I went up Lhotse or down to Base Camp, Mr Lee would still be dead.

There was some noise at the edge of the site and I saw someone arriving. It was Mike Roberts, with his Sherpa, Tendi. We'd just been with them on Everest, and it turned out he was attempting an Everest–Lhotse double-header, but using slightly different tactics. He was going to climb from the South Col, and so had spent all day at the col rather than moving camps. His was another friendly face, as I've known Mike for quite a long time; but crucially he's a physio and also wilderness-medicine trained. So Mike poked his head inside the tent and said in his Kiwi accent, 'Yes, he's definitely dead.' I remember thinking, 'No shit he's dead.'

Mike's arrival helped me cement a decision. I was going to

203

climb Lhotse and finish what I'd started. 'I'm going to lean on you guys a little bit,' I said, 'because I've been up pretty much all night, I've just done two hours of CPR, and mentally I'm wiped out.'

Dorje's handsome face split into his broad smile. He didn't have to utter a word. And he climbed straight back to our tent to start breakfast. We agreed that we would leave in an hour. Now normally you don't leave to climb an 8,000-metre peak at eight or nine o'clock in the morning – that's way too late – but this time I had no choice.

I knew it was the right thing to do after what I'd been through. I needed to spend some time with my friends, doing what we all enjoyed. Dorje has been a great friend for eight years, and Mike had been there in 2004 when I first went to Everest. 'These are my mates,' I thought, 'and this is what we do. And you know what? Those bastards didn't even wait for me! I was knackered and so I was the last to leave (because I was trying to get all my shit together), and off they went. I took a picture to prove this to them later: in it Dorje's 50 metres away, and Mike and Tendi are in the bottom of the couloir already.

I called out, 'Oi, assholes! Bloody wait!'

The four of us started up in the couloir and it went really smoothly, so much so that I was surprised how easy the climbing was. After a while we caught up with the two Australians, because they were climbing without oxygen, and as a result were going slowly. They asked about Mr Lee, and I said, 'He's dead, I'm afraid.' That was the first time I'd said it out loud.

I continued to find the ascent of Lhoste a struggle, although not physically. I had heard all sorts of horror stories about the climb, but I actually found it straightforward. I was tired, of course, but the climb was mostly up fixed lines, which made it easier. But I was finding the emotions raging within me hard to cope with; I couldn't shake the thought that I could have done more for Mr Lee. And then there was the anger – a man had died on the mountain when he could have been saved.

We climbed higher and higher and I made myself focus on the task at hand. Mike was in front, and I could see something, just down from the summit, although I didn't realise what it was until we got closer. 'Oh God, it's another body.'

It was the body of a European climber from a number of years earlier, just hanging awkwardly on the ropes, and we literally had to clamber past him. I found myself looking at him, but all I could see in my mind was Mr Lee, so cue more tears.

It is tragic to see a body left hanging like that, it's so lonely; but it's a desperately difficult thing to retrieve a body so high up the mountainside. It requires a big logistical team to do the job, and, of course, you're asking people to go into the Death Zone to retrieve a body. It is horrible for friends and relatives, but that's the reality. Before I left for the Himalayas one year, I had a frank conversation with Jazz on the subject. I told her that in those circumstances I would want my body left on the mountain, that I wouldn't want anybody putting themselves in danger to bring my body back.

But Jazz saw things from a completely different perspective: 'Well, you're not the one that's left behind, so who are you to say what happens?'

So we've agreed to differ on that for the time being; not that I ever intend to die in the mountains.

Finally, I made it to the top of Lhotse, only to find Mike was already on his way down. On the last third of the ascent the wind picked up – that short six-day weather window was closing. Base Camp had been keeping us informed, and we knew we had until early afternoon before the weather deteriorated. Luckily, we'd climbed really fast. We had left at about 9 a.m., and we were on top sometime after midday, taking about three and a half hours. Mike was not taking any chances though, he had tagged the summit and headed down without lingering.

By the time I got to the summit, I couldn't see anything, there was clag (misty, cloudy, wet weather) everywhere. This strangely really upset me: everybody says the view of Everest from Lhotse is sensational, and I've always wanted to see it for myself, but it wasn't going to happen that day. I was so upset that I began to blame Mr Lee, but then I stopped myself. Of course if we had got there earlier in the day I might have seen the view, but who could know for certain? The odd thing about it for me, though, was how much of an anticlimax it felt at the time. I had just completed my goal, I'd achieved the Triple Crown, the first person to do so, and yet I didn't feel anything at all. Dorje and I hugged, exchanged a few words and we left. I simply wanted to get back down as soon as I could.

By this time visibility was poor – the mist was swirling and it was snowing heavily. Snow was building up on the rocks on the side of the gulley and then cascading down over our heads. It began to feel serious, and I knew we needed to get down off the mountain quickly. On top of everything else that had just happened, I felt close to breaking. It wasn't just one thing. It was climbing Nuptse, climbing Everest, then being up all night with Mr Lee, and now the weather had broken. 'God, what else can you throw at us?' That's when I just let it out. 'You know what, throw anything at us, we can deal with it. We've dealt with a lot worse the last couple of days – you bring it on.'

Despite the fresh falling snow, there wasn't a whole lot of snow in the couloir in 2013, so there was exposed rock, much of which was shattered and loose. I was acutely aware that the two Australians underneath us weren't wearing helmets. We started down on the ropes, moving swiftly but trying to be as careful as possible with the loose rock. We passed the Aussies halfway down. They were still making slow upward progress, we chatted for a moment and headed off. Finally we popped out of the cloud and we were back at the High Camp in no time at all. It had taken us only an hour and a half from the top . . . or maybe even less – my concept of time had been totally lost. At the camp, Dorje started to pack the tent, I moved to help.

'Just go, carry on down,' he said. 'I'll pack up here and catch you on the ropes.' So I did just that, arriving back at the tent where Mr Lee's body was just as the Sherpa rescue team got there.

I had a quick word about the situation, finishing with: 'Hey, it's out of all of our hands now.' I was far too exhausted to be able to do anything helpful. Before departing, I unzipped the tent and took one last look at Mr Lee, who was in exactly the same position as when I'd left him that morning. I don't know what I thought I'd achieve by sitting next to the body but that's what I did for a few quiet moments. Pulling myself back to the present, I realised I needed to get down, to get some rest; I wanted to try to leave what had happened behind. I was told there had been some confusion about Mr Lee's whereabouts when he'd first become ill. A helicopter had been called in, but nobody knew where to send it, which explained the chopper we'd seen making a couple of sweeps of the face as we climbed over the Geneva Spur on our way up to Everest. Plainly, somewhere along the line there had been a breakdown in communication. It had only been forty-eight hours ago but it now seemed like a different life.

You can never know this for sure, but if there had been a Sherpa team on the spot the day before, when Mr Lee was first in difficulty, maybe he would have survived. I can't know that for sure, no one can; but if he'd been part of a team with a back-up plan – a team that recognised that problems might occur and had contingency plans in place in case they did, a team that actually cared – then I can't help thinking he might have survived. Might.

I started heading down the lines. Dorje caught up with me really quickly, a sign of just how tired I was. We bypassed Camp Three. I waved to my friend Heather on my way past but didn't stop to talk: I knew that everyone would have heard what had happened to Mr Lee and I couldn't face talking about it. I was feeling pretty fragile, still trying to work through what had happened, and I felt a deep physical tiredness. We got down onto the upper section of the Western Cwm, where it's flat, then we trudged back. That part of the descent always seems to take for ever, but on that day it felt never-ending.

As if we hadn't had enough already we came across an exhausted climber in the Western Cwm. I don't know what she had been doing, but she could hardly move. Despite what he'd already done that day, Dorje dropped his rucksack, lifted her onto him piggyback-style, and walked with her on his back down into the top section of the camp. I was blown away by the power, resilience and stamina of the man. It was unbelievable. After all we'd just done, he was not only piggybacking somebody else, but then he would have to go back and get his own rucksack which was sat on the glacier. Despite this, he caught me up before I had the time to stumble into camp. I was knackered by then, utterly exhausted.

I felt satisfied at what we'd achieved, but we still had one last stage to do the following morning. We had to walk down through the icefall back to Base Camp. I wasn't going to make the mistake I'd made the year before, when I'd walked back from the summit of Everest to BC in one day, having taken an Olympic gold medal to the summit. I left it too late and found myself wandering through the icefall exhausted, lost and in the dark. It was a nightmare, but oddly a memory that I cherish at the same time.

When I arrived at Camp Two I chugged back some tea with

them; no matter how tired I was I knew I had to hydrate. Then I crawled into my tent on my own, which with hindsight was a bit of a mistake. I crawled in thinking, 'God, I'm going to have the sleep of kings.' Of course, I didn't sleep a wink. I lay there, tossing and turning, plagued by demons. 'What if . . . ? Did I do . . . ? Could I have . . . ?' I didn't even think about the three climbs, which is a shame, because that was the great part, the reason I was there among the mountains.

I finally got some fitful rest, but when I woke up in the morning I was in agony. It felt as though I'd been beaten up: every joint, every muscle, every bone was aching. My face was sunburnt, I was dehydrated, and my lips were cracked. Everything hurt. It was a fight just to get up and get moving. I was really keen to get through the icefall before the day warmed up, making the journey down like walking through a furnace, and in the state I was in, I needed all the help and ease I could muster.

Dorje and I went back through the icefall together. Unlike my previous descents that season it seemed to go on for ever, ceaselessly trudging along. Whenever we got onto a flat bit in the lower section I'd think, 'Now we're close,' and I'd redouble my efforts: all I could think was, 'Let's get this done, just let me be there.' As each footstep sank into the ice, I just wanted to sit down and sleep. Finally we reached the end, and I could see the tents ahead.

Finally stumbling into Base Camp, I was handed more cups of sweet, restorative tea, and immediately went to see Henry Todd. We cracked open a beer or two, and I did some more crying with Henry. I said, 'I've got to go and see Rachel. I need to go and thank her.' I walked across to HRA, and I immediately burst into tears again: 'I'm so sorry, I let everybody down, and he died.'

Rachel then said something that has stuck with me ever since. I didn't really pick up on it at the time, it was only a few days after that it sank in. She said: 'You did the best that you could possibly have done, you couldn't have done anything else. The chances are we were never going to keep him alive, but we had to try.' I think about what she said a lot, and, when I am asked to give talks to schools, I try to use those words – do the best that you can do. Those words have a lot of power.

Meanwhile, Jazz was wondering what had happened to me. 'Right, I'm off to climb the Triple Crown,' I'd told her before setting off. 'We've got a great forecast, I'll be gone for a few days, so I'll speak to you when I'm back down.' Of course, a few days turned into seven days. I used the term 'few days' loosely – I knew what I meant but poor Jazzy didn't . . . Back at home, Jazz was going a bit crazy. That's that selfish climber again; I was completely oblivious.

It didn't help that the first call she received was not from me but from Henry Todd: 'Jazz, it's Henry. Don't worry, everything's fine. He's about to enter Base Camp. He's taken so long because he tried to save this guy's life; it has not quite worked out and he's emotionally in bits.'

Henry had the best intentions, of course, but I had spent years instilling in Jazzy that no news is good news, that bad news only comes with unexpected calls and visits. And here, suddenly, was just such a call. It took some minutes for Henry to get the whole story across, conveying that although I was exhausted I was totally fine, and in the meantime Jazzy was going frantic. Putting myself in her shoes, the whole situation must have been terrible: first no news and then, out of the blue, a strange number from Nepal, followed by a familiar voice but not one that was expected . . . One can only image the thoughts.

I called Jazzy as soon as I was back down. Of course she was relieved to hear my voice, yet at the same time tore strips off me for generating the situation and confusion. I couldn't argue, partly because I was too tired to, but mainly because I knew she was right.

I spent only one full day at Base Camp before I managed to secure a seat on a helicopter out. During that day I thought a lot about what I'd done, trying to process what the last eight days or so meant. On the one hand, I realised that I'm actually quite good at climbing at high altitude; on the other my bubble of immortality had been burst. To climb like I had done since my university days requires a strange detachment – something akin to going to war, I guess: the notion that it's the guy next to you that's going to die, not you. It's a strange, illogical belief in your own specialness. For the first time I realised, almost viscerally, that climbing is dangerous. I also spent most of the afternoon sat with Dorje, the two of us drinking tan and chatting. It was a lovely couple of hours with my friend.

People at Base Camp knew what I had done; it went up on one or two blogs, and before I knew it – you know what the Internet is like – the story had spread. First it was the climbing press who were interested – after all, it did represent a climbing first. It may not have been up there with the greatest achievements, because I'd accomplished it with fixed lines and while using oxygen, but to paraphrase the words of Rachel from the HRA at Base Camp, I had done the best that I could do. There was a great piece in *Outside* magazine by Alan Arnette, and then, all of a sudden, *The Times* wanted to do a piece on it.

What pleased me was that at last there was something to celebrate about that bloody mountain. There had been so much bad news over the previous few years: the punch-up between climbers and Sherpas; the queues at the summit that drew so much criticism the year before; and, of course, the furore over David Sharp's death in 2007. For once there was something good to say, and I felt proud to be part of that.

My generation were quick adopters of a new ideology in climbing that came with the equipment and information. News spread fast and ethics became more important – it was less what one climbed, more how one climbed it. Standards exploded as climbers specialised in certain aspects of the sport. I was at the very start of this explosion, straddling the previous generation and the new one.

EPILOGUE

In the twelve or so years that I have been climbing in the region, Everest has changed significantly. The romance that I experienced in 2004, on my first summit, has now gone – partly because one cannot recreate the excitement of something new, but mainly because of how commercial it's become over those years. Of course, there have always been aspects of climbing that by necessity are to do with commerce. You have to bankroll a trip in one way or another. Even as far back as 1922, on that first attempt to climb Everest, there were two people on the expedition who had paid over the odds to be on the team.

Today, if you take into consideration both the north and the south side of the mountain, there may be up to five hundred people looking to summit in any one season. If you add all the support staff into the mix, this means Base Camp can be housing up to a thousand people.

There are two climbing seasons on Everest, pre- and post-monsoon, but, traditionally, pre-monsoon is the time to go. Pre-monsoon is springtime, and that's when all the commercial teams set up. In spring the jet stream is less fierce, and you do not have to deal with the tail end of the rains or the onset of winter and the brutally cold weather it brings with it.

It's worth taking a look at what it costs. First there's a peak fee of $10,000, which allows an individual onto the mountain and to attempt to climb it, although the Sherpas don't have to pay this fee. Then there are the fees to the SPCC (Sagarmatha Pollution Control Committee), who oversee waste management, an environmental bond to pay per team, which works out at $4,000. This fee is paid back once your time on the mountain is over, provided you have met with the SPCC's requirements. There is also a fee to the SPCC for the fixing of the ice-fall. In addition, each team is required to pay the fees of a liaison officer, which again can run to a couple of thousand dollars. The LO is an interesting case. Most teams, myself included, don't particularly want an LO at Base Camp. They don't really help a team in the manner that they are designed to; more often than not they become a drain on resources. What will often happen is that they are paid off by the team so that they don't even come to Base Camp; then the expedition leader and the LO will simply meet at the end of the expedition before the final debrief, the leader of course gives a glowing report back to the ministry.

In addition you will need to buy your kit, and this means not just your own personal clothing but also some specialised high-altitude kit that you'll require for climbing 8,000-metre peaks. A suitable pair of boots and a down suit can set you back close to $2,000 in total.

Without doubt the biggest decision, and the area where saving pennies can mean the difference between life and death, is the choice of your logistical team. Depending on what you want to pay, you'll get all your food, Sherpa support if you want it, oxygen delivery systems and bottles, as well as guidance to help you make a successful climb. There is a huge range of services on offer, from the bare bones through to constant hand-holding; the important thing is for the climber to know what he or she is buying into, and being honest about the level of support that they will need. Once you reach the top, you'll also be expected to pay a summit bonus tip, which is about $1,000 for a successful summit with a Sherpa; and of course tips for the Base Camp staff are another few hundred bucks. All in all, someone with reasonable mountaineering experience, using a good and reliable outfit, could expect to pay around $60,000 to join an expedition. For a bespoke trip you would pay a great deal more.

If the thought of paying $60,000 seems excessive, look at, for example, the logistics of getting food and equipment to where it needs to be. Base Camp is at best a forty-minute fix-wing flight followed by a ten day trek from Kathmandu. So it doesn't take a rocket scientist to work out that the cost of even the cheapest item escalates dramatically. In an effort to keep porterage down to a minimum, most teams store much of the heavier equipment – tents, stoves, kitchen supplies, mess tent furniture, etc. – as close to Base Camp as possible, but even then it can be a couple of days on the back of a yak to get things in each season. And when the last day of the expedition comes round . . . it all has to be taken out again. Russell Brice, the head of Himalayan Experience, who may be guiding up to thirty people each season, has a colossal amount of equipment there. When he decamped all his equipment from the north side of Everest to the south side in 2008 (after repeatedly being messed about by the Chinese Mountaineering Association, and the closure of the north side in 2007 for the Olympic Flame to be taken up), it reputedly cost him in excess of $60,000 to move the equipment. That's not the cost of the equipment: it's just the cost of moving it from Tibet, through the border, and back up to where he needed it to be.

There are predominately two types of people that come to climb Everest these days. The first are time-poor and cash-rich, the second time-rich and cash-poor. The latter might be students who have beaten out the fundraising path to get to the Himalayas. Last year there was a young climber who raised all the money through sponsorship, but pretty much lost it all because of the Sherpas' strike; then to his credit he raised all the funds again, only to caught up in the earthquake of 2015; one has to feel a little sorry for the poor guy. Of the former there are people like bankers and hedge fund managers, with oodles of cash. These people, who will pay top dollar, sometimes expect everything on a plate. The mountain is a goal for them but they're not prepared to reach it in stages, they want to fly in, learn how to climb to the top on the job, so to speak, and reach the summit. I'm generalising, of course, but I constantly get emails from people with no climbing experience whatsoever asking me to guide them up Everest. To get the most out of the adventure people need to put the time in.

But of course, there are great people who go to climb Everest. Base Camp attracts some really nice folk, but it also attracts some utter idiots, and indeed everybody in between. Perhaps that's one of the great things about Everest. You can rub shoulders with doctors and dentists, or students, or rocket scientists, or hedge fund managers, or guides, all getting along with the Sherpas. I don't think you find that eclectic mix of people anywhere else. Climbing brings people together with a common goal. It's a place where everybody's equal, where everybody has the same aim: to summit and get back down. Everest doesn't know whether you're a student or you earn a million pounds a year, you're just another person to Everest, and that's what I love.

More people have now climbed Everest than have circumnavigated the globe by sail. In fact, climbers now have a 65–70 per cent success rate, certainly on the south side. A number of factors lie behind this success. The technology is better, for a start; and the weather forecasting has vastly improved. Sixty-two years ago, the BBC World Service might have said at the end of the news, 'And for the 1953 Everest expedition, the monsoon is still down in the Bay of Bengal,' whereas now on a summit push we can order forecasts that come in hourly, which will give wind grams indicating speeds on the mountain at every 500 metres, the likelihood of precipitation, and temperatures. But above all, it's the increase in our knowledge that helps people achieve the summit in the numbers they now do. We know how to approach the mountain in the most efficient way. The Sherpa teams that we work alongside are more professional. Not only do they have a much better understanding of how the mountain works, they also know what the Western client needs to facilitate an ascent. Huge amounts of fixed rope get put on the mountain each year; Everest gets climbed through manpower – throw enough men at it and you're going to get to the top. Everest gets essentially beaten down to her knees, and then we ascend.

Everest has – maybe had; after the avalanche this year, we'll have to wait and see – become a little bit like going elephant hunting with a rifle that can take one down from 2,000 yards. Is it really sport? I'm not so sure. Now, some purists might say I'm one to talk. Let's face it, I've never *properly* climbed Everest because I've never climbed it without oxygen, but, apart from the time in 2013 when my client didn't turn up, every time I've climbed Everest it has been for work, and as such I've had a duty of care to my client. But it is still Everest. It still holds that cachet and that romance for me.

For some people, summiting Everest is simply a box to be ticked. They're not interested in the romance; they just want the trophy, the picture on the boardroom wall, bragging rights in the office. Others often have very personal reasons why they want to do it, and I respect and totally get that. It means something emotional for them at some particular point in their life, and I tend to like those people more.

People who want to climb with me will pay far more than the $50–70,000 it costs to climb with a commercial team; but one of the reasons why people pay so much is that I only work one-on-one – I don't work in groups. I will meet my client's family, have dinner with their wife or girlfriend, husband or boyfriend. I want to know what their daughters and sons think about it all. Everybody in their family has got to be onside, because there is a chance that Daddy or Mummy, or whoever's climbing, may not come home. Everybody has to understand that, and everybody has to understand the reasons why that individual wants to go. The main reason that people don't summit Everest is because they are not mentally ready. If there is any doubt at home about why that individual wants to be on a mountain for six to eight weeks then this is likely to be a constant source of stress between all parties which won't be of any help in achieving the end goal of a summit.

I don't think there's enough of that kind of due diligence taking place. I make sure my clients understand the risk, and that they are as fully prepared as possible for the ordeal ahead. Most of the decent companies will have a checklist: *Have you any previous experience . . . ? Have you ever climbed . . . ? Can you navigate across an ice field . . . ? Can you straddle a ladder across a crevasse . . . ?* If there's any doubt, they may ask you to do a course. You'll remember that when Sir Ranulph Fiennes contacted Jagged Globe asking to climb Everest, they weren't happy with his climbing résumé, so off he went to the Alps and then South America, just to gain a little bit more experience. I think that's the right thing to do; you need to be sure your clients know the potential hazards they're going to be facing up there, and to have some experience of climbing at height so that they are not dealing with things for the first time when they try to summit Everest.

There are other companies out there who don't do that due diligence. They're looking to do little more than to put bums on seats. As a result we see people arriving at Base Camp with hardly enough experience to attempt Mont Blanc, let alone Everest.

Only four years ago, I was on Everest, and came across a woman who had clearly never climbed a mountain. She had no romantic interest in mountains, she had never worn crampons or a harness before, and she treated her Sherpas like dirt, even though they were the ones keeping her alive. Not only was she putting herself at risk, she was also putting others at risk. To this day, I have no idea what possessed her to think that she could go to Everest and climb to the summit. I had a stand-up shouting match with her on the Lhotse face, and I told her to go back down. She wouldn't listen to me, so then I demanded that her Sherpas just leave her, thinking that this might shock her into seeing sense; that she might realise what a stupid and selfish thing she was attempting to do. The Sherpas being Sherpas with their hugely loyal values wouldn't leave her, and they somehow got her down the mountain. She didn't summit that year; but she came back the following year and she summited, Lord knows how. If you cut the Sherpas out of the equation, she probably would have died.

Sadly, stories like that are not uncommon. People are doing their rope training when they arrive in the Himalayas at the start of the season in the pinnacles, which are part of the lower section of the icefall. The team set up ropes to make sure that they can go up a rope, across a rope and down a rope. Well, if you don't know how to go up a rope, across a rope and down a rope by the time you get to Everest, why the hell are you there? I would never walk into a hedge fund and think I could run a multi-billion-dollar fund; I would never walk into a hospital operating room and think I could perform surgery; I would never jump into a Formula 1 racing car and race a bloody Grand Prix. So why do these idiots think that they can come to Everest and pretend to be climbers? It's sometimes farcical.

That said, as I've always maintained, part of the beauty of mountaineering is that there are few written rules, no regulations. If you want to go, then nobody's going to stop you.

With all the people associated with the mountain each season many armchair critics seem to think Everest is just a high-altitude tip, but that's not my experience! Rubbish-wise, it's a very clean mountain, Base Camp especially so. Everest has to be clean, because the commercial teams have a vested interest in maintaining it – don't forget that they have, after all, paid that $4,000 environmental bond to keep it so. Higher on the mountain, where the icefall is, you can see the old ropes in crevasses and bits of tent here and there, but again, it's pretty clean. Camp Two is getting a bit messy, more with human waste, as the waste management there isn't the best. A lot of teams are now starting to bring the human waste down off the lower reaches of the mountain. I have already mentioned what the Rangers in Denali National Park insist on, and perhaps Everest is heading in a similar direction. All the human waste from Base Camp is already carried down into the valley in large blue 100-litre barrels. The people who carry it down the valley get paid very well, about $100 a load, which isn't bad when you consider the average national salary in Nepal is $400 a year – although it's not exactly a job I'd relish.

But here's the issue as far as I'm concerned. I totally understand the reasons why the waste is carted down off the mountain, but you then have to think about where it goes to after that. Is it fair to the people of Nepal to cart our rubbish to them? People are being paid to bring down not just human waste but also batteries, oxygen cylinders and gas cans; but there's not a single recycling plant in the whole of Nepal. So what happens to this stuff? Do they bring it back down and then toss it into a landfill site in Kathmandu (where the recent earthquake has shown people live in an already fragile city anyway)? What happens to the people living there, when it starts to affects their lives as the alkaline seeps out of the batteries into the rivers? Do you bring all the human matter down and dump it in Gorak Shep, where it would pollute the water supply? There's nothing you can do with it, because you can't recycle any of these things unless you export them back home. But how much CO_2 does a 747 kick out, transporting an empty gas cylinder back to the UK so that it can be disposed of in an 'environmentally friendly' way?

In my view, there needs to be some common sense applied. Perhaps once much of this waste could have been disposed of by hurling it down a deep crevasse, where it wouldn't be seen until it emerged bashed into a pulp, or squashed into powder after it's been scraped along the bottom of the crevasse for a couple of hundred of years. But with the numbers on Everest today this is not a viable solution. We have to think long-term. It's all well and good saying, 'Aren't we environmentally forward-thinking because we're bringing all our poop down the mountain?' But what are we doing with our poop once we've done that? A lot of the time I see this as a marketing stunt by some of the guiding companies – it certainly doesn't do anything for the local people. I'm not saying that we shouldn't be looking for solutions – of course we should, and not just on Everest but in every mountain range – but we shouldn't be holier-than-thou just because we bring rubbish off the mountain and by doing so create an even bigger issue for someone else.

Western climbers on Everest generate a lot of income for the Nepalese economy – last year (2014), peak fees alone raised over $3 million – but not all of that money goes where it should go, unfortunately. Even the money that does go to the government doesn't always trickle down to those people or departments that need it the most. It's a desperately poor country, as has been shown in the aftermath of the 2015 earthquake, and in such situations there are always individuals who look for personal gain at the expense of others.

To anticipate whether anything will change in the way the mountain is managed after the earthquake and avalanche this year, we can look back at the events of 2014. The icefall collapse that killed sixteen Sherpas carrying loads up to Camp One and Two on Everest was early in the morning of 18 April 2014. There are huge hanging ice cliffs close to the west flank of Everest, and, on one of my earlier trips, we nicknamed it 'Darwin's Corner', as we could see it was dangerous even then. Russell Brice pulled his whole expedition, including the high-profile Walking With The Wounded team in 2012, as he deemed it too dangerous – a very brave move, but he knew that the conditions on the mountain had deteriorated and it was only a matter of time before something fell off. Every other team stayed there, every other team summited that year, which you would have thought made a mockery of Russ's decision, yet I've got a huge amount of respect for him for making that decision. He decided what was safest for his team and his clients, regardless of what anyone else was saying. There's always going to be somebody willing to accept the level of risk, in the same way that there's always somebody willing to accept somebody's dollar to climb Everest, even though they don't have the experience.

The unfortunate thing is that the serac fell off during the start of the climbing season. If it had happened a month earlier or a couple of months later, when there was nobody there, then none of us would have been any the wiser. If it had occurred a week later, there would have Western fatalities, which might have made for an altogether different response in the aftermath, but at the time it happened the Westerners weren't sufficiently well acclimatised to be on the hill.

It was a huge serac fall, meaning a whole ice cliff broke off, as opposed to a snow avalanche. Not snow but ice, tens of thousands of tonnes of ice. So it would have pulverised anything in its path. That's one of the risks of mountaineering, known as objective danger; it's a constant threat that we can do little to mitigate, apart from choosing not to climb. I know that sounds very callous, but that's one of the dangers of mountaineering yet one of its allures.

We're paying the Sherpas to carry loads up to facilitate our whimsical Western dream of climbing Everest. So how do we feel when the Sherpas risk their lives for us, the paying customers? That for me is a really difficult question. The Sherpas work incredibly hard, they don't really gain the recognition that they deserve, but they do get paid very handsomely, comparatively speaking, for what they do. Dorje, my friend and my number-one Sherpa, earns approximately $6,000 a season, plus summit bonuses. Compared to the average annual salary of around $400 a year, that means he earns a lot of money. In UK terms, based on the average salary, that would mean earning roughly £400,000 a year; but don't forget that he earns that in a scant two months (albeit it two months of very hard and dangerous work). Once he's finished working on Everest, he'll work on Cho Oyu in the autumn, getting paid around $3,500 and then a possible Ama Dablam trip later still in the year.

So the Sherpas earn a lot of money, working incredibly hard exposing themselves to a lot of risks and carrying huge loads. It's

223

brutal, unrelenting work, and they all do it with a smile, with a laugh and a joke, and I admire them so much for it. However, nobody makes these people do the job, it's their own choice. If they don't want to work on Everest, they don't have to work on Everest. They can work on other mountains, they can run tea houses, they can herd yak, they can trek, they could porter up and down the valleys, they could go back to tilling the land; but they've made the choice to work on Everest. These guys are well rewarded financially. At the same time, I totally get the moral issue. If I had been there last year and watched one of the Sherpas I was employing die, what would I do? Since I first started writing this book I have sadly lost some of my Sherpa team. Pasang Temba and Kumar, both of whom have worked for me over many years, passed away in the disaster on Everest this year (2015). It's made me stop and think about the way that I operate on Everest.

Death is not uncommon on Everest; an average year would see about three to five fatalities. The north side is roughly the same, although I have never worked on the north side. Russell Brice tried to persuade me to go one year but I turned the offer down. Although I'd love to explore the north side of the mountain, to visit some of the valleys that the 1921 Everest reconnaissance explored, I have little desire to climb from this side. I think it's the dust and desolate nature of the Tibetan side of the mountain that makes the area feel cold and unwelcoming compared to the warmth and welcome nature of the Khumbu Valley of the south.

Sherpas die every year on the mountain while working; they fall into crevasses, they get avalanched, they succumb to exhaustion. Maybe one or two of the Western paying clients might die a year, and then possibly as many as three or four Sherpas a year, sometimes more. Occasionally the Sherpas make mistakes, going across ladders without clipping into the ropes, or falling down ice cliffs when they are meant to be clipped into fixed ropes. These mistakes are essentially caused by corner-cutting, trying to save a few minutes here and there. Every year the big commercial teams attempt to drum into their staff the importance of safety, but health and safety is often flounted, just as it is on building sites all over the world, sometimes with dire consequences.

Following the sixteen deaths after the icefall in 2014, the mountain was shut for a few days for a period of mourning. Some of the Sherpas returned to their villages to pay their respects in their monasteries, and no Westerners could climb – or indeed wanted to – until it was lifted. While that was happening, things shifted behind the scenes. There had previously been four main stakeholders on the mountain: the paying clients; the predominantly Western commercial outfits, like Jagged Globe, AAI, IMG and guides like me; the Ministry of Tourism, essentially the government; and the Sherpas. Now there were five: a new, very small group of militant Sherpas had appeared, a group of young Turks. They were very outspoken, not only about the avalanche but also about the incident with Ueli Steck and the 'fight' of 2013. Some of them have their IFMGA (International Federation of Mountain Guides Associations) qualification, and they are ready to change things. They look at the guide owners and want a bigger slice of the pie. I know some of them. They're very talented in their own way, and they want better working rights, which I'd agree with them on. However, they don't have the attention to detail, they don't have the logistical planning, they don't have the flow-through of clients. The reason why some of the organised outfits are multi-million-dollar companies is not just because of their work on Everest. It's because they organise climbs on mountains all over the world – only the top 5 per cent of their clients come to Everest.

It was this group of Sherpas that essentially shut down the mountain in 2014, through a series of strikes and then systematic intimidation of some of the Sherpas who were willing to work. It was a scene that horrified me: that something that should be so pure and majestic becomes nothing more than a commercial power struggle.

So things do change and are changing. Will we, or can we, make the mountain too safe, so that it is no longer a challenge? Many already say that the challenge has gone, that the commercial teams beat the mountain into submission, and although I'd be inclined to partially agree, one only needs to look at the events of 2014 and 2015 so see that no one can ever tame Everest. She will bite, and hard.

There's a term in climbing: 'climbing by fair means'. It's a very hard thing to define. One person's fair means is not necessarily somebody else's fair means. I have a problem in that my fair means is with no aid. Nothing. So have I climbed the mountain by fair means? In my view, not really. Again, in my purest view nobody has really climbed it by fair means since Reinhold Messner in 1980. Messner and his Austrian climbing partner Peter Habeler became the first people to climb Everest with no supplementary oxygen in 1978, famously describing the experience later as like being 'a single narrow gasping lung, floating over the mists and summits'. Two years later Messner returned to the mountain and solo-ed it by a new route, with no one else on the mountain, no oxygen, no Sherpa support, no fixed ropes; he hadn't even set up a camp on the mountain before he set off. It was a truly visionary ascent.

The British team made famous by George Mallory reached 8,300 metres without oxygen in 1922. In theory almost anyone should be able to exceed what they did back in 1922 when one considers all the equipment and technology that we have today.

Ninety years ago they climbed in tweed and vast fur- lined leather boots, and I for one won't be trying to emulate that. I've been to that height on Everest's flanks without oxygen, within 500 metres of the summit. But the change in the environment over that final distance is exponential; the last 500 metres could easily be 500 miles.

Everest is the one mountain everyone knows. If I go to a dinner party and tell somebody that I've climbed Everest eleven times, they think, 'Wow, that's amazing.' Very rarely does anybody say, 'Have you ever climbed it without oxygen? Have you ever climbed it without Sherpas? Have you done a new route on it?' Nobody ever asks me that, they're just in awe that I've been up Everest eleven times. For me, though, climbing Annapurna III was light years ahead in terms of difficulty, complexity and the level of commitment needed, both physically and mentally. The stuff I was doing in Alaska was way more challenging than on Everest, with the proviso that at no point was I climbing in the Death Zone. For me, what I managed to achieve in 2013 with the Everest Triple Crown represented a big step forward in my development as a high-altitude climber, and although retrospectively I could have played a fairer game, it still represents the best it has got for me on Everest so far.

I still have a nagging feeling about my climbs on Everest, but I'm trying to work out what it is that nags. I've climbed it eleven times, so that sets me apart from 99 per cent of the other people who have climbed it, but so what? If I'd climbed it without oxygen, that would set me apart. But it's colossally dangerous. I could start training today for an ascent next year, and I am confident I would be able to climb Everest without oxygen, come back down without significant frostbite (one of the things that oxygen does is help keep you warm), and climb it in relatively good time. But climbing without oxygen at that height can permanently damage your brain. Is that a risk that I'm willing to take with a young family? Most of the time I dismiss the notion of attempting it sans O$_2$, yet some mornings I'll wake up and think, 'It is really important that I give it a go. The mountain deserves that I at least attempt to climb her by fair means.'

I've had this discussion at Base Camp with Henry Todd, Bill Crouse and one or two other colleagues whom I respect, and the general consensus was 'There's no need for you to climb it without oxygen. We all know that you are capable of climbing it without.' Well, it's one thing being told that 'we all know', and there's another thing actually proving it to yourself.

Why should I bother? Because somehow it does matter. Why do I climb at all? Why do I set myself seemingly impossible challenges? Why, for instance, do I choose to do a particular route, usually the hardest one up to the summit? It short, it doesn't matter to anyone, but it does matter, it matters to me.

I ask myself all the time what motivates me. I'm still not sure I have my answer. It's not just about being in the high places of the world, or being the first to reach them a certain way, or being alone with a glorious view. It might be that, but it's so much more, and maybe the day I do have my answer is the day I no longer want to go climbing.

Some of what I do, some of the things I've written here, must seem more than extreme to a lot of people – I realise that. Like climbing fifty hours straight, with just one four-hour period of disturbed sleep when Ian Parnell and I climbed Denali – that even sounds a bit obsessive to me now that I think about it. At the time it was happening, though, it seemed perfectly normal. As a young climber, I was lucky to be part of a fantastic scene, and I couldn't help but get swept along with everyone's enthusiasm. The hushed tones when you heard people discussing climbs that others had achieved. 'Oh, so-and-so's just done this.'

'Wow. I wonder if I could do that.' 'Oh, they've done that.' 'I had my eye on that one – bugger.' I was competitive, but probably more with myself and what I thought I should be achieving than with any of my fellow climbers.

I've always said I was the yes-man, by which I mean that I wouldn't necessarily come up with the ideas but if somebody said, 'Fancy doing this?' I'd say, 'Yes, I'm all over that.' The reason is because I had this constant fear of missing out. I still have it, although it smoulders rather than roars. That's why I did so many expeditions. Maybe that is why I climbed – for fear of missing out? I was doing two or three expeditions a year at one point, purely because someone would ask me. Then, once I had committed, I felt I could not back out. I believe you can't let your friends down. That led to there being an expectation amongst my peers that that's what I do: 'Why don't you ask Kenton? Kenton's up for anything.' I would go to these far-off places and be successful on the climb, so that led to the self-inflicted pressure of expectation: I started to think I had to say yes, because I'd said yes before. No one was deliberately putting the pressure on me; I put the pressure on myself.

I wasn't part of any formal group when I broke through as a climber. Climbing has always had extraordinary groups within its ranks, throughout its history. There was the Golden Age of Alpinism, from the 1850s through to the 1880s. Then in the 1950s, of course, came the conquerors of all the 8,000-metre peaks. Things went lightweight in the 1980s, with the likes of McIntyre, Scott, Boardman, Tasker and Baxter-Jones, climbers who brought a new level of commitment to the high Himalayas, climbing in Alpine style rather than the older heavyweight siege style. So what did we – my generation – bring to the table? Ian and I certainly didn't bring high levels of fitness to the game. Today climbers train methodically, whereas I was still

229

too much into beer and dancing on a Friday night – a familiar refrain when you talk to my generations of athletes, in any sport.

We were lucky in that the equipment was evolving quickly, which enabled us to climb lighter and therefore faster, and with it came a different ideology, a different way of approaching the mountains. We were no better, we were no more talented, than any generation before us, who had paved our way. They showed us what was possible, and what we accomplished we did because we were lucky enough to have the equipment to really exploit what the generation before had done. We were truly standing on the shoulders of giants'. I think what best illustrates this is the ascent of the west face of Gasherbrum IV by Schauer and Kurtyka in '85. The face is a huge technical wall, and they approached it with the same mentality one might climb an Alpine peak. Climbing very light and fast, they totally committed themselves to the wall; today it's still considered one of, if not *the* benchmark Himalayan ascent of all time.

Only five, maybe ten years later it had changed again. The really great climbers (of which I was never one – I am not really a great climber, though I am certainly a determined one) brought with them an Olympic fitness combined with the vision that perhaps came from the generation before us, with the equipment that we were the first to have at our disposal. Climbers like Ueli Steck and Steve House before him have taken things to the next level. Ueli Steck has this innate talent, combined with amazing commitment and extraordinary fitness levels (he trains at the Swiss Olympic training facilities), and he utterly dedicates himself to the sport.

For me, certainly during the period when I was climbing in Alaska with Ian, it was always a hobby. I wasn't making any money out of climbing in those days; in fact, it was draining my resources. I was coming back from every expedition utterly broke. Today there is the possibility of making a lucrative career out of adventure in one way or another. Over the last couple of years, with responsibilities of family, I have made the conscious decision to make what I do more of a profession. It's not so glamorous but I can do what I love and earn money from it. Unfortunately it's not an attitude that endears me to some of my colleagues.

Today in all sports – and climbing is a sport – everything is more professional and focused. The mental efficiency, and the focus, combined with how pristine you are physically, is constantly on a knife edge with the ability to tip one way or the other at any moment – that's something that's really been honed over the last ten or fifteen years. One only needs to look at what the likes of Clive Woodward in rugby and Dave Brailsford in cycling have done for those sports, and the levels of professionalism that came about as a result. It's no longer good enough to be the plucky amateur, and perhaps that is what climbing needs to break through to the next level. But by even saying that climbing could get more professional is to enrage a large proportion of the community, although who could possibly say that the likes of Steck, House or Arnold aren't totally professional?

The Golden Age of Alpinism was predominantly driven by middle-class English people going across to the Alps, as amateurs, then hiring local crystal hunters to guide them. The 1953 Everest expedition was essentially a bunch of amateur climbers, though highly professional in their organisation mostly due to the leadership of John Hunt. It's always been like that. There have been one or two exceptions, such as the likes of Chris Bonington, who was not only a brilliant climber and an exquisite leader but also a full-time professional mountaineer – there was very little that was amateur about how he went about his career – but the silly attitude still exists today in certain parts of the climbing fraternity:

you're considered a sell-out if you make money through climbing.

Doug Scott once said to me, 'You are wasting the best years of your climbing career shuffling up Everest taking paying clients.' Well, Doug, you may be right but I've got to put food on the table and I've got to pay the mortgage. 'Pay the mortgage?' some would reply. 'Why don't you live in a van and strip away any materialistic wealth? If you live in a van then you don't need to pay a mortgage and you can focus on your climbing and leave your mark all around the world.'

There is some strange stigma within climbing attached to having a nice house and being financially secure; as though this is somehow not being true to the values of climbing because it means that that the amount of climbing done is affected.

Many in the climbing world scoff at those who have ambitions outside of climbing. Years ago I also would have struggled to see the importance in life other than climbing, but the more I travel, meeting new people, seeing more things, the more my horizons broaden. If you were to ask me, I would still reply that I was a climber. But now I also have other things in my life; I enjoy different things, I strive to be successful in other areas. I'm still in love with climbing and the mountains, as much today as that first climb at Subliminal, but I realise now that there are other lives that can be led.

Live and let live. If you want to climb from a van and climb 24-7, go do it, and I'll be the first to doff my hat to you. But don't judge those who want to do something else.

For me it has never been about how hard I climb, it is all about the experience, having a day out in the mountains, hills or countryside that makes me feel totally alive, and being able to share that experience with friends. That is what the foundations of memories are made from.

Some put climbing above all other things, call it selfishness if you want. Ten years ago, 100 per cent; yes, I got that, I felt that way myself. But let's ask ourselves a simple question: what do you gain from climbing? Self-satisfaction. That's about it. You don't get fame and fortune. You get to stand on summits and see incredible views and have incredible journeys with incredible people. Climbing was, for me, everything; anything else was sacrificed for climbing. I needed to climb.

But today, when I have to walk out of my front door, it's almost exclusively for work. I love what I do but I've not done an expedition just for me since 2007, when I attempted the north face of Kalanka with Nick Bullock. Completing the Triple Crown was only possible because a client dropped out; that expedition started as a work trip. My priorities have changed. It's not all about me and climbing; I'm now having an incredible journey with three other people: my wife Jazz, and my children Saffron and Willoughby. This journey is at least as incredible as any mountaineering adventure I've ever been on. When I'm at home I get up at the crack of dawn, 5.30 a.m. most mornings, so that I can drive to the gym to train and then drive back to be in time to get the children out of bed, because above all else I want to spend time with them. People will often talk about the risks I take on a mountain, questioning how I can justify them with a family. Well, working away from my family – stepping out of the door and leaving my family behind – is the hardest thing I do in my life today, so I make damn sure the risks are manageable and the return worthy. Yes, it's difficult, but risks are a part of everyone's life – cycling to work, taking the train, driving a car, they're none of them totally safe. I calculate the risks I take. Everything I do when I close that front door is calculated. But in the end you have to gauge what's right for you.

When I was younger, I wanted to leave a legacy on a mountain, but it would probably end up being some far-flung mountain across the world that no one ever went to, where nobody would repeat the route. Now, I want my legacy to be two beautifully rounded children from a stable home who then take something forward into the world. Do I get to climb as much as a person living in a van? No. Would I want to climb as much? Maybe, I don't know. What I do know is that I still love my sport as much as any person living.

It is, I believe, all about risk, and management of that risk. Knowing my limits, being objective and knowledgeable, training my body and brain, and knowing the difference between taking my own risks and assessing risk on behalf of a client *and* my family. Touching the tip of the summit of Nuptse with my nose is an example of that. I took the risk because I was by myself, and because I knew I could trust my own abilities. If I'd been guiding a client, I wouldn't have got that far; I'd have turned back before the summit, because I wouldn't have taken the risk on their behalf.

Sometimes I lie awake at night, worrying about the consequence of my actions high on a mountain – not just for me and my fellow climbers, but also for my children and wife far away and safe at home in Gloucestershire. The fact that I'm even thinking about it perhaps indicates that maybe I shouldn't go, because it might cloud my judgement. I've always been good at shutting off from what's at home once I step out that door. I can build a barrier, but as the children get older, they're knocking that barrier down, and I find that increasingly hard to build it back up. How long will I be able to keep on doing this – until I physically can't cope, or will my will give up before then?

We are all very much aware that time is the single most precious commodity that we have on this planet. Nowhere is this clearer to me than at home. As I watch my children grow older, I wonder how they'll cope when they understand the length of time I'm away and why I'm going and the potential dangers. A couple of years ago I was going bike riding on Boxing Day – a training ride up and down some Gloucestershire hills. I said to Saffron, 'Daddy's going on his bicycle,' and she burst into tears. 'No, Daddy. Don't go. Don't go.' I comforted her: 'No, sweetheart. I'm going on my bicycle, just for a little hour and a half, and then I'll be back. I'll be back before lunch.' She said, 'No, no, no. Daddy, last time you went, you were away for ever.' I'd forgotten all about it, but I'd raced across the Pyrenees earlier that year. By the time we drove down there and got acclimatised and did the ride, which was seven days, and then spent a day bumming around in Biarritz before driving home, I was gone almost two weeks and my absence had clearly made an impact on Saffron. At the moment, the way Jazz and I deal with my random departures is to say, 'Daddy's got to go to work,' but what happens when Daddy's not going to work? What happens when Daddy's going on a selfish adventure, which has nothing to do with putting food on the table, but everything to do with fulfilling Daddy's ambitions?

Inside me there's a hunger to face new challenges; I don't know if it's wrong or not to acknowledge that, or to want to do something about it. A famous book called *Feeding the Rat* by Al Alvarez was published back in 1988, about the climber Mo Anthoine. The 'rat' is the need inside a climber to climb. It's a hunger that has to be constantly fed, for if it isn't it will consume the climber from within. Everyone has a rat of some description, the craving probably varies from person to person, but nevertheless it is there, always slowly gnawing away. I have tried very hard to cage my rat, to throw him into the nearest stream and let the little bastard drown, but he is cunning, resilient and tenacious, in it for the long haul. Over the years I've realised that it's not good to ask myself 'Is this going to feed the rat, or leave the rat wanting more?' because I don't know. Hopefully, one day, I'll feed my own inner rat to the point where he's satisfied, and then I'll understand my motivations, but I don't see that happening any time soon.

Even when I don't want to admit to that gnawing inside me, it doesn't help that I see so many pictures and videos now of climbs that I could be going on instead of being sat at home, thanks to the ubiquitous smartphone. Pictures can be uploaded quicker than Ueli Steck can set a pitch in the Alps. Recently I was supposed to travel up to Scotland for a day of winter climbing, for nothing more than the sheer pleasure and indulgence of it. It would have been the first time in a very long time for me to have done something like that; but it didn't happen in the end, which turned out to be a huge blessing, because the children and Jazz all came down with some nasty bug. I was more than happy to stay at home playing nurse, yet the frustration of missing a trip to Scotland was amplified so much more by the stream of information that is constantly fed to us, real time information that wasn't possible even ten years ago. Social media is nothing short of fantastic in stirring the rat to life, like some super steroid that makes him gnaw faster and harder than ever before.

I'm a little envious. The pictures remind me of days that hold a significance in my life, days that weren't simply ordinary. I'd heard recently that it is very hard, almost impossible, to remember something – anything – from a day that was simply ordinary. It's true, and those photos help me realise that. To treat a day as ordinary is nothing short of criminal when there's so much life around us – in our own homes, surrounded by our families, let alone being amongst the beauty of our wild places. Looking at pictures of Scotland, or Wales, I'm reminded what I'm missing out on. Having been there myself so many times in the past, I know the feeling intimately. In many ways I can only assume it's like being addicted to drugs: it's hard to know how to stop when the thing that you seek makes you feel so good.

So the rat inside gently chews away inside me, slowly consuming my very being from inside out. I know it's futile to let it do this to me, but at the same time it's impossible not to. On the face of it, travelling all the way to climb in awful conditions while my children toss and turn in their beds and my feverish wife tries to get some work done is completely illogical but climbing – like any passion – isn't logical, it doesn't follow rules.

That thought always makes me wonder how it would be if I didn't come back at all. I've seen death in the mountains, I've sat next to men as they've breathed their last. I've had moments on the mountains when I've thought, 'Wouldn't it be horrendous if I left Saffron and Willoughby without their Daddy?' I try to put myself in her mind: how would a five-year-old process the fact that she has just been told that Daddy's dead. I'm sure she would say, 'But Daddy always comes back. He's just gone for a long time and then he comes back.' Jazz would have to tell her, 'No. Actually, Saffron, Daddy's not coming back this time; he has gone to be with Grandpa in heaven.' My God, how selfish is that?

When I received emails and posts from friends and watched news broadcasts from the Himalayas after the avalanche swept through Base Camp in the spring of 2015, I was shocked. I wonder if it will change people's attitudes to turning up there and trying to climb the mountain? Will they now realise how dangerous it really is?

The sight of a devastated Base Camp at Everest should always remind us how fragile life is at the top of the world. Recently I experienced an emergency of the kind that I had faced with Mr Lee on Lhoste, only this time I was there at the start of the incident and so was able to influence the outcome in a far more successful way. It was quite a high-profile incident, because, although it was at the much lower height of just under 4,500 metres, as it took place in the Alps, it involved Sam Branson – son of Sir Richard.

Sam had asked me to lead him and his group to the top of the Matterhorn, on the last stage of a fundraising endurance challenge, (for his own charity, Big Change Charitable Trust) during which they'd already run three marathons, rowed across the English Channel and cycled all the way to the Alps. But when everyone arrived at the Matterhorn, where I met them, the mountain refused to play ball: adverse weather meant no one, not even the local guides, was climbing it. We waited a few days for the weather to improve, before finally the forecast looked favourable, although the climbing conditions were still questionable. The teams set off at 3 a.m. I had mixed feelings about our chances of a summit, but felt we had to give it our best attempt. I thought that if we made the Solvay hut, about halfway up, then that would be a good result. As is often the case when one waits under a mountain in bad weather, we had built the Matterhorn into something she wasn't. The route to the Solway hut went quickly and efficiently, and when we reached it everyone was feeling confident. I was happy with how things were going.

Until, that is, we got to within 200 metres or so of the summit, and Sam started to slow up before soon slowing to a crawl. It was obvious that he had lost colour in his face, and his breathing was laboured even at rest; I was concerned. 'I don't feel good, I feel nauseous,' he said. It was clear that he was starting to feel the effects of altitude sickness. It had come on very suddenly, but we had spotted it right away.

It was imperative, I thought, to get him off the mountain as quickly as possible. The question was how to do that: should we climb back down the mountain, enduring the long and tricky descent of the Hornli Ridge, or press on to the summit where a helicopter evacuation would be easy? I had to get Sam to understand that carrying on, while it might seem like the wrong thing to do, was actually right, for him as well as for everyone else there. He bravely accepted this.

We got the team to the top, where Sam collapsed; it was the culmination of an extraordinary physical achievement for them all – just to get to the mountain alone from the UK had been something of a feat, let alone the months of planning that went into the challenge. So understandably Sam was very emotional on reaching the summit. I wasted no time in getting him winched on board the helicopter that we'd radioed for, and he was taken down to safety.

Of course some of the climbing community felt that they had to comment on this, mostly in a manner that was, well, less than positive. At no stage did they mention the huge sums for charity that Sam and his team raised; it was more focused on how, because of who he was, it was no surprise that a helicopter was used to descend the mountain. Personally I'm tired of fighting the tide of naysayers. I can only say that I conduct myself in the way that I see fit, hoping that I stay true to the morals and values that my parents instilled in me all those years ago. Striving to be the best that I can possibly be, while trying to stay true to my personal beliefs and values.

Sam's story ended happily, but for many others things aren't as straightforward. At the time I'm writing this, no one is yet clear what will happen on Everest as a result of the devastation seen there in the past months; only one thing is sure: it will have to be different from how it has been run in the past few years, and I can only think of that as a good thing.

While it's impossible to peer into a crystal ball to have any insight into how Everest will play out next year, one can't help but think that it has to be business as usual. All the stakeholders need the season to unfold as normal, none more so than the Sherpas who rely so heavily on their Everest season for their existence. Personally I plan to be on the mountain again – I'm too much in love with her not to be. I can feel the pull to go back as strong now as ever. My hope is that there will be something to celebrate rather than a hideous news story akin to what we have seen in the last couple of years.

And what of my own personal ambition? Well, there is a saying: 'To tell the devil your dreams is to risk their loss . . .' and while I agree with that I do feel that I owe it to you the reader to at least give a glimpse of what they may look like.

My dream is to link the three highest mountains of the world, in a single climbing season: Everest, K2 and Kanchenjunga, the epic, dark and mythical summits of the Himalayas. Not simply to climb the mountains but to embark on the journey of a lifetime by linking them with a colossal 2,800 miles overland drive, and do it all within three months. I hear you mutter, 'Why?' Why leave the family again on what may prove to be my hardest test to date? The answer isn't simple: partly it's the bloody rat, partly it's that part of me that still does want to leave a legacy in the mountains; but there is also a more valuable reason. I truly believe that adventure represents the classroom of the future. My dream is to inspire and motivate the next generation of game-changers through the power of adventure. The ingredients are all present for something very special, and while we think that we are immortal and can still instigate significant change in this world, we can't, our time to do that is long gone. It's the next generation, our children that hold the key to our own futures. In the same way I was inspired by the likes of Scott, Bonington and, of course, Sir Ran when I was young, I feel the need to attempt to do the same. By encouraging future generations to take risks in the pursuit of learning, to savour adventure, to love the mountains and outdoors, I hope we can instill a sense of leadership, team-work and humility that they will take to adulthood, so that when they are faced with key decisions in their lives they make the right choice, not just for themselves but for us all. The project will take me to some pretty dark places, it will be a real test of human endurance and a huge mental challenge. But when it's all over I can come home, hug Jazz and the children, shut the door and look foward to the next time.

GLOSSARY

Abseil
The process by which a climber may descend on a fixed rope using a friction device. Also known as rappling.

Alpine climbing
Generally, climbing in the mountains; will often include a mixture of snow and ice climbing and rock climbing.

Alpine style
Alpine-style climbers are totally self-sufficient, carrying everything needed for the ascent on their backs. They do not use fixed ropes or Sherpa support.

Altitude sickness
A medical condition that is often observed at high altitudes. Also known as acute mountain sickness, or AMS.

Anchor

An arrangement of one or (usually) more pieces of gear set up to support the weight of a belay or top rope.

Approach

The path or route to the start of a technical climb – generally a walk or, at most, a scramble.

Belay

1 A place where you attach yourself to the rock. This can be done either briefly (during a climb, you put in protection to create a 'running belay', which the rope is clipped to) or more long term, between pitches. In the latter, the belay should involve many independent connections to the rock (or other immovable objects) that can bear a shock-load of one or both climbers falling off.

2 To protect another climber by preventing the rope from slipping, either with a belay device or with a body belay.

Bivy (or bivvy)

From the French *bivouac*. A camp or the act of camping overnight while still on a climbing route off the ground. May involve nothing more than lying down or sitting on a rock ledge without any sleeping gear. When there is no rock ledge available, such as on a sheer vertical wall, a portaledge that hangs from anchors on the wall can be used.

Bold

Term for an unprotected – that is, no protection – or a sparsely protected climb.

Bolt

An expansion bolt fixed permanently into the rock face to protect a climb. Climbs that only use bolts for protection are known as sports climbs. According to Reinhold Messner, bolts are the 'murderers of the impossible'.

Closed-circuit oxygen system
Commonly known as a rebreather, it is a piece of breathing apparatus that absorbs the carbon dioxide of a user's exhaled breath to permit the rebreathing (recycling) of the substantially unused oxygen content of each breath. Oxygen is added to replenish the amount metabolised by the user. This differs from an open-circuit breathing system, where the exhaled gas is discharged directly into the environment.

Clag
Slang for bad weather, often involving low cloud and drizzle, or rain.

Crag
Any expanse of rock that is climbed on.

Karabiner
Metal rings with spring-loaded gates, used as connectors. Usually oval or roughly D-shaped. Also known as crab, krab or biner.

CO_2 scrubber
A device that absorbs carbon dioxide. In this context it would be found in a closed-circuit oxygen system, which removes CO_2 from the air that is exhaled by the climber.

Cornice
An overhanging edge of snow on a ridge.

Couloir
A steep gully or gorge frequently filled with snow or ice.

Crampons
Metal frameworks with spikes that attach to boots, allowing the climber to walk on or to climb snow and ice.

Crux
The most difficult portion of a climb.

Cwm
(Welsh) A hanging valley, or *cirque* – a steep-walled semicircular basin in a mountain – sometimes containing a lake; also known as a corrie.

Dexamethasone
A drug used in the treatment of high-altitude cerebral oedema as well as high-altitude pulmonary oedema. Commonly known as 'dex'.

Exposure
Empty space below a climber, usually referring to a great distance a climber is above the ground or large ledge, or the psychological sense of this distance due to being unprotected. Exposure can also refer to exposure to the elements, like wind, snow or sun.

First ascent
The first successful completion of a route.

Glacier travel
Walking or climbing on a glacier; a rope is usually used to prevent falls into crevasses.

High-altitude cerebral oedema

A medical condition in which the brain swells with fluid because of the physiological effects of travelling to a high altitude. It generally appears in patients who have acute mountain sickness and involves disorientation, lethargy and nausea, among other symptoms. It occurs when the body fails to acclimatise while ascending to a high altitude.

High-altitude pulmonary oedema

A life-threatening form of non-cardiogenic pulmonary oedema (fluid accumulation in the lungs) that occurs in otherwise healthy mountaineers at altitudes typically above 2,500 metres (8,200 feet).

Harness

A combination of sewn nylon waist loop and leg loops, with belay loop and gear loops that climbers wear when not soloing. Designed to allow the climber to safely hang suspended in the air.

Haul bag

A large and often unwieldy bag into which supplies and climbing equipment may be thrown. Often called a 'pig'.

Ice axe

A multi-purpose hiking and climbing tool used by mountaineers in both the ascent and descent of routes that involve frozen conditions with snow and/or ice.

Ice tools

The collective name for a pair of ice axes used for climbing.

Ice screw
A threaded tubular screw with teeth used to protect a climb on steep ice or for setting up a crevasse-rescue system.

Jumar
1 A type of mechanical ascender (a device for climbing rope).
2 To ascend a rope using a mechanical ascender.

Lead climbing
A form of climbing in which the climber places anchors and attaches the belay rope as they climb (traditional) or clips the belay rope into preplaced equipment attached to bolts (sport).

Move
The application of a specific climbing technique to progress on a climb.

Nut
The simplest form of protection. A metal wedge threaded on steel wires, intended to go into rock cracks. The name comes from the practice of 1950s climbers, who used motorcycle nuts.

Objective danger
Danger in a climbing situation that comes from hazards inherent in the location of the climb, not dependent on the climber's skill level. Most often these involve falling rock or ice, or avalanches.

Open-circuit oxygen system
The traditional breathing systems as used by high-altitude climbers deliver a continuous flow of oxygen into a mask that

the climber breathes in, then breathes out, into the surrounding air. The system is fairly wasteful of oxygen, requiring the climber to carry reserve bottles.

Peg
A piton.

Pitch
The portion of a climb between two belay points.

Piton
A flat or angled metal blade of steel that incorporates a clipping hole for a karabiner or a ring in its body. A piton is hammered into a thin crack in the rock and removed by the last team member.

Protection
1 Process of setting equipment or anchors for safety.
2 Equipment or anchors used for arresting falls. Commonly known as 'pro'.

Quickdraw
Two snap-gate karabiners linked by a short sling equals one quickdraw. Used to connect protection to the rope when leading a traditional route or to clip bolts when sport climbing.

Serac
A large ice tower.

Sherpa
A person of the ethnic group of the same name that is located in the Himalayan Mountains. Also a generic term for mountaineering

porters in Nepal (usually those working at or above Base Camp) regardless of their ethnic group.

Technical climbing
Climbing involving a rope and some means of protection, as opposed to scrambling or glacier travelling.

Technical
A term often used as synonymous with requiring precision and control, as in a very technical sequence of moves. Difficulty ratings of climbs are often a combination of the technicality of a climb and the endurance or strength necessary to complete it.

Traverse
1 To climb in a horizontal direction.
2 A section of a route that requires progress in a horizontal direction.
3 A Tyrolean traverse is crossing a chasm using a rope anchored at both ends.
4 A pendulum traverse involves swinging across a wall or chasm while suspended from a rope affixed above the climber.

Wire
Another name for a nut.

ACKNOWLEDGEMENTS

There are literally hundreds of people that I could mention. I do feel so very lucky that throughout my travels I have met so many people who at various stages in my life have been important to me, but what I have tried to do is acknowledge those who have been part of this small section of my life, the book. That said, there are a few folk who do need a special mention.

You aren't mentioned very much in the book; I've tried to keep it a little private while still trying to be honest to myself and to my family, but I owe almost everything in my life to two very amazing people: my mother and father. Dad, unfortunately, will never read this, as his mind has been lost to dementia. His loss pains me more than anything. These two people taught me that you don't need money to be rich; they instilled in me my strong values and morals. They were there for me in the dark times, and let me celebrate the good without interfering. They are my heroes, my role models and my inspiration all in one . . . I can't begin to thank you.

Mark Georgio, who over that last five years has constantly

asked every time we have spoken, 'When is the book out?' I essentially wrote the thing to get you off my bloody back.

Trevor Dolby, my editor and now friend. I hope our time together doesn't stop here.

Henry Todd, an unlikely mentor. A man with a big heart, even if it's sometimes disguised. I thank you for your unwavering support over the last fifteen years in the mountains.

Ian Parnell, the partner that was always there, the shoulder that was always solid, the friend that I often needed. Thank you for the photographs over the years.

Andy Fowkes, if for nothing else than saying yes to taking me to Brunel University all those years ago. You have a lot to answer for my friend.

Simon Lowe, the man who first had faith in me to climb Everest. Who could have guessed where it would lead?

Andrew Eggleston, a constant source of advice and friendship.

Nick Bullock, for the shared memories in the mountains, for your endless rants about nothing which kept me entertained all those years, and for stepping up to the task of being my best man.

Dorje Gyalgen, the machine of a man at high altitude. Thank you for being there every time I've ever needed you.

Bo Parfet, for being my wingman.

Jo Davies, for reading this through with such a brilliant eye.

Tim Williams, for help with the map which appears on the endpapers.

Alun Powell, Corry Taylor, Tim Gilling, John Varco, Sir Ran Fiennes, Jon Bracey, David Long, The WWS'ers, Dave Morten, Russel Brice.

To my sponsors over the years but in particular:
Sherpa Adventure Gear
Bremont Watches
Land Rover
Lyon Equipment
Power Traveller
Black Diamond

Photographic acknowledgements
Section One

p1 top: Simon Grayson; middle: Andy Fowkes; bottom: Steve Lewis
p2 top: Andy Fowkes; bottom: Stu Rose
p3 top: Kenton Cool; middle: Stu Rose; bottom: Ian Parnell
p4 Ian Parnell
p5 Ian Parnell
p6 Ian Parnell
p7 Ian Parnell
p8 Ian Parnell

Section Two

p1 Ian Parnell
p2 Kenton Cool
p3 Ian Parnell
p4 top: Kenton Cool; bottom: Ian Parnell
p5 Kenton Cool
p6 top: Dorje Gyalgen; bottom: Land Rover, Nick Dimbleby
p7 top and middle: Keith Partridge; bottom: Kenton Cool
p8 Neil Grasham

INDEX

Benegas brothers 183

Benson, Andy 68, 71

Benson, Pete 68, 71

Bettembourg, Georges 173

Bhim (cook) 102

Blitz, Johnny 76

Bonington, Chris 66, 165, 231, 240

Boko Haram 169

Bourdillon, Tom 117, 127

Brailsford, Dave 231

Branson, Sam 237–9

Branson, Sir Richard 238

Breithorn, Pennine Alps 149

Brice, Russell 103, 173–4, 177–8, 179, 183–4, 190, 194–5, 203, 215, 222, 224

British Antarctic survey 47

British Mountaineering Council 12, 69–70, 70*n*

Brooke, Nick 7

Brown University 139

Brown, Gordon 99

Brown, Joe 70*n*

Bullock, Nick 99, 233

Cairngorms, Scotland 20, 66*n*

Capel Curig, Wales 12

Carolyn (KC's girlfriend) 11, 14, 15, 16, 17, 34–6, 42

Cartwright, Jules 72, 75

Castor, Pennine Alps 149–50

Cave, Andy 69

Chalfont Heights Scout Camp 201

Chamonix 26, 27, 79, 143, 148, 151–7, 171

Chèré Couloir, France 158

Cheyne-Stokes respiration 187

Chinese Mountaineering Association 215

Cho Oyu, Nepal 6, 223

'climbing by fair means' 226

Colossus Wall, Wales 13

commercial expeditions 4, 74–5, 77, 91–2, 128–9, 173, 195, 196, 197, 213–14, 218, 220, 225, 226

Cool, Jazz (wife) vii, 7, 99, 141, 182, 202, 205, 210–11, 233, 235, 236, 237, 240

Cool, Kenton:

accident and injuries sustained to heels climbing 'Major Head Stress', Wales, 1996 11–18, 31–7, 39–48, 54, 68, 69–71, 91

amateur climber, end of period as 89–90

ambitions 240–1

attitude toward climbing, evolution in 231–6

breaks wrist climbing 'Right Wall', North Wales 12

childhood 18–21

climbs *see under individual area, climb, mountain or mountain range name*

cost of climbing with 218

deaths of friends and 136, 137

Everest and *see* Everest

fast and light approach to climbing and 73–5, 79–80, 229, 230

Fiennes and *see* Fiennes, Sir Ranulph

Index page.

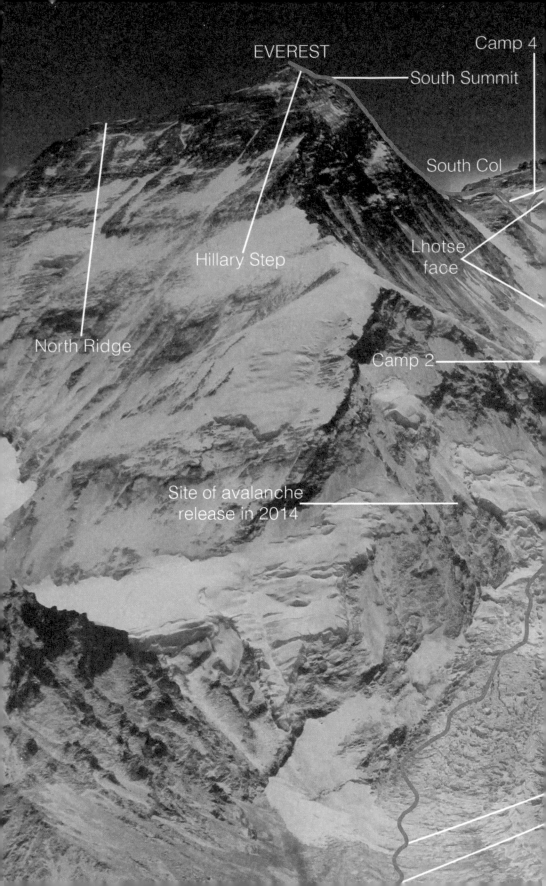

EVEREST

South Summit

Camp 4

South Col

Lhotse
face

Hillary Step

North Ridge

Camp 2

Site of avalanche
release in 2014